Rememberings

Pauline Wengeroff
(ca. 1908)

Rememberings

THE WORLD OF
A RUSSIAN-JEWISH WOMAN
IN THE NINETEENTH CENTURY

Pauline Wengeroff

Translated by Henny Wenkart
Edited with an Afterword by Bernard D. Cooperman

UNIVERSITY PRESS OF MARYLAND

LIBRARY OF CONGRESS CATALOGING-IN-PUBLICATION DATA

Wenkart, Henny.
    Rememberings : the world of a Russian-Jewish woman in the nineteenth
century / Pauline Wengeroff ; translated by Henny Wenkart ; edited with
an afterword by Bernard D. Cooperman.
    p. cm. — (Studies and texts in Jewish history and culture ; 9)
    An abridged translation of the German, 2nd ed. of: Memoiren einer
Grossmutter.
    ISBN 1-883053-58-7 — ISBN 1-883053-61-7 (pbk.)
    1. Wengeroff, Pauline, 1833–1916. 2. Jews—Russia—Biography. 3.
Jews—Russia—Social life and customs. 4. Russia—Biography. I. Cooperman, Bernard Dov, 1946– . II. Wengeroff, Pauline, 1833–1916. Memoiren einer Grossmutter. III. Title. IV. Series.

DS135.R95 W328 2000
947'.004924'0092—dc21

                                                              00-043945

Paper cuts © 2000 by Tsirl Waletzky

Cover photograph of Pauline Wengeroff ca. 1908
Cover design by Duy-Khuong Van

ISBN: 1883053-58-7 (hardcover)
       1883053-61-7 (softcover)

Portions of this translation by Henny Wenkart have appeared in the 1980s
and 1990s in *Lilith*, *The Jewish Advocate–Boston*, *The Cleveland Jewish News*,
and *The Canadian Jewish News*.

STUDIES AND TEXTS
IN
JEWISH HISTORY AND CULTURE

The Joseph and Rebecca Meyerhoff Center
for Jewish Studies
University of Maryland

IX

General Editor: Bernard D. Cooperman

UNIVERSITY PRESS OF MARYLAND

Translator's Dedication

My translation of this book from the German, my native tongue, is dedicated first of all to the memory of its author, Pessele Epstein Wengeroff. It was her wish to convey the light and warmth of her life in Eastern Europe to succeeding generations—and to give us some idea, as well, of its hardships.

In addition, my own work is dedicated to three men:

My friend, Rabbi Ben-Zion Gold, Director Emeritus of Harvard-Radcliffe Hillel, who called the book to my attention twenty years ago and asked me to make it the first volume of the translation project he was planning, to preserve the record of Jewish life in Eastern Europe.

My dear husband, Henry David Epstein, whose loving virtuoso nagging over these twenty years has finally inspired me to translate the entire book.

My editor, Professor Bernard D. Cooperman, who has trimmed the work to its svelte, accessible proportions, at the same time illuminating it with the historian's insight.

TABLE OF CONTENTS

A NOTE TO THE PRESENT EDITION

This translation from the German is based on the second edition of Pauline Wengeroff's *Memoiren einer Grossmutter. Bilder aus der Kulturgeschichte der Juden Russlands im 19. Jahrhundert* (Memoirs of a Grandmother. Images from the Cultural History of Russian Jews in the Nineteenth Century). The two volumes of that edition, published in Berlin around the time of the First World War (1913 and 1919), contained some 434 pages. In the present abridged version, we have tried to preserve both the tone and the content of the original while making this delightful work accessible and convenient for English readers—both students of the period and the general public.

As her subtitle makes clear, Pauline intended her book to be an evocation and celebration of a lost world, and she therefore included lengthy descriptions of events that she herself had not witnessed, drawing her information no doubt from eyewitnesses, newspapers, and history books. For this edition, we have chosen memoiristic passages that seemed to reflect Pauline's own experiences and that we hoped would be most interesting to today's reader.[1]

The transcription of Hebrew and Yiddish words in this book presented us with an unexpectedly complex historical and editorial challenge. Pauline tells us her family spoke "Russian-German," which was different from Lithuanian Yiddish (below, p. 127). Still, we cannot be sure how she pronounced many words if only because even as a child she would switch between languages and dialects according to context. Moreover, her transcriptions that reflect western (rather than the more commonly recognized eastern) Yiddish were intended for Ger-

---

[1] The complete and unedited translation by Dr. Wenkart may be consulted in a number of libraries and archives around the world and will also be available on the website of the Joseph and Rebecca Meyerhoff Center for Jewish Studies at the University of Maryland.

man readers, and the grammar and spelling of the Yiddish may have been somewhat "Germanized" by her or her publisher to suit the needs and expectations of that audience. Trying to recapture the sounds of the original, therefore, seemed an impossible task, or at least one that required sophisticated linguistic techniques well beyond the scope of this volume. In the translation we have generally followed her spellings, deviating only where we felt an English reader would have difficulty recognizing what she intended. (Thus, we use "ch" as she did to transcribe both *ḥet* and *khaf*, but changed her "w" to "v", "sch" to "sh", voiced "s" to "z", "j" to "y", and so forth.) We have similarly followed her representation of Hebrew/Yiddish vowels. The reader may be most surprised by "au" where "oy", "o" or even "u" might have been expected (*kausses, moraur, shaul*). We have also felt free to use commonly accepted English spellings where appropriate, even when this has meant some degree of inconsistency. Each non-English word is translated the first time it appears in the text. The glossary lists all such words along with modern Hebrew equivalents in brackets where these are appropriate.

Many people contributed their time and expertise to the production of this book—too many to list by name. For special help at crucial moments the editor would like to mention Mordechai Breuer, Irene Laclair, Ben-Zion Gold, Gershon Greenberg, Michael Grunberger, Marvin (Mikhl) Herzog, Steven Lowenstein, Yelena Luckert, Meyer Katzper, Peggy Pearlstein, Robert Rothstein, Sol Sobel, Shaul Stampfer, Michael Terry, Electra Yourke (Pauline Wengeroff's great-granddaughter), and especially Dianne, Avital, and Yael Cooperman. We would also like to thank Ms. Liz Ferris for her patience and for her excellent, professional transcription.

AUTHOR'S INTRODUCTION

I was a quiet child. Every event, whether happy or sad, made a deep impression on me. To this day, many events remain so fresh and lively in my memory that they seem to have happened only yesterday. Every year my desire to write down my experiences has grown, and now, in my old age, when life has become so lonely, I find my most beautiful and comforting hours those I spend with the rich material I have gathered together. These are hours of celebration for me, when I pick up these writings and leaf through them, sometimes with a quiet tear or a suppressed smile. I am no longer alone; I am in good and beloved company. Seven decades of storm and stress pass before me like pictures in a kaleidoscope, and the past becomes a living present: my cheerful, untroubled childhood in my parents' house; later, more serious moments; the sadness and joy of Jewish life in those years; and many scenes from the home that I myself made. These reminiscences help me through lonely, difficult hours as I face the bitterness of life's inevitable disappointments.

In such hours the hope steals into my old heart that perhaps this work is not in vain. In these yellowed pages I have gathered and preserved the more important events and the enormous cultural changes that affected me and all of Jewish society in Lithuania in the 1840s and 1850s.[1] Perhaps the youth of today will be interested to hear how things used to be. If even one of my readers gains something from all this, then I am richly rewarded.

I was born in the early 1830s in the Lithuanian city of Bobruisk.

---

[1] Wengeroff used the term "Lithuania," as did other nineteenth-century Jews, to include the areas of the Pale of Settlement east of Poland and north of Volhynia. Thus the Jews of Brest-Litovsk, Pinsk, Minsk, and Bobruisk were all "Litvaks" even though they did not come from the core Lithuanian provinces of Vilna and Kovno.–ed.

My parents were strictly religious, intelligent, spiritually advanced people. They raised me in a way that made it possible for me to follow the changes that entered Jewish family life through the introduction of Western European culture and education.

I have come to the conclusion that it was easy for our parents to raise their children, but very difficult for us, the second generation. In our youth we became acquainted with German and Polish literature, but we also studied the Bible and the Prophets with great energy and application, for they filled us with pride in our religion and in our tradition, and tied us closely to our people. The Bible's poetry made a deep impression on our fresh spirits. It gave our souls purity and clarity, rapture and enthusiasm. How difficult for us, then, was the time of the great transition of the 1860s and 1870s. We had already acquired a certain degree of European culture, but we realized that great gaps remained in our education.

We strove to see that our children would have what we had missed. But unfortunately, in our great enthusiasm we forgot the ultimate goal and the wisdom of restraint. It is our own fault that a chasm opened between us and our children.

For us, obedience to the commands of our parents was sacred. But now we find ourselves required to obey our children and submit ourselves completely to their will. In the past we were required to hold our tongues and keep silent before our parents. Now we have to remain silent before our children. This is even harder. We listen silently, filled with joy and pride, when our children tell of their lives and their ideals. Our admiration for our children has made them egotists and tyrants. The medal of western culture has an obverse side for us Russian Jews; in taking on Western European civilization no other people has given up all remembrance of its tradition so irrevocably.

It was much easier for our children than for us to attain a higher level of education. It gave us satisfaction that we had smoothed their way, removing obstacles from their path through heavy sacrifices. They had everything: governesses, kindergartens, libraries for the young, children's theater, celebrations and suitable games. All we had was our parents' home where we played with the poor children in our neighborhood, tossed our skirts over our heads and sang "God, God, send rain/ For the sake of the little children." A lot has changed, and I have tried to picture these changes here.

I ask the readers for their indulgence. I am not an author nor do I wish to appear as such. Think of this work as the writings of an old woman who, in the quiet twilight of her life, simply tells about the eventful times through which she lived.

To the youth of today, this family chronicle will seem covered with thick mold and dust. Still, I hope that learning about Jewish life in those days, as different from today as heaven is different from earth, will hold some interest for people who like to dip into the past, to test and to compare. And so I have found the courage to publish this spiritual child of an old woman, what in Hebrew would be called my *ben zekunim* (child of old age).

I cannot send this little work into the world without thanking my friend Louise Flachs-Fockschaneanu for her generous support.

Pauline Wengeroff

Foreword to the Second Edition

My old heart is so full of sincere, grateful joy to find my modest little book of memories received so much more widely than I had expected. May this second edition also find generous readers and provide them with an hour's pleasure. This would lend joy to the evening of my eventful life and reward me for my painstaking labors.

The Author

My Childhood
in Lithuania

Tsirl Waletzky

MY PARENTS AND MY FIRST HOME
[ca. 1840]

Summer and winter my father rose at four o'clock in the morning. Careful not to move more than eight paces from his bed, he washed his hands so that he could pray, then serenely recited the early morning service, and went off to his study without so much as a bite of breakfast. Row upon row of folios awaited him there, the various talmudic volumes arranged close beside other rabbinic and Hebrew works. He was very proud of some of his rare old editions. The furniture consisted of his desk, a tall, narrow table called a *shtender,* his easy chair and a footstool.

My father settled in his chair. Very early in the morning a servant had lit fresh candles for him. He drew the candelabrum closer, opened the great folio, which he had left ready the night before, and began *lernen* (to study) in the familiar singsong. So the hours passed until seven, when he took some tea and left for the morning service in the synagogue. At our house the time of day was referred to by the names of the three daily services: We said, "In the morning before (or after) *davenen* (praying)"; the afternoon was called "before (or after) *mincheh* (afternoon prayers)"; dusk was "between *mincheh* and *maariv* (evening prayers)." In the same way, the seasons of the year were "before (or after) *Chanukkah*" or "before (or after) *Purim,*" and so forth.

The business day began after my father returned from synagogue at ten. Many people came and went, Jews and Christians: managers, salesmen, business acquaintances. He dealt with them all by dinner time, which was one o'clock. After dinner he took a short nap and a cup of tea, and soon after that his friends began to arrive to chat with him about Talmud, about various literary questions, about the news of the day.

In the early 1840s my father wrote a contribution to the *Ein Yaakov,* which he called *Kuntres Kinmon Besem.* In the early Fifties he published a large collection of his Talmud commentaries under the title *Minchas Yehuda.* These works he never gave to a publisher to sell.

He just gave them to his friends, acquaintances, and children and distributed them especially to many *botei midrashim* (houses of study) all over Russia. [1]

In times past Jewish authors and publishers unfortunately did not give dates of composition for their works. My father actually included a family tree in his last work and listed many rabbis and great scholars, beginning with his grandfather and going back more than ten generations. But he gave no dates of birth or death. Of what importance was the life of the individual except as fruitful ground for Talmud study. Like his ancestors, my father dedicated himself faithfully to study and to the service of God.

Mincheh gedoleh (afternoon prayers) he usually said at home very early, and *maariv* again in synagogue, returning home at nine o'clock. Then we ate our supper, and after the meal he would sit at the table and chat with us about this and that. He took an interest in everything in the house, everything about the children, especially our progress in our studies. (My mother was in charge of actually hiring our teachers—the Jewish *melammed*, as well as the tutor for Russian and Polish.) We told him what was happening in the house and the town, and he shared with us what they were saying in synagogue. That was our favorite amusement: our father's stories were the best imaginable newspaper. Such oral transmission was called *gazeta pantoflowa* (unofficial newspaper; word of mouth). There were very few actual printed newspapers in those days, and they were hard to get hold of.

My father's impulsive nature was deeply stirred by what went on around him, and he transmitted his enthusiasm to all of us. Father also explained Jewish Law to us, and we loved, treasured, and revered him above anyone else we knew. Intently we listened to all he had to say about famous men, about their great deeds, their religious way of life.

---

[1]   On these works, see the Editor's Afterword, p. 265f.

alone. Irritably he asked why I was crying, but I was too full of grief to speak and only sobbed harder.

My father flew into a rage. "You wait. The switch will teach you to answer me."

He grabbed my hand, yanked me into the house, and had a switch brought to him. As he prepared to beat me, I had gone quite still and looked up at him in amazement. I was convinced that he was taking me for someone else, for I was never beaten.

"But I'm Pessele!" I said.

Everyone burst out laughing, and through their giggles they all begged him to spare me. It was my confidence that he must be making a mistake that saved me from the beating. *confidence*

My pious mother was very exacting in the fulfillment of every regulation. One of my favorite things was to dig up potatoes and other root vegetables with a spade or rake I borrowed from one of the half-frozen women in the garden, until the sharp winds of autumn drove me inside. After all our own produce was safely down in the cellar, a lot more was bought in the market. Then the very important work of putting up sauerkraut kept many women from among the poor busy for a full eight days every fall. In accordance with Jewish Law all the little worms that nest in fruits and vegetables, and particularly in cabbage, must be carefully removed. Each cabbage was pulled apart, leaf by single leaf; each leaf was held up to the light and examined closely for worms. If the cabbage was especially well grown and of the best sort, so that it had very few worms, she gave a prize for every worm the women found. She lived in fear that their search would not be meticulous enough.

I loved to be around them and to watch this work, because here as in the vegetable garden these women sang the most marvelous folk songs, which always moved me deeply. Sometimes to tears, sometimes to laughter. I still remember many of those precious songs.

That was a slower way of living. It seems to me that in our present age of steam and electricity we live much faster, and the driving haste of the machines seems to have altered the human spirit as well. We grasp things more quickly and find it easy to understand many com-

• Women working in vegetable gardens

* Femininity vs Masculinity

plicated things, while years ago people had difficulty mastering the simplest facts.

In the 1840s, for example, my grandfather was commissioned by the Government to construct a highway from Bobruisk to Brest. Because of mountains, swamps and valleys, it normally took a wagon two days to traverse the distance. The new road was to cut this to a comfortable one-day trip. Naturally this undertaking, a very big one for its day, was the topic of conversation everywhere. And even at the highest levels of society there could be found skeptics who would say, "Within human memory it has always taken two days to get from Brest in Lithuania to Bobruisk, and along comes *Reb* Ziml Epstein and tells us he's going to shorten it to one day. Who is he? God? Is he going to stick the rest of the trip in his pocket?"

A WEALTHY HOUSEHOLD

My parents were honest, God-fearing, generous people, gentle and refined. This was the dominant type among the Jews of that time. The chief task of their lives was to love God and their neighbors. The greatest part of their day was devoted to the study of Talmud. Although my father's business often involved sums of hundreds of thousands of rubles, only certain restricted hours were given over to business affairs. Like my grandfather, Shimon Ziml Epstein, my father belonged to the *podriadchiki* (entrepreneurial class), very important in the Russia of the first half of the nineteenth century. They built new fortifications, roads and canals for the government and supplied the army. My father and my grandfather were among the most highly regarded of these entrepreneurs; their absolute honesty in business was known to everyone. It is a documented fact that my grandfather, who bore the title of Honorary Citizen, was called to Warsaw from the provincial town of Bobruisk in the 1820s by General Dehn, Chief of Works at the fortifications in Medlin near Warsaw. Work of the same kind brought my father, Yehuda Halevi Epstein, to live in Brest.

There we lived in a large, richly furnished house; we kept carriages and many costly horses. My mother and my grown-up sisters had a

Lived In Brest

great deal of jewelry and beautiful, costly dresses. To get to our house, you drove out of the city and across the long bridge spanning the Bug and Muchawiecz Rivers, past a lot of small cottages, then to the right, then straight ahead about six hundred feet—and there you were! Our house was yellow, with green shutters. A large Venetian window in the facade was flanked by two narrower windows, under a tall shingled roof. A wooden fence surrounded a narrow flower garden in front. Tall silver poplars around the whole establishment, including the vegetable garden, gave it the air of some residence of the Lithuanian aristocracy.

Sometimes we had some high military or civilian official billeted upon us. Since the fortifications at Brest contained no palace at that time and our house was richly and comfortably furnished, Commandant Piatkin, who was a friend of Father, used to put up important guests with us.

I remember some of them very well. There was Prince Bebutov of Georgia in the Caucasus, who later held a very high post in Warsaw. He lived with us for a long time. He was always very nice to us children and pleasant to everyone. When we were playing in the flower garden in front of his windows he would give us candy and honey cake and would chat comfortably with us in Russian.

He had a tall, skinny servant named Johann, who had a hooked nose and black glowing almond-shaped eyes. That man could climb like a cat to the outermost branch of a poplar tree. And he could ride the *dzhigitovka burdiuk:* leaning down from his fiery galloping stallion he could pick up coins from the ground. Johann had a violent temper. It was very dangerous to get in his way when he was excited, or to tease him. He always carried a dagger. One time he split a dog that got in his way in half with that dagger. Another time, he caught a rooster in flight and ripped off its head. We children were very much afraid of him.

The other guest I still remember was Doppelmeyer, the Governor of Grodno, who often came to Brest and always stayed with us. He was a very genial, heavyset, blond gentleman who was received in our house as a friend. Every time he was in town he felt obliged to pay my

Johann the servant → scary.

parents a visit. If it happened to be on a Friday evening he always got a piece of pepperfish, which he considered a great delicacy. He also paid ample respect to the braided *shabbes* (Sabbath) white bread. It must have been a lovely sight to see all of us rosy-faced brothers and sisters around the table with our parents. The Governor often complimented my parents most cordially on their family. He discussed many serious subjects with my father, and remained chatting till the end of the meal.

At that time the relations between Jews and Christians had not yet been poisoned by anti-Semitism.

Among the guests who stayed in our home there was one little Jewish man who came every year in the middle of the summer and remained with us for several weeks. He belonged to the sect known as *dovor min ha-chai*, "to eat nothing living," who are now called vegetarians. He was so strict in his observance that he would not eat from any dish that had ever been used to serve meat. My pious mother used to prepare his meals with her own hands: soup made of sour beets or sorrel, porridge without fat except for a bit of vegetable oil, nuts with honey, or radish cooked with ginger in honey; tea and black coffee. He was a quiet, very modest man and very much revered by us all, especially by my father, who used to sit with him in his study bent over the folios of the Talmud, discussing points of Law.

Good highways were the prerequisite for improvements in transportation, and the contracts for such construction were let by competitive bidding; in late autumn the Government would organize *torgi* in Brest, auctions for the assignment of work and supply contracts. *Podriadchiki* arrived from many distant cities. Among them my grandfather would come to us from Warsaw.

Great preparations were made for his arrival. Every day my father was apprised of the progress of his carriage by express messengers, riding especially fast horses, which they changed at every station. When the appointed day had come at last, everyone in the house, especially the children, was filled with anticipation. We took up our stations on the balcony or in the portico, each picking out the best

spot among the columns to catch grandfather's eye *first*. All eyes were fixed on the bridge. The suspense mounted.

Finally we heard the rattling of the bridge, and Grandfather's great four-seater drew into view pulled by four post horses (and by our impatient eyes). Each girl stood ramrod straight and brushed the hair out of her eyes, heart pounding.

The carriage stopped by the porch. A tall, bony, blond footman dressed in livery with a profusion of overlapping collars jumped from the box, opened the door and helped Grandfather down—a stately, venerable old man, still rather fit, with a long gray beard, high, wide forehead and large, expressive eyes. Though habitually stern, his eyes rested with tenderness and pride upon his son. The old man's heart rejoiced that our father found time to apply himself with diligence to the study of Talmud, despite his many business obligations. Often I heard him say that he envied our father his great learning, and the leisure he had to pursue it.

First my Grandfather greeted my mother, without shaking hands. He embraced my father, my elder brother and my brothers-in-law. Then he turned to my elder sisters and to us younger ones, and said, "What's new, children?"

These few words made us hop and skip for joy. Surrounded by the entire swarm of us he made his way across the porch and into the house. We smaller children were not allowed just yet into the festively decked-out front rooms. Through the door on the left we went back into the main corridor to our part of the house. My elder sisters had arrived at an age and position to remain with Grandfather and my parents and participate in discussions of business.

Our mother took us little ones to him the next morning. Tenderly he stroked our hair and our cheeks. Sometimes, very seldom, he kissed us. Then he got his footman to give us all the good candy and oranges he had brought for us from Warsaw, and our brief "audience" with him was over. We kissed the strong white hand that he held out to us, wished the beloved old man good morning, bowed, and left the room without addressing a single superfluous word to him.

For the whole time that Grandfather remained with us there was

11

a running to and fro in the house, noise, the coming and going of friends and business contacts, continuous arrival and departure of carriages and coaches in the courtyard. The mid-day meal was served later than usual. The big dining room table was moved into the yellow parlor and set with the best silver, crystal and china. Long meals, consisting of many courses, were served daily to multitudes of guests.

There was no room for any of us children—from my eldest sisters to the youngest, at that table. To our great delight, however, a separate table was set in the same room and our *nyanya* (nursemaid), Mariasha, served us there. She was a buxom, rosy-cheeked girl with thick black braids and a red turban. My older sister Chashe Feige fetched us tidbits and cakes from the main table, and we enjoyed not having to obey the usual strict table rules.

In the evening more guests arrived, including many Christians— military officers of the highest ranks, engineers, construction commissioners, with whom Grandfather played a card game called *préférence*. A rich dessert was served, and we would ask Mother to let us take our portions into the dining room where we could eat sitting on top of the stove. It was so snug up there, full of shadows even at mid-day. Way in the back corner lived our dolls with all their paraphernalia—dresses, beds, dishes. Mariasha always kept us company, and she told wonderful stories.

Mother really did not like to let us go up there. It was a dangerous climb. You had to put one foot into a special indentation in the stove and swing yourself up by the other. Sometimes we slipped, and crashed head first onto the floor. Even once safely up, we sometimes leaned out and fell. But often we did receive permission to spend an entire evening up in our favorite roosting place, sitting or lying flat. There was no room to stand beneath the low ceiling.

In the rooms below it was pretty lively. Lots of business was discussed after tea and dessert. The commotion continued every day until Grandfather had completed the transaction of his business. He had undertaken the construction of the new fortifications at Brest; my father was to deliver many millions of bricks from his factory, each stamped with his initials, "J.E."

Interactions w/ Christians

As a farewell present we received many beautiful silver and gold coins. Then Grandfather departed, and the house was suddenly quiet again.

I loved the winter time. Especially when it was snowing hard, I used to love to walk outdoors. Then at dusk, beginning to shiver, I crept into the wing of the house where my married sisters lived with their husbands and little ones, looking for Chainke, the *nyanya* who took care of my sister's baby son. She would tell me fascinating tales and sing beautiful songs.

Usually I found her rocking the cradle with her foot while her wrinkled blue and yellow hands worked away at her knitting. She was always knitting stockings of coarse dark gray wool. I would climb up on the bed beside her and flatter her and beg her to let me help a little with her knitting.

blue + yellow hands?

"No," she would grin. "You'll drop a stitch, like you did yesterday. Go away."

"Chainke, Yubinke," I would start again, "if you won't give me the stocking, then sing me some of those wonderful songs that you sing to put Berele to sleep."

Crankily she'd say, "I don't feel like singing."

"Are you sick, Chainke?" I would ask, full of concern.

"Leave me alone!" she would scream, jumping off the bed.

I never allowed these fits of hers to frighten me away. I kept begging her, kissing her wrinkled cheeks, stroking the folds of her neck.

"*Mishelaches!* (Plague from God!)" she would cry. "Just to be *poter* (rid) of you, I'll sing."

Pattycake, pattycake, buy new shoes,
The child will run to cheder.
Properly he will learn.
He will learn some shures [*lines of Talmud*].
Of him we'll hear good bsures [*news*].
To the world he'll give advice,
Good advice to all the world.
He will pasken shailes [*answer ritual law questions*]:

13

What to do, what not to do.
He'll give learned droshes [*talmudic talks*]*.*
They will send him a golden box,
And a big fur shtreimel [*Holy Day hat*]*.*

"Ah! Wonderful! Beautiful!" I would cry. "Now sing me a second song, Chainke."

"What a plague has fallen on me today!" she screamed. She jumped up roughly, dropping her knitting needle into the cradle so all her stitches slipped off. Now I was sure I would hear no more songs that day. But I sat quite still while she organized her stocking, grumbling all the while, looking at me sideways as if to say that of course it was all my fault. She could see from the look on my face that I "admitted" my guilt, and so she forgave me. It may also be, of course, that her mood improved because I promised to bring her part of my supper.

She sang me another song, "just to get rid of me."

Sleep my child, peacefully,
Close your kosher eyes.
Under the child's carriage
There stands a little white goat.
The little goat has gone to trade,
To trade in raisins and almonds.
This is the best stock in trade—
Berele will learn Torah.
Torah, Torah in his head,
Kasha, kasha in the pot.
Butter for his bread,
Daddy and Mommy will lead Berele to the chuppeh [*wedding*
      canopy]*.*

Jewish cradle songs are unlike those of other nations. Jews spin dreams of learning Torah, going to school—not of hunting, dogs, horses, war and daggers.

Enraptured by her own singing, Chainke sang me several more songs. There is one more I would like to offer here:

Little goat, little goat,
In a jug red nettles are growing.
When the Daddy beats the Mama
Kiddies tear their clothes in kriyeh [*mourning*].
Little goat, little goat,
In a jug red oranges grow.
When the Daddy kisses Mama
Kiddies dance with great relief.

Darkness had come on by this time, and I hurried back to the main house, where my siblings were already eating supper. Mariasha was still not finished slicing bread and spreading homemade gooseberry jam, our favorite treat. I got my portion and, quick as a wink, I was heading back to the other wing, where I was received in a much friendlier fashion than before by the now favorably disposed singer. Together we ate up the tasty tidbits with pleasure.

Springtime also had its special charm for me. It enticed me out into the meadows near the house, where I skipped about in great spirits all morning with my constant companion, Chaya the tinsmith's daughter. Rejoicing in every fresh blossom, we picked buttercup after buttercup, added the delicate forget-me-nots that grew on the riverbank, wound thick garlands about our heads and wore them home.

Often I joined the children of our poorer neighbors on their forays behind the house, where they gathered deep red berries from the bushes at the foot of the mountain. We'd string long chains of berries to wear around our necks. Then I often forgot to go home, which worried my mother. The whole family would be seated around the dinner table and people would have to be sent to search for me.

One of my favorite places was the hayloft. On top of the great, fragrant piles of hay I would dig myself a hole and play with my kitten. I taught her to stand on her hind legs and to sit, wrapped her in my apron, pulled her ear and screamed at her, "Kitten, do you want *kasha* (buckwheat cereal)?" The tortured creature yanked her ear out of my hand and shook herself. That was "No." So I grabbed her other ear and screamed into it, "Maybe you want *kugel* (noodle pudding)?" Then she meowed, and that was "Yes."

15

If I tired of this game, I would lean way out, push fresh hay down in front of the horses below, and watch them gorge themselves.

I START SCHOOL

My mother decided it was time to put an end to all my adventures and send me to *cheder*, to the same *melammed* (elementary teacher) who was teaching Hebrew to my older sister.

One beautiful afternoon, in the middle of a lively game, she suddenly called me into the dining room. There *Reb* Layzer the *melammed* sat waiting for me.

Mother turned to him.

"This is my Pessele. Tomorrow she will come to *cheder* with Chavehleben (my sister)."

I was too shy to raise my eyes.

"But don't bring your kitten," he said.

Well! Half the novelty of visiting the *cheder* lost its charm right there. Glumly and full of resentment I sat wondering what would happen to my kitten now, and what would happen to all the other splendors of life.

I heard *Reb* Layzer say to Mother, "Well, then, on Tuesday my *behelfer* (assistant) will pick her up."

Then he said goodnight and disappeared into the dark.

So now it was farewell to Chaye, the tinsmith's daughter, who used to bring along such pretty little dishes to play with. And to Peyke, who was so good at making up doll games. And to Yentkeh—how many times did we two sit together on the big log at the end of the garden fence and tell sad and funny stories, making each other weep or giggle! It hurt to have to give all this up.

The first day of school! Mother had made me go to bed early so I could get up with Chaveh and go to *cheder* with her but I hadn't slept well. I was up earlier than Chaveh, and our *nyanya* washed and dressed me first, so that in the end I was the one kept waiting.

The junior *behelfer* who came to collect me and Chaveh turned

16

out to be a long, thin youth with long, thin blond curls dangling in front of a pair of donkey's ears. He had a very wide mouth. It wasn't often that you could see his eyes, because even in the hottest weather he wore his quilted *kutshmeh* (a high, tapering fur cap) pushed down low as though it had put down roots in his head. His shoes were often mismatched: one was so large that he came close to losing it at every step; the other was so tight that he dragged his leg. His name was Velvel and he came from a backwater town called Zabludeve (Zabludów).

Velvel was "eating days." Every day he was fed by the parents of a different pupil. Tuesdays he ate at our house.

As I watched him get his breakfast, he made me laugh. He plumped his long body down on one end of the bench. The other end immediately rose up in the air, and the *bocher* (young man) fell full length to the floor. Even our grouchy cook had to laugh. But this accident did not prevent him from wolfing down his meal.

Then Velvel blessed my first day of school by calling out, "Now, right foot first!" As we went along he brought up the rear, probably on account of his uneven footwear. Suddenly a stray dog attacked us. We looked for Velvel, our protector, but he was the first to scream and, despite his shoes, he managed to run so fast we were left behind to face the dog.

Chaveh grabbed my hand, and breathlessly we repeated the magic verse:

Doggie, doggie, want to bite me?
There will come three teivolim [*demons*].
They will tear you limb from limb.
Doggie, doggie, want to bite me?
There will come three teivolim.
They will tear you limb from limb.
I am Jacob, you are Esau.
I am Jacob, you are Esau.

17

You have to recite this very fast, without moving from the spot and all in one breath. We knew that this would calm the dog, and it would let us pass.

When we finally caught up to our true blue guardian, our procession was back on its way. My sister pointed out all the remarkable sights and explained everything to me. We pressed our way through crowds of people, passed the booths and stands with dry goods for sale, and arrived at the *cheder* about eight o'clock.

Once long, long ago the little house must have had a coat of yellow paint. Now it stood deep in the ground, its tiny window panes admitting little light, surrounded by a mound of earth on which my new classmates and my sister's friends were playing various games.

They all opened their eyes wide and stared at me.

At the entrance we stopped—it was not so easy for the uninitiated to find her way there.

My sister led the way. She opened the door, jumped down into the room, and held out her hand to me. I grabbed at it and put down my leg, feeling in the dark for the sill, which turned out to be a rotting chunk of wood buried in the mud floor. I had to feel a long way down to find it. Then I let down my other leg and bravely took a step into the room.

Chaveh warned me not to trip over a ladder that half barred the way. Another step, and there we were at the water barrel with a great ladle suspended from its rim. There was also a pitcher, and a broom.

On the left I glimpsed a door whose wooden handle was rubbed smooth as glass. Chaveh opened it and stepped into the school room and I followed her. There was not room for both of us to stand up straight in the cramped space between the door and the school bench, which was attached to a long table covered with prayer books and other sacred texts. Across the table a second bench backed right up against the other wall. You can imagine how wide that room was!

Reb Layzer, the *melammed*, reigned over this domain, seated at the head of the table. He was a powerfully built man whose heavy shoulders completely obscured the window beside him. His large, watery-blue, protruding eyes, with two small *peyes* (earlocks) in con-

18

stant motion before them, his long face, his pointed gray beard, all exuded self-confidence and pride. The strong swollen veins in his forehead were evidence of his great energy. His clothes were typical for the time and for his station: short trousers fastened at the knee over thick gray stockings; gigantic shoes; shirtsleeves of dubious cleanliness; a colorful, dark cotton *arba kanfos*[1] that took the place of a jacket in summer. (In the winter he wore a quilted jacket.) A small black velvet cap sat on his large head, completing his uniform of office.

At the other end of the table sat his chief assistant, his head always bowed, holding a long, thin wooden rod called a *deitelholz*, with which he pointed out, letter by letter and line by line, the passage the children were reading. His job was to repeat with us the lessons taught by the *melammed*. He was always serious. His nose was shaped like a spade, his eyes were small and melancholy. His two long black *peyes* moved continually.

We stood still. We had to stand still, since there was only that one spot to stand in. When he caught sight of me the *rebbe* cried out, "Ah!"

He got up, grabbed me under the arms, lifted me up, and sat me down beside him. The other girls came running in to inspect this new phenomenon—me—and to compare notes. My sister, who felt at home here, sat down at her place but kept looking over at me protectively.

Fear, embarrassment, the many strange faces, the muggy air in the house, the low ceiling at which I kept glancing nervously, all this and probably the after-effect of the angry dog, choked me until I knew nothing better to do than to start crying.

I was ashamed, I was furious with myself, but I couldn't help it. *Reb* Layzer tried to quiet me. I would not have to start learning today. I could just play with the others at recess. But the more he talked the more I cried. Finally he guessed that what was frightening me most were the many curious eyes.

[handwritten margin note: Started crying in school]

---

[1] A four-cornered piece of cloth in whose corners the *tzitzis* (ritual fringes) were tied. It had a large hole in the middle for the head.

He stamped his enormous feet and shouted, "Out! Into the street, *shiksehs!*[1] What are you staring at, have you never seen anything like this before?"

At this command they scattered in all directions. Finally they resumed their games outside. I did quiet down, but was afraid to stir from my place. My sister went over a paragraph with the *rebbe*, repeated it with the chief assistant, and then tried to take me outside to play. But I wouldn't budge.

Finally it was time for lunch. I had been too absorbed in myself and in my new surroundings to consider the question of where and when we were all going to eat. It turned out that Velvel, that morning's knight in shining armor, would bring us our food, but he was late. Finally he appeared carrying bread and cooked food in pitchers, pots, bowls, glasses and spoons of various kinds and sizes. The pots and pitchers were tied to his waist by means of his wide belt, hanging down over his hips; the bread had been stored by the resourceful *bocher* next to his chest between his shirt and his caftan; the full bowls were piled one on top of the other, pressed against his chest with one arm and held fast with the other hand. The dessert of nuts, apples, cooked beans and peas was weighing down his deep thief's pockets. Thus laden the ship of state made slowly for the *cheder* port.

It was literally impossible for Velvel to sit down.

He arrived. The *rebbe* scolded him for his tardiness. In reply he explained exactly how and where and for how long he had been kept waiting for each item.

"Hurry up. Hand out the bowls and spoons," the Rebbe commanded.

He poured all our food together into one large bowl. I received a spoon with a little hole in the handle to signify that it was *milchig*—that is, for use with dairy food. I turned it this way and that, unable to plunge into that bowl.

---

[1] Wengeroff explained in a footnote that the term was a derogatory epithet meaning "young girl." The term derives from Hebrew and is used in Yiddish to refer specifically to non-Jewish girls.–ed.

I was thinking, "With this spoon I'm supposed to eat? And not from my china dish?" *spoiled*

The tears started back into my eyes and my throat constricted.

The *rebbe* looked at me in astonishment. This time he could not imagine what the cause of my distress could possibly be.

My sister was more practical. (She has had this advantage over me all of our life.) She dug in and ate one spoonful after another with pleasure. Once she had taken the edge off her own appetite she inquired why I wasn't eating. I gave no answer. I felt that as soon as I tried to talk I would burst into tears again. But I forced myself to take a spoonful and choke it down, together with my tears.

Once the meal was over, the *rebbe* helped me down off the bench. Despite my vexation I began to go over in my mind all the many ways in which this kind of meal was better than the kind I was used to: Here we could talk, or take a drink during the meal whenever we felt like it, while at home we had to wait until after the roast. Here we could get up whenever we liked, while at home we had to wait until Father had risen from his place. *Jewish customs*

When I wanted another drink after lunch, someone showed me the big ladle by the water barrel. Then my sister took me by one hand, another pupil by the other, and I finally did go out to play until seven in the evening. We were called back into the schoolroom for the evening prayer. The assistant stood in the middle and we watched him and repeated every word after him. Then we hurried home.

I was so exhausted by the events of the day that I could not tell my *nyanya* much about them. I drank my tea and fell asleep without any supper.

But in the morning I was eager to get back to those other children whose faces had frightened me only yesterday. Most of all I was eager to take up our games where we had left off. This time my behavior was quite different: I learned with the *rebbe*, and later I played with the children. In less than a week I was quite at home, familiar with every nook and corner of the school. In addition to the long, narrow school room there was also a long, dark crawl hole—no other word will describe it—containing the beds of the *rebbe* and *rebbetzin*. In front of

home meals different than school meals.

their beds, suspended from a beam, hung the cradle of their only daughter, Altinke. Whoever came and went down this passage knocked against the cradle and set it swinging for a long time.

You couldn't say that this room, or the linen on the beds and in the cradle, were clean. But the inhabitants of this hut were content in the true sense of the word. They wished for nothing more. Their only concern was for Altinke, the last remaining child of the four they had produced. Although she was more than two years old, she was unable to stand or walk. They tended and protected her as the apple of their eye. She wore an amulet around her neck—a leaden square engraved with bits from the Kabbalah—and a little *mezuzeh*. These, as well as a wolf's tooth, were suspended from a ribbon that was pasted to her quilted shirt by means of filth and spit.

This unhappy little creature spent most of her time lying in the cradle, since *Rebbetzin* Feige operated a number of cottage industries: She baked a special honey cake containing an herb to drive out worms; she cooked the peas and beans the pupils bought from her every day for snacks; and she tended a hen and her chicks. All this left her little time to carry the child in her arms.

Every day she chose one pupil to help her. I was soon her willing and obedient helper. Sometimes I rocked the baby (I loved doing this), sometimes I floured the paddle with which the *rebbetzin* pushed the loaves of bread into the oven, sometimes I found the egg, which the hen would lay every day. If the egg was still warm, I loved to rub it across my eyes.

The shape of the *rebbetzin* was reminiscent of a beanstalk. She had unusually long arms, a long, thin neck, and a horse's head in which small eyes scurried this way and that. Her cheeks were bony and her thin lips had surely never smiled since the days of her childhood. Her hooked nose hid half of her mouth, giving her face the appearance of a predatory bird. Her speech was unpleasant, partly because of her horse teeth and the spaces between them. This did not prevent her from giving frequent proof of the unimpaired condition of her vocal chords.

It did not pay to fool around with the *rebbetzin*. Her hand was not

22

Altinke:
Rabbe & Rabbetzin's daughter

gentle. I had had to leave my kitten at home, but at first I made substitute pets of the *rebbetzin*'s chickens. I would sit by the *pripetshek* (the lower part of the stove) and watch the brood hen sit carefully on her eggs with her wings spread, her eyes filled with an almost human tenderness. Patiently the bird sat waiting to be picked up and fed.

One day the *rebbetzin* saw me bend down to take up the hen and feed her. She misunderstood and, afraid that I would frighten the hen away from her eggs and that they would cool off and fail to hatch, she rushed over, grabbed me by the shoulder and screamed at me.

"What are you doing? What do you want? *Meshuggene, aveg*! (Crazy person. Get away!)"

She was gasping with fury. Now the chicken did tear out of my arms and flutter over to *Reb* Layzer's domain, where she settled on a corner shelf near him, announcing with loud cackles that she liked it there. Then she proceeded to the top of *Reb* Layzer's head and ducked, leaving a souvenir of her brief visit. Next she flew to the shelf where the tin plates and bowls were kept and knocked them all down, making a huge racket, and then finally returned to her nook under the *pripetshek* to calm down.

Reb Layzer, however, was not able to calm down quite so readily, since the pupils around the table were all laughing and pointing at his head. Scolding and cursing aloud, he pulled off his hat and cleaned it. He swore to his helpmate that he would slaughter all her chickens. Tomorrow.

Our fearless *rebbetzin* was of another opinion and protected her charges, arms outspread. She argued that I was really the chief culprit. Furthermore, her husband had no authority to pass a sentence of death upon her chickens.

Apparently her oration for the defense was of a brilliance to silence the arguments of *Reb* Layzer. He reversed the sentence and pardoned the hens.

Both in the *cheder* and out in the alley this incident was the topic of a great deal of discussion. Spectators gathered to peer in at the windows and some nearly got involved in the fight. That evening I had a lot to report to my *nyanya*.

When *Reb* Layzer at last fell silent before his wife, he did so with the air of a man whose dignity was unassailable come what might. To this he was fully entitled: in his own school room, in his neighborhood and even on the peninsula across the lake he was a very popular man. They came to *Reb* Layzer the *melammed* whenever a child was sick with fever. He was a healer who knew how to drive away the *ayin ho-ra* (evil eye). He would take a piece of the victim's clothing, say a stocking or a shirt, whisper a secret word and spit on it three times. This sufficed for a cure. He had no need to see his patient in person. The piece of clothing was returned to the messenger with these words: "He'll get well."

If you had a toothache, *Reb* Layzer would go out into the moonlight with you, and at midnight sharp he would stroke your right cheek, and your left cheek, all the while whispering his magic words. He was certain that now this had been done your pain would stop— of course, it might take a while; sometimes until the tooth had actually been pulled.

For a severe backache, all you had to do was stretch out on the floor. *Reb* Layzer, a *bchor* (firstborn son), would stand upon your back for a brief moment and you were cured!

One word from the lips of *Reb* Layzer could accomplish much. People were convinced that when *Reb* Layzer participated in the purchase of a cow, for example, his haggling assured them of a larger output of milk.

Reb Layzer made almost as much from the *shadchen* (matchmaker) business as from his school, with the added advantage that matchmaking was usually accompanied by a glass of whiskey. Depending upon the success of the resulting marriage, each deal increased the number of his friends (or enemies). There were more enemies than friends, but *Reb* Layzer got no gray hairs over it. All matches were the same to him. This business was conducted Saturday evening between *mincheh* and *maariv*, when the Jews of those days, rested after their twenty-four hour respite from work, were in the mood to speak of such things. It may have been a good thing that he had so little time to devote to this.

24

The incident with the hen soured me on life inside the *cheder*. I concentrated on the outdoor games. I got very good at some of them, especially a dice game that we played with bones shaped into primitive cubes, a nut game, and a pin game, singly or with a partner. One of my friends was so good at the pin game that she made me quite jealous. She could hold a large number of straight pins under her tongue and talk at the same time. We played so much we often forgot the real reason we were at school.

THE SYNAGOGUE

Soon I had come to know the whole *cheder* neighborhood and was on good terms with all the neighbors. My special favorite was the little *shaul klopfer* (synagogue knocker), a haggard, bent little man with a goat face of a greenish-yellow complexion. His dull goat's eyes were filled with anguish. All his life he seemed to suffer from a wheezing cough. He would stand in the street near the synagogue and call the community together before morning and evening prayers, shouting with all the lung power he had left: "To *shaul!* To *shaul!*" Each time he completed his cry, he would dig his fists into his sides and cough, fighting for breath. Whenever we saw him in the street, my friends and I would follow along behind him, shouting "To *shaul!*"

Another of his duties was performed on Friday afternoon, when he would run from one Jewish merchant to another to remind them to close before the onset of the Sabbath. And during the week before New Year he roused the community at dawn for *sliches* (penitential prayers).

The synagogue of Brest was a beautiful, majestic structure, built in the old style with a circular glass tower whose windows poured daylight into the building. Inside there was a vaulted ceiling, painted sky blue and sprinkled with silver stars, and hung with many chandeliers. Tradition had it that the building dated back to the time of Saul Wahl, who was elected king for a night by quarreling Polish factions, and that he had built it in memory of his wife, Deborah.

I was always afraid to step inside much beyond the entrance. Once

25

when my playmates pushed me into the men's section (which at that hour was deserted), I was terribly frightened by the large hall, the benches and tables, the raised rectangular area in the middle surrounded by a low, carved railing (where the Torah was read), and by the tall *oren ha-kodesh*, the Sacred Ark, curtained in red velvet with an embroidered Star of David and a pair of life-size bronze lions standing guard on top. My friends assured me that from inside the Ark a tunnel led underground straight to Jerusalem. On Friday evenings all the *resho'im* (sinners) freed from *gehinom* (hell) for the Sabbath would gather here to carry out their mischief.

Perhaps what frightened me most was the story that a clay *goylem* (statue) rested up on top of the Ark. A *goylem* could do anything that a real person could if it was activated by secret kabbalistic amulets, hieroglyphics and other special signs and magic formulas. As everyone knew, instructions to a *goylem* had to be given with absolute precision in every detail: "Go to the door, take the doorknob, turn it, open the door, close it, go into the house on such-and-such a street, go into the first room, go to the table where my friend is sitting, tell him to come to me today with the book." And the way home had to be described just as precisely. Otherwise he might bring your friend's whole house back with him on his shoulders. He was a true imbecile. To this day Jews insult each other by saying: "You are a clay *goylem*."

One other time I ventured into the great hall, but I ran out screaming and weeping, shaking in inexplicable fright. *Reb* Layzer forbade me to go in there unaccompanied, ever again.

When the City of Brest was demolished in 1836 and turned into a fortress, the synagogue was torn down as well.

goylem = statue

26

THE CYCLE OF
THE JEWISH YEAR

Tsirl Waletzky

PURIM

Purim, which arrives just before earliest springtime, meant presents and excitement. All we did for feverish days before the holiday was needlework, needlework. Every one of our many cousins and nieces had to have a handmade present for *shlachmones* (presents exchanged on *Purim*). All through the days and late into the evening we worked, imagining how each recipient would admire (or envy) our skill and artistry.

The day before the festival, *Estertanes* (the Fast of Queen Esther), all the grown-ups fasted. My sisters spent the day preparing the baked delicacies of *Purim*. Most important were the *hamantashen* (three-cornered poppyseed pastries), but there were also *mohnelach*—poppy-seeds cooked in honey and then allowed to harden. If these turned out well, it was a sign of a good year to come. We children were allowed to help and nibble as much as we wanted, because there was no regular meal that day.

Evening prayers were recited in our house, and then company came in from all around the neighborhood for the reading of the *megilla*, the Book of Esther. At every mention of Haman's despicable name the men stamped their feet and the young people set up a great din with their *graggers* (noisemakers). My father tried to forbid this, but every year it happened anyway. Finally, at about eight or nine in the evening, the adults broke their fast at the heavily laden table in the dining room.

We children awoke very early the next morning. Unable to go back to sleep, we called to each other from our beds:

"What's today?"

"*Purim!*" came the jubilant reply from every corner of the house.

We got dressed as fast as we could and then we waited through the endless morning, joyous anticipation turning bit by bit into plain impatience. If only the afternoon would hurry up and come, the time for sending (and for receiving!) *shlachmones* (holiday gifts).

My father and the young men of the house returned from the synagogue, where the festival service had been recited and the *megilla* read again. We had our dinner, consisting of the traditional four

29

courses: fish, soup (of course with *hamanohren*—three-cornered *krep-lach*), turkey and vegetables. On this day we dined very early so that we could begin the *sudeh* (festive meal), the central and most important part of the festival, before nightfall. At that meal each Jew is required to abandon himself to the real or pretended joy of his heart, even to the point of getting really tipsy. As I remember it, every Jew was always full of joy on that day, treating himself to good food and drink and expending considerable effort to raise the money.

We children thought of nothing but sending and receiving *shlachmones*. At last the important hour had arrived. We placed all our gifts on an enormous tea tray, and drilled the maid on the recipient of each gift. In voices trembling with anxiety and excitement, we forbade her to stop anywhere along the way, even to exchange casual remarks with anyone, even in passing.

She must go straight to the homes of our aunts. We gave precise instructions for every move. Just so must she set the tray on their tables, in such-and-such an exact manner must she distribute our gifts. In our imagination we heard the exclamations of delight that our handiwork was bound to evoke. Repeatedly we pointed out each piece. At last we sent her on her way.

She arrived all right, but then she was overrun by our cousins.

"Do you come from our aunt's children?"

"Yes," she stammered. Pursued into the living room by their noisy questions, she lost control of the tea tray, which was snatched from her and plundered. Our cousins took possession of their gifts, inspecting, comparing, judging. The clumsy girl had no hope of obeying our careful instructions.

Within the next quarter hour they would be sending their gifts to us. But our poor messenger, after her overwhelming welcome, crept from their house almost unnoticed. She got home only to be questioned again, impatiently, this time by us. Just how had each gift been received? Exactly how had each cousin looked? What were her exact words as she inspected our handiwork?

Soon the presents they had prepared for us arrived, far exceeding our expectations—or not. In any case we must exercise restraint in receiving them. Before their servant, our mother forbade any show of impatience or curiosity. We were expected to behave with quiet *well-behaved* decorum.

Meantime all sorts of *Purim* players arrived to perform for us. The first scene was always the story of Achashveros (King Artaxerxes), Haman, Mordecai, and Esther. Usually a young fellow in a lady's dress played Esther, whom we admired with great sympathy and emotion. The clothing of the other performers was not exactly distinguished by cleanliness or elegance. Their three-cornered hats, epaulets and so on were made of dark blue and yellow cardboard.

For over an hour we gave this performance our undivided attention. It was followed by a play about Joseph. Each play included many songs, all of which I can still recall word for word. I remember a funny dance performed and sung to us in Yiddish by Zirele Wans, a lower-class woman, and Lemele Futt the pauper. It was all angular steps and movements, rather grotesque. We giggled, but discreetly.

What we loved best of all was the song of the *kozeh* (goat). The pelt and head of a goat bounded into the room, leaping into the air and shaking a multitude of little bells and coins and glass beads till they jingled merrily. Upon its two horns, augmenting the music of the rest of the goat, two larger bells sounded shrilly at every move. The good man inside the pelt whirled around the room while his companion, the goatherd, offered the following song in a hoarse, funny voice:

> *Up on the mountain, on the green grass,*
> *A couple of Germans with long whips.*
> *We are tall men,*
> *We wear short clothes.*[1]
> *Our Father, our King,*
> *Our hearts know no grief.*
> *Jolly we'll be,*

---

[1] Possibly the verse alludes to German Jews who wore coats that were shorter than those of their East European coreligionists.–ed.

31

And wine we'll drink.
Drink wine and eat kreplach,
And of God we'll think.

The singer was a tall blond fellow nicknamed Kozeh, who moved clay around in our brick factory all year long. We small children were delighted with this show—but scared as well. Soon we fled to the top of the stove in the dining room. From this safe corner we watched the goat guzzle the brandy Mother pressed to its lips, and gulp down a whole *hamantash*. We never could arrive at a settled opinion about this goat: *was* it really a goat, or only a man in goat's clothing? The matter seemed thoroughly puzzling to us.

Over and over again the performances in the dining room were interrupted by messengers bringing *shlachmones*, waiting for Mother's orders, and leaving with her reciprocal offerings. On the long table all sorts of precious wines were set out along with English port, the best liqueurs, rum, brandy, candy, oranges, lemons, marinated lox. All afternoon my mother and my grown-up sisters kept filling plates with all these things. There was no set measure or number. Generally, a gift for a gentleman would consist of a bottle of wine or port and a piece of lox, some fish and a few oranges and lemons. To a lady they might send cakes, candies and fruit. People of lower station received honeycake, nuts and apples on a plate tied into a red kerchief.

I have a very vivid memory of one incident: It was the custom for the younger of two friends to send his gift first; on this occasion, my mother had forgotten to send a return gift to a young friend of our family. When she remembered it, late that evening, she got no sleep all night. First thing in the morning, she hurried to his house to apologize for the oversight, and as it turned out, she was right to go. He had indeed felt hurt and insulted.

The afternoon of coming and going of messengers, of sweets and delicacies for us children, was observed by our father as time for his nap. When he awoke, a steaming samovar of fragrant tea awaited him. He said the afternoon prayers, and then it was time for the great feast, the *sudeh*, which must begin before evening.

The great chandelier in the yellow parlor sparkled with candles, augmented by cheerful little candle flames in sconces all along the walls. The table was set with various chilled delicacies. Most particular attention was paid on this day to the drinks, quite an unusual thing for our household. It seemed almost as though Father considered it an especially pious act to get a bit tipsy on *Purim*.

One year, my sister and I played a trick that evening. We borrowed dresses from *nyanya* and the cook—too long, of course, and dragging on the floor—and came to the door as a poor woman and her daughter. I, the daughter, had been abandoned by my husband with an infant. We begged all good people to help us find the husband, so that I might not remain an abandoned woman, an *aguneh*, forbidden to remarry all the rest of my life.

They asked us where we came from.

Disguising our voices, we said, "From Krupziki."

Our demeanor was so quiet and serious that at first not even Mother recognized us, never mind the guests.

"What kind of imposition is this?" Father shouted. "How dare the butler let these people into the dining room?"

We begged for alms—either money or food—for we were hungry and had had nothing to eat all day. (All this in purest Yiddish.) We were invited to take places at the table, which we did with well-feigned shyness and reluctance, gawking at everything, admiring everything, heaving such deeps sighs, that the whole table rocked with laughter.

So effective was our disguise, so low the headdresses pressed over our foreheads down to our eyes, that we were able to carry the joke to its very conclusion.

My recollection, from earliest babyhood to the very end, is that there was food and drink and laughter at our house every *Purim* until daybreak. This once in the year, all kinds of pranks and hijinks were permitted, even encouraged. There seemed to be no boundaries at all—even at table all discipline was abolished.

Purim left you with the best memories, and also with tangible mementos. It might be a pretty neckerchief; or a little perfume bottle, to turn this way and that in your hand, reading the inscription over and over to yourself, although you knew it by heart—to be hidden away in a drawer and taken out on a suitable occasion.

PESACH

On the very next day, on *Shushan Purim*, my mother and the cook held a long conference concerning the great preparations for *Pesach*. The most important food—the beets for the borscht—must be put down on *Shushan Purim* in a kosher barrel. And only a few days later Vichne the flour merchant appeared in her inevitable fur coat, bringing samples of different batches of flour for our *matzehs* (unleavened bread).

My mother conferred with my eldest sister, the flour was examined, the various samples were baked into thin little crackers, until the specific type of flour had been selected.

My mother was so meticulous in every detail of her *Pesach* preparations that the cook was often beside herself, and got downright rude. My sisters prepared new finery for the holidays, in accordance with the latest fashion. Tailors, shoemakers and milliners were often in the house at that season. Voices were raised, sometimes very loud, about the "in" finery of the year.

The day before *Rosh Chodesh Nisan*, the first day of the spring month of *Nisan*, my eldest sister must sew a sack (my mother didn't trust the cook to be scrupulous enough as to its cleanliness). This sewing must be done a certain distance away from any bread or other leaven.

Very early in the morning Vichne had appeared with a bag of flour under her fur coat, on this occasion covered all the way up to her throat with a white apron. My sister brought the white fine linen sack into the dining room, followed by Vichne. We children, with devout concentration, helped count the measured pots of flour. So and so many pots of flour were counted off; then the sack was tied at the top and stored in a corner of the dining room, covered with a white linen cloth. We were forbidden to go anywhere near it with bread or any other kind of leaven.

Finally, on *Rosh Chodesh,* the *matzeh* baking began, with every member of the household, even Father and Mother, taking part. Our old retainer, Meshia Chetzicheh, would show up. She lived with her husband in a mud hut near our brick factory, where he worked transporting clay; but she spent most of her time at our house where we valued her knowledge of such things as pickling cabbage and putting up vegetables. A faithful soul, she would cheerfully have sacrificed herself for any one of us children. I never saw her wear anything other than a ragged dress of blue-striped cotton, and a pair of very large shoes, which slopped off her feet at every step. Even in mid-summer her feet seemed nearly frozen. Her bluish-brown, frozen face was wrapped in a cotton scarf, which once, long ago, had been white. A narrow band of red wool was tied about her forehead, and two ends of netting floated about her neck like wings. Sunk deep into her face, her small, dim eyes were always full of good will and gratitude. The repertoire of her thin, enormously wide lips appeared to consist of a single sentence, "Good people, warm me up and give me something to eat." Every fall my sisters had a quilted skirt made for her, as well as other warm things, but every attempt to warm up this thoroughly frozen creature failed.

Well then, Meshia Chetzicheh came. First she was given a plate of hot gruel in the kitchen. When she had eaten her fill and felt a little warmer, she crept to the half-open door of the dining room, poked in her head and reported for duty. My mother ordered her, first of all, to have a thorough wash. Then the spare figure, clothes and all, was covered with a long white shirt. Over her headdress a clean white cloth was wrapped, hanging all the way down to cover her chin and mouth, lending her a ghostly appearance. She sifted the flour for the *matzehs.*

Before she began she blessed my mother: "May you live this coming year with your husband and children in great joy." Then she sifted measure after measure of flour onto a specially prepared table. We children stood at a distance and watched awestruck as this apparition worked. Meshia Chetziche was strictly forbidden to utter a word, lest a stray drop from her lips moisten the flour.

When she had finished she spent the night in the kitchen; first thing in the morning she scrubbed the great red wooden chests in which clean linen was kept all year. Although these had had no contact with food of any kind, she went at it with her strong hands, scrubbing them to make them pure and fit to hold the *matzehs*. Next the wooden tables and benches had to experience Meshia Chetziche's powerful scrubbing brush. Nor did she spare the many dozen rolling pins and the baking pans, nor the enormous brass cauldrons: red hot iron rods were placed in these, and first boiling and then cold water was poured in to overflowing, to make them *kosher*. Later they were scrubbed once more till they glittered.

The most important part of baking *matzehs* is fetching the water from the well or river. It counts as a great *mitzveh* (meritorious deed). The *matzeh*-water utensils include two large wooden vats covered in gray linen, a pail with a big ladle, and two long poles.

First the great kitchen in the courtyard was thoroughly cleaned and the bricks of the baking oven made red hot and *kashered*. Next a great quantity of dry, resinous wood was brought in, which had been specially gathered and set aside over the course of the long winter by our trusty old watchman Feivele. And then finally, on the eve of *Rosh Chodesh Nisan*, a peculiar drama was enacted—sometimes in the courtyard at our well, other times all the way down at the riverfront! My father and my brothers-in-law betook themselves in person, the wooden vats hanging from poles across their shoulders, to the well or river. They drew the water, and with purposeful step carried it into the big kitchen and set it down on hay-covered benches. Merrily and cheerfully the young men stepped along; but Father's face was solemn. For him these customs were a sacred, serious matter, as they were especially pleasing to God.

The carefully wrapped and guarded sack of flour was also brought into the kitchen by my brothers-in-law. Meshia Chetziche was spending the night there so she could light the oven first thing in the morning. We all turned in early in order to be present when the baking began.

The next morning I pressed right close to the oven, admiring with fascination the skill of an old woman who pushed in the thin round *matzehs*, moved the half-baked ones to one side, gathered the finished ones in both hands and tossed them into a basket standing nearby, never breaking a single one of the brittle things.

Soon I was given my assignment: to hand the cut-up morsels of dough to women with rolling pins who stood around a tin-covered table.

Every year my older sister managed to be up ahead of me. This year she informed me proudly how many *matzehs* she had already rolled—some of them were even baked already. Furious with myself for getting up so late, I worked all the harder at being useful. I was somewhat consoled only after I had thoroughly worn myself out with running and standing around.

I washed my hands and went into the next room, where the dough was prepared. There a woman stood bent over a sparkling brass basin, kneading one piece of dough after another from the measured portions of water and flour without emitting a single sound. Here too I made myself useful. I begged the little boy who ladled in the water to let me take his place, and carefully and quietly I did his work. Now and again I glanced up at the kneading woman, who wore a long white shirt over her clothes just like Meshia Chetzicheh, and over that, an apron left untied at the waist. I helped until I was completely overcome by fatigue.

The baking took almost two whole days. My mother made tireless rounds to inspect the rolling pins of the women and scrape off the dough, which was considered to have become leavened and must not come in contact with the unleavened dough for *matzehs*. My brother and my brothers-in-law helped her with this work, using bits of broken glass. The young men also helped prick the *matzeh*; it occurred to no one that this might not be "men's work." Anything to do with *Pesach*, and especially with *matzeh*, is sacred work.

Next day my mother inspected each of the several thousand *matzehs*, discarding as *chometz* and unfit for the festival any that were bent or not completely baked through. Then the perfect *matzehs* were laid in perfect rows into the great red wooden chests, which were covered with a white cloth. Without looking, her eyes shut tight, Mother drew out one *matzeh* from under the cloth and broke off half, murmuring the appropriate blessing. Still without looking she cast the half *matzeh* back into the flames. She had "taken *challeh*"—to remind us of the share due to the priest.[1]

The remaining days until *Pesach* passed in endless preparations of the household and of our clothes and finery, rising nearer and nearer to peak intensity as the day of *Erev Pesach*, the eve of the festival, approached.

The night before *Pesach* is the time for removing all leaven. Mother went to the kitchen and made Cook hand over her wooden spoon and several goose feathers. She wrapped these in a white cloth, added a little wax candle, tied the whole thing with a ribbon and brought it to my father's room, where she put it on the window sill.

Following the evening prayer Father lit the candle and handed it to my brother, who was to be torchbearer, launching the year's campaign against *chometz* throughout the house. Every window sill, every corner where it was suspected that food might be lurking, was illuminated by my brother and inspected by my father. Pronouncing the appropriate blessing, he used the feather to brush any crumbs he found onto the spoon. We kids sometimes went around the house ahead of him, distributing crumbs on the window sills. These always moved him to expressions of the greatest astonishment, for on this day window sills had been dusted with special, meticulous care.

The next day the dishes were washed and under Mother's direction Shimon the server brought them into the dining room. Topsyturvy and in gay confusion, all over the floor, the table, the window sills, was everything from the precious porcelain service down to the last little copper casserole. It all had to be packed into enormous chests and taken up into the attic, so that the chests filled with *Pesach* dishes could be brought down.

---

[1] "Several thousand *matzehs*" seems exaggerated. Possibly several families baked their *matzehs* together.–ed. On this manner of "taking *challeh*," see the Editor's Afterword, p. 258.

Now the dining room was thoroughly cleaned once more and the window sills covered in white paper. The large dining table was pulled out to its full extension and covered: first with white cloth or paper, next a thick sheet of felt, then a layer of hay, and finally a quantity of gray linen. Only now could the *Pesach* dishes be unpacked. We waited eagerly for this moment, for each of us possessed a beautiful silver goblet that was in one of those chests.

But in addition there were other fascinating activities to watch, indoors and out, especially in the yard where the wooden tables and benches were set out to be "kashered" (made kosher): you poured boiling water over each of the pieces of furniture, rubbed it with a glowing iron, and then poured on cold water.

And there was a greater spectacle even than this. Father appeared at the kitchen holding yesterday's *chometz* crumbs in his right hand and ordered Feivele to bring bricks and dry wood. Quick as lightning the old man had it all there. He built a little oven of the bricks and laid the wood ready. My father placed the spoon with the crumbs upon the funeral pyre and ordered it lit. We ran back and forth trying to find a way to be helpful.

The wood caught at once, little flames showed on this side and that.

"Look, look, watch the feathers singe!" we shouted.

"The rag is on fire!"

Finally the flames combined to devour the spoon as well, and within ten minutes the auto-da-fé of the *chometz* was completed.

My father remained on the spot until every last wisp of ashes had been removed. It is forbidden even to step on the ash, so as to have neither pleasure nor use of it.

We skipped back into the dining room, where Shimon the *meshores* (servant) was busy unpacking the *Pesach* dishes, to help and to take possession of our *koyses* (wine goblets). But that *bocher* (young man) gave us a roguish smirk and informed us that we were not yet fit to receive them. We were dumbfounded.

In answer to our shocked question he said casually, "You haven't been kashered."

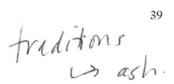

traditions
↳ ash.

"How do you mean 'kashered'?"

"Oh yes," replied our tormentor. "You've got to take some glowing pebbles in your mouth and roll them around. Then you rinse your mouth with cold water, then spit it out, and then you can touch the dishes."

Sobbing we burst into the kitchen where Mother was hard at work. She and Cook were discussing the preparation of the enormous turkey, which had already been slaughtered, plucked, singed, salted and given three thorough rinsings. Now it was lying on a board held fast by Cook as though she expected it to fly off, while Mother made the main incision with a large kitchen knife.

A golden-scaled pike, fresh from the Bug River, lay stretched to its full length on a freshly planed slab of wood. To the left was the freshly scrubbed kitchen table with various bowls, plates, forks and spoons; also a large basket of eggs and a pot of *matzeh* meal that my sister was sifting to get ready for the tarts, almond cake and so forth that would be baked later.

We were burning to ask Mother if Shimon was right; but her nonstop activity held us spellbound, while the horrifying prospect of those glowing pebbles drew from our breasts timid, choking sobs of fear. At last my younger sister begged me at all costs to ask Mother the question.

We sobbed out our tale of sorrow. At first she could make nothing of it. Then suddenly she thought she understood.

"What glowing pebbles?" she screamed. "Who put them in her mouth? Who has scalded herself with boiling water?" Only after lengthy explanations did she finally understand our trouble. Then she sent for Shimon and strictly forbade him to prattle such nonsense to us ever again.

Soon Shimon brought out a bowl of hard-boiled eggs, a plate of freshly grated horseradish (this is called *moraur*, and is meant to remind us of the bitter circumstances of our ancestors' lives in Egypt), several pieces of roast meat (the *zro'a*) as a reminder of the Paschal sacrifice in the Temple in Jerusalem, and a plate of salt water.

He also brought in the *shmureh* (guarded) *matzehs*, prepared from flour harvested in the presence of a rabbi and several Jewish witnesses, and guarded ever since against contact with moisture.

Mother covered all these foods with white cloths, leaving only the green salad to contrast with the unrelieved gleam of the white table cloth. Sparkling red wine in the crystal decanter was mirrored in the high polish of the silver candelabra and mirrored again in each crystal tumbler.

While she set the table and prepared all these symbols, Father kept popping in to make sure that nothing was being left out. To crown her labors, Mother sent for several feather beds and a white piqué blanket and prepared an elaborate armrest called a *hesebet*[1] to the left of Father's seat. For the young men similar armrests were prepared on two chairs beside their seats. (Was this a symbol of freedom from slavery or, possibly, a vestige of an oriental custom to eat festive meals half-reclined on cushions?)

The whole house breathed cleanliness and comfort.

And now it was time to dress up. Very shortly Mother appeared decked out in her best to light the festival candles. At that time she was young and pretty, her bearing modest yet self-confident. Her manner, her eyes, expressed the deep calm and peacefulness of a truly religious soul. She gave thanks to her Creator for His grace in permitting her and her loved ones to attain this festive day in good health.

Her costume was that of a wealthy patrician of the time, her bearing aristocratic. Aristocracy among Jews derives from the life of the spirit: study of the Talmud and love for God and man. To these, worldly wealth and honor were often added.

When Mother had lit the candles she recited a brief prayer, covering her eyes with both hands as is the custom. This gave us the opportunity to admire the precious rings sparkling on her fingers, reflecting the light of the candles in all the colors of the rainbow. One

---

[1] A shortened form of *hesebeh bet*—a "bed" on which to lean.–ed.

41

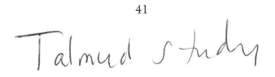

ring especially remains in my memory—it had a large yellow stone, surrounded by three rows of little diamonds.

Now my married sisters came in, richly dressed. Instead of narrow, gold-embroidered skirts it was the fashion in the 1840s to wear wide pleated skirts, but without those hoop skirts or bustles that do so little to enhance a youthful figure. My four unmarried sisters, down to the very youngest, were all wearing jewelry too.

From the age of twelve we girls had the obligation to light candles on the eve of every Sabbath and Holy Day. We gathered about the table, and all the candles were lit. At my father's place there burned two spermaceti candles, called *mah nishtanah* candles after the four questions that would be asked by the youngest at the table.

We were waiting for the men to return from the synagogue. Soon we heard Father's great "gut yom tov" (happy holiday) from the front door, filled with festive joy. He sent my brother for the *Haggadahs* (prayer books that tell the story of the exodus from Egypt), and blessed each one of his children. That night, Shimon the *meshores* (servant) ate with us, sitting proudly in a new caftan at the corner of the table, in fulfillment of the patriarchal tradition which makes everyone equal at the Seder—servant and master alike.

Father settled comfortably into his seat. He laid his magnificent snuffbox down beside the foulard handkerchief to the right of his place and began to read the *Haggadah*, asking Mother to hand him the individual dishes as needed. The younger men followed his example. When he asked for red wine, she filled his goblet, and my married sisters filled the goblets of their husbands. Our older unmarried sister filled the cups of all the other people at the table, including the children and Shimon the *meshores*. Each of the men had a complete *seder* plate and three *shmureh matzehs* at his place, all covered by a white napkin.

Father took his goblet in his right hand and made *kiddush*. (Every Jew is obligated to say this prayer at the onset of every Sabbath and Holy Day, over a cup of wine which must be of a certain size and most of whose contents are sipped at the conclusion of the prayer.) He drained his cup. Everyone at the table said "amen" and then followed

42

his example. Mother refilled his cup and the other women did the same for their husbands. The cups of everyone else at the table were filled with sweet raisin wine.

And so the *seder* ritual continued. I never lasted to the very end. I would wake up briefly in my room as my *nyanya* tucked me into bed, come bolt awake for a moment and then go blissfully off to sleep, awaking in the morning in the best mood in the world to a house decked in vernal splendor everywhere, revelling in the holiday and in glorious springtime. I got some tea with *matzeh,* and was put into a fresh dress so that I could run out into the meadow where my friends were waiting. That lovely, golden childhood in my parents' home .... It is still precious to me!

The women and men of the house had been in the synagogue since early morning, praying for dew. The Jewish people is by nature conservative. They still pray for dew even though they haven't had grain, grass and mead to worry about for nearly two thousand years. As Lord Beaconsfield once said, a people like this who still pray for dew and rain twice a year will surely possess their own land again. It does show how deep in their souls Jews carry their love for the land. The Law orders us first to plant a vineyard, then to plow a field, then to build a house, and only then to marry.

The noon meal consisted of four traditional courses. There had to be stuffed turkey neck. Next came the best and tastiest vegetables of the season, something a poor Jew could only dream of. These, accompanied by pepperfish and huge *kneidlach* (dumplings), made people very thirsty, and so there was lots of old brandy, red wine and *kvas* (applejack). After the meal there was all kinds of snoring in the bedrooms, the kitchens, and even the hayloft. The children played for walnuts and ran in the fields and meadows. Quiet reigned until six or seven when it was time for tea.

After tea, people went for a walk in the fresh air, the men with their men friends and the women with their women friends. Then back to the synagogue for the evening prayer. My mother did not go since she had to prepare a second *seder* table. Supper was not ready until about ten since nothing could be cooked that day until the stars

43

were out. We had bouillon or borscht and boiled chicken. (There was no roast served in the presence of the *zro'a*, symbol of the burnt offering in the Temple.) We were given apples and nuts to play with, and great efforts were made to keep the children awake so that the youngest could ask the Four Questions and all would be involved in a more detailed discussion of the Exodus from Egypt. The meal had to be completed before midnight, and so Father kept calling for the food and the details of the *seder* were followed more rapidly than the night before.

For my mother, the work continued for eight days, guarding the *shmureh*, the *matzehs* and the dishes. More than once there was trouble with servants who mixed up the dishes. I remember one incident: It was the eve of the last two days of the festival, which are again Holy Days. A goodly number of chickens and turkeys lay already *kashered*—ritually slaughtered, plucked, singed, soaked and salted. My mother came to the kitchen, took a big knife, and examined each fowl to make sure that no feed grain had remained inside to make it unfit for *Pesach*.

Sure enough! She found a grain of oats in the gullet of one of the turkeys. He and all his companions in misfortune were therefore *chometz* and must not be served. My mother was very annoyed. With a look full of mingled reproach and triumph she shouted at the cook, "Here! Here's the disaster, then, you clumsy thing. Where were your eyes? Were you blind when you were *kashering*? You wouldn't have caught it now, either. I thank God in His mercy that He helped me find the grain—you'd have fed us all *chometz*!"

All expense and effort had been wasted upon that batch of fowl. They were removed and a new batch was slaughtered, cleaned and *kashered*. Imagine the annoyance of the housewife. The day was well advanced, it was near supper time—but she could console herself with the feeling that God had preserved her from a sin. Strict observance of all the rules of *Pesach* is doubly important, for their violation is punished by premature death. And so the sentence of death fell upon another equal number of chickens and turkeys, though they raised a noisy protest in the courtyard.

Another time the serving man had handed the cook a plain *matzeh* instead of a *shmureh matzeh* to stuff the fish. A quarter hour before the meal my mother noticed it as she was arranging the fragrant slices. She fell into a passion of rage at the serving man, and the whole house rang with her righteous anger; neither my parents nor the *melammed* touched the delicious fish. Mother, Father, and the *melammed* ate only *shmureh matzeh* and had their own special set of dishes, while the rest of the household ate ordinary *matzeh*.

The last day of Passover had arrived. All the trouble and special precautions were at an end. In the dusk, the young people shouted in the synagogue courtyard, "Come for the *chometz borchu*" (*borchu* is the first word of the Evening Prayer). My father returned from the synagogue and made *havdoleh*, asking a blessing for the coming workdays over a cup of wine and thanking God for separating the workdays from Holy Days, darkness from light. He emptied the cup, pouring the last of the wine onto the table. Then he took a deep sniff of the cloves in their special container, held up his hands to the little braided candle and let its light shine through his fingers, and finally doused the candle in the puddle of wine.

Now we were free of the constraints which *Pesach,* with all its splendor, had imposed. Spring, and all our outdoor games, could begin in earnest.

In the house, however, there was still lots of work. All the Passover dishes, pots and pans had to be located and then put away. Shimon the *meshores* brought down the great chests and packed everything away again. Not even the leftover *matzeh* could be eaten.[1] In some Jewish homes a single round *matzeh* was hung on the wall by a little thread and left there all year as a memento.

---

[1] I have not been able to find any source for this notion.–ed.

COUNTING THE *OMER* AND *SHVUOS*

Right after the festival all the various kinds of grain in the storehouses were examined for mildew, which might develop while they were shut up for eight days, since it was quite hot in our region by that time of year. At our house we never ate last year's grain, called *yoshen*, but waited for *chodesh*, the new grain.[1]

For the first few weeks of spring our home lived under the cloud of *sfireh*. All concerts and visits to the theater were prohibited, as were weddings and the wearing of new shoes or dresses. Even if there was a heat wave, we were forbidden to soak our feet in cool water. Only on Friday afternoons was it permitted to take a warm bath, in the interest of cleanliness. All our jewelry, all our pearls and embroidered headbands, were put away. We wore simple, old, used clothing. My parents and siblings all refrained from their usual jokes and laughter during the entire time of *sfireh*. Often my mother promised to give us handfuls of nuts if we would remind her to count the *omer* at night. These reminders were completely superfluous, of course; she never forgot to count how many weeks and days of the *sfireh* had passed.

Rosh Chodesh Sivan (the first day of the month of *Sivan*) was followed six days later by the beautiful festival of *Shvuos* (The Feast of Weeks or Pentecost). This holiday, as we were told in *cheder*, commemorated the day on which Moses received the sacred Tablets of the Law on Mount Sinai. This is the only one of the Three Major Festivals on which you can eat anything anywhere. That's why Jews say *Shvuos* lasts only two days!

Three days before *Shvuos*, the *sfireh* mourning period ended and joy took its place. *Cheder* went on half-day schedule, and roasting and baking began again in the kitchen—especially buttery pastries since dairy products are favored on *Shvuos*. What was *Shvuos*, after all, without cheese *blintzes* with sour cream?

---

[1] On this custom, see the Editor's Afterword, p. 285 n. 9.

On *erev yom tov* (the eve of the festival) all the rooms were decorated with fresh greens and brightly illuminated.[1] We children were decked out in our party best, as was the table. When the men returned from synagogue we went in to supper. Warm, fresh spring winds blew into every room through the open windows. After each course the men read aloud a section of the *tikun Shvuos* (the special readings to be studied that night). Afterwards my brothers-in-law and their teacher withdrew to their study, where they spent the rest of the night completing the reading. The eldest did this without complaint, though the younger probably preferred to be doing something else. It didn't matter. The religious atmosphere in our house overruled any personal preferences—and this would continue even after the spirit of Lilienthal had already begun to buzz in young people's heads.

Early in the morning it was off to synagogue, for a festival service and the recitation of *Akdomus*, a festival hymn in Aramaic in honor of the Torah, chanted alternately by the cantor and the congregation. On the second day of *Shvuos*, the biblical Book of Ruth was read aloud, often until noon. Good cheer reigned at home—we drank fragrant coffee with our butter cakes and blintzes, and then went for walks outdoors.

SUMMER FAST DAYS

The days between *Shvuos* and the seventeenth day of the month of *Tamuz* were the most enjoyable, the most beautiful of the whole summer for a Jew of the first half of the nineteenth century. But there must not be too long a chain of festive days allotted to him—lest in an excess of high spirits he forget his Maker. I think that this is why a Fast Day follows every period of relaxation. The seventeenth day of *Tamuz*, at the height of the summer season, is a Fast Day. It inaugurates the "Three Weeks," which end in the Fast of the Ninth of *Av*

---

[1]   On the custom of decorating the house with greenery on *Shvuos*, see the Editor's Afterword, n. 9.

(*Tisho be-Av*) commemorating the destruction of the Temple in Jerusalem.

One Friday morning preceding *Shabbes Chazon*, the Saturday before *Tisho be-Av*, we were at the breakfast table when my mother appeared in the dining room carrying a wooden bowl in one hand and a brush in the other. She seemed solemn and at the same time deeply moved. Her bowl was filled with some kind of black stuff. Full of curiosity we watched her climb on the sofa and paint a black square right on the beautiful red wallpaper. We asked her what she was doing, and she explained to us that this spot was to serve us as *zeicher le-churben*, a reminder of the destruction of the Temple in Jerusalem: we lived in *golus* (exile), under the yoke of strangers.

I still remember how my father and the young men of the house took off their shoes on the eve of the ninth day of *Av* and sat on low footstools. Before them a servant set a low bench with the meal for the eve of the fast: hardboiled eggs rolled in ashes and eaten with hard ring-shaped rolls. There they sat, serious and full of emotion, their eyes as full of grief as though they personally had been among the witnesses to the destruction of the greatness and glory of the Temple. To this day, the past is alive for the pious Jew and he mourns deeply the loss of his old home. Then, in their stocking feet, they left for synagogue.

My mother and elder sisters remained at home with us. Low benches were brought in; candles were set on footstools and on chairs. We sat around my mother on the stools and read the Book of Lamentations. Mother wept, and quietly we wept with her. When some of the *kinos* (poetic laments) were read, our tears really flowed.

Of course the boys had their own special activities. *Kundesim* (street urchins) followed the grieving men on their way to synagogue and tossed burrs the size of small potatoes at their hair and at their stocking feet.

One year, there were special games to mark the day. My brother had arranged with a friend of his own age (he is now Dr. H. S. Neumark) to bring several hundred *cheder* boys out from the city to our suburb, Zamuchawicz, in order to observe the day in a fitting and dignified manner, using the empty lot next to our house to re-enact the battle over Jerusalem two thousand years before.

The "soldiers" arrived singly and in groups, varying wildly in size, age, and social position. In this army things like that were irrelevant. Each boy brought along his red-painted wooden sword (every Jewish boy had one), a bow and arrow set, a club or even a whip. (The bravest simply used their fists.) Generals and officers were chosen; the rest were foot soldiers.

My brother and his friend were elected kings. The generals wore paper stars and oak leaves and had wide, shiny paper ribbons diagonally across their chests in blue or red or white. Dark blue sugarloaf paper was twisted into pointed helmets, called *kreplach*, and trimmed with bunches of cock feathers. Strings of red berries worn around one shoulder served as the colonels' braid. Officers of lower rank wore cockades of big yellow camomile flowers in their hats.

The whole army was split in half, and each king took command of his forces and arranged them in battle formation.

The royal costumes were in striking contrast to those of their armies: One of the kings had a bath towel, the other a bed sheet across his chest, decorated with countless medals plucked from the fields and meadows: sunflowers, various white, yellow and red blossoms of all sizes. Each royal brow was adorned with a crown of hemp.

The two armies were roped off from one another, awaiting the signal to attack.

But which side should start?

One side began to scream, "*Shlach, shlach, shlach!* (Send out your men!)"

"My people are all sick," replied the other.

Then one warrior approached the king of the opposing army, took his hand and, raising an index finger, said to him, "The *malach* (angel) has sent you three places. Do you see fire? Do you see water? Do you see the sky?"

On hearing this last question the king must look up at the sky, while the messenger made good his escape across the cordon between the two lines.

If he reached his lines without being captured, his side began the battle. The war began with bows and arrows, and swords; but as these broke under the first clash of arms, the soldiers depended mostly upon their fists. A quarter of an hour passed without a decision, but with a tremendous increase in howling and yelling.

Then one of the kings waved a white handkerchief on a white stick, shouting, "Enough! Stand! Cease fire!"

But the wild youngsters ignored him and kept on beating on the backs and heads of the weaker side. The game was turning nasty, and it took some serious doing to get the boys to stop. Most left the field of battle with marks of honor—black eyes, nosebleeds or bruised shins. The kings comforted their brave heroes, and we girls who had witnessed the battle ran to the house for fresh water, towels and tablecloths to perform the role of Sisters of Mercy, washing and drying the wounded limbs.

Once quiet was more or less restored the leaders began to organize the triumphal march. Back into the house we went to provide the necessary: a great brass cauldron, the brass tray of the samovar, some copper casseroles.

The soldiers stretched paper over their combs for a makeshift wind instrument; some had little wooden penny whistles.

The whole army was drawn up again, though many a soldier was hard put to it to stand upright. No one wanted to miss his share in the ceremony.

The marching band was recruited; the kings took up a majestic posture. Acknowledging the ecstatic "hurrah" of the crowd, they inclined their heads most graciously.

Then the procession began. Beaten by someone's mighty fist the brass cauldron made a deafening racket, accompanied by the booming of the casseroles. The shrill squeaks of the penny whistles sounded like a faint protest, contrasting with the odd sound of the massed combs. The voices of the troops singing with all their might added to the harmony. Slowly, stepping to the music, the triumphal march moved forward. The two kings had acquired the commanding presence to rule over their fellows.

We girls accompanied the parade, clapping delightedly. The march went along our garden fence and past the house and then dispersed. The "battle" was the main topic of conversation in town for days afterwards. Despite the bloodied heads, our parents were very pleased with our observance of tradition with such war games.

It seems that the customs of the Jewish people are designed to keep a balance between joy and sorrow. Each day of fasting is followed closely by a season of happiness. Thus *Tisho be-Av* is followed by *Shabbes Nachmu*, the Sabbath of Consolation.

My parents believed with an unshakable faith in the prophetic promises that the Temple would rise again in even greater glory. Mother Jerusalem would rise in youth and beauty out of the midst of ruin. Hope and illusion were their shield against despair— in those days, suicide was very rare among Jews. The word of God and their faith in the hereafter were their consolation. Here is one of the songs our mother taught us:

> *The Jew, the Jew, a thing of wonder!*
> *Knock him to the ground, you can't keep him under.*
> *His people least numerous, it is clear,*
> *Yet you'll find him there, you'll find him here.*
> *Climb to the heights, there he'll appear,*
> *Plunge to the depths, he's there, never fear!*
> *Retreat into your castles, still he'll be near.*
> *Creep into hovels and you'll find him there!*
> *Persecuted, tortured, bloodied, in pain,*
> *Faithful and steadfast he rises again.*
> *Pay him honor, value him!*
> *One thing his heart keeps telling him.*
> *As, frightened, he rises, he will always say:*
> *Whatever my suffering, God will repay!*

Another song she taught us was an allegory in a mixture of Polish and Hebrew. The latest theory proposed by Russian Jewish scholars has it that Russian Jews originally spoke only Russian with an admixture of Hebrew, and similarly that Polish Jews mixed Hebrew into

51

their local language. This theory is proposed in the recent collection of folksongs published by Saul Ginzburg in St. Petersburg.[1]

The recurrent theme in each of these songs was that at present Jews were expiating the sins of their fathers, and that God would raise them up again. As my mother sang these songs her eyes shone, and she assured us with deep serenity that the prophecy would one day be fulfilled. Only in my own maturity did I learn to appreciate how fervently she prayed, and to understand the reviving power of such pure, total faith in God. I see her standing before me, her eyes closed in deep contemplation, her arms relaxed at her sides, removed from all trivial earthly cares, softly reciting the *Shmoneh Esreh* (Eighteen) prayers. Her lips hardly moved, but her whole face was alive with the emotions of her praying soul: devout submission, consciousness of sin, entreaties for forgiveness, and faith in the mercy of the Lord.

ROSH HASHONOH

Shabbes Nachmu restored a cheerful mood to Jewish life; now we made up for the privations of the period of mourning. Amusements and weddings had been forbidden; now everyone rushed to bind their sons and daughters with the golden chains. There was no time to waste, for the month of gaiety would be followed by *Elul,* the month of the withered leaves and rising storms of autumn, the season of blowing the ram's horn every day following the morning prayer. The ram's horn was a call to concentration and introspection, examination of the deeds of the year, confession and remorse. The month was filled with fasting and castigation, fervent prayers to the Creator and pious undertakings.

In most Jewish homes a row of covered tin boxes was hung on the wall, usually near the dining-room *mezuzeh.* One of these was called the *Eretz Yisroel pushkeh* (box for the Land of Israel), and the money went to support Talmud academies in Palestine as well as the old peo-

---

[1]   On this collection, see the Editor's Afterword, p. 281.

ple who had emigrated to Jerusalem. They intended to die there and be buried in hallowed soil which was said to preserve the body from mortal decay. When the Messiah came, it would arise fresh and strong from the grave. (Observant Jews who lived in Europe would have little sacks of this powerful Palestinian earth scattered into their graves.) The money was collected once a year by a *meshulach,* a messenger from *Eretz Yisroel,* who traveled throughout the Russian Empire. Whenever he came to Brest he would stay with us. A sturdy man with a dark, sunburnt face and intelligent eyes, he would tell us all about Palestine at the dining table. For us these strange stories were like fairy tales.

The second box was the *Reb Meir Baal ha-Nes pushkeh* (charity box of Rabbi Meir the miracle maker). If any potential misfortune loomed or if someone was ill, you put in eighteen kopeks, rubles or other coins depending on your means and the occasion—eighteen is the numerical value of the Hebrew letters of the word *chay* (life).

We children were not particularly troubled by the heavy days of repentance. We enjoyed the beautiful autumn days and gobbled down the ripe fruit that we bought by the apron-full for the copper coin our mother gave us each day. In our own garden the fruit was ripe as well, tree branches hung low and the vegetables grew high, in the most wonderful colors. The cabbage was ripe. My eldest sister had a great knack for making what looked like a tallow candle from the stem. She cleaned it, rounded it off, and stuck a splinter of wood, blackened with soot, into the top, so that it looked like a candle. Late in the afternoon she would give this to the cook or the servant to light. We children watched from afar and giggled as the splinter of wood caught fire for a moment, but then went out, much to the person's disgust.

Such indoor hijinks were our chief pleasures once it was too cold to play outside for long. The days became shorter and grayer. We went to *cheder* later in the mornings, and often we had to play indoors there, driven inside by the autumn rain. At home it became quieter; our parents and grown-up siblings got more and more serious the closer the end of the month of *Elul* approached, bringing the troubled period of

53

sliches, when penitential prayers are intoned before the first light of dawn.

The New Year Festival was very serious and holy, but it was celebrated with joy. All sorts of puddings were baked, sweets and honey and sugar were prepared. The white bread was baked in a round shape to represent the round year. The women had white dresses that they wore only at New Year's and on the Day of Atonement.

On the eve of *Rosh Hashonoh* the women of the family lit and blessed many candles. The mood was festive, though a certain seriousness lay on all spirits. People cried at the evening prayer in synagogue; when father came home, his voice was hoarse with weeping. But soon the holiday spirit was restored. He blessed us cheerfully and made *kiddush*.

We all poured plenty of water over our hands, dried them, sat down at the table in silence and kept up with our father while he said a blessing over the two large loaves that waited under a cover. He cut one of these in two, and from one part he cut a slice which he dipped in honey and softly mumbled a blessing. Until he ate the first bite neither he nor anyone else could speak at the table. Now the children each got their share of the *mautzi* (the piece of bread over which the blessing was said) with honey, and then we enjoyed a rich holiday meal. No matter how early I got up the next morning, I don't remember a single time that I saw my mother or the others who were going to the synagogue. They were all already there, coming back at one or two o'clock in the afternoon exhausted but in a lofty mood under the influence of the lofty *piyutim* (poetic hymns) specially written for that day. My father and the young men used to sing these prayers again at table, crying as they sang. On this day the afternoon nap was omitted, for on this Holy Day there must be more prayer than eating and sleeping. After *mincheh* we went to *tashlich*, down to the river, said a short prayer and cast bread crumbs—our sins, as it were—into the water. My father didn't take this custom seriously and did not take part in it.

From the river, again to the synagogue to say the evening prayer. At home the women lit the candles again. Father came from the synagogue, blessed us again and made *kiddush* over the cup of wine and recited the *shehecheyanu* blessing over a piece of fruit. This is a blessing over some fruit of a kind not yet enjoyed in the course of the summer. My mother usually bought watermelon or cantaloupe or pineapple for this purpose, fruits very rare in our region.

YOM KIPPUR

I still think back with awe and wonder to *Erev Yom Kippur* in the home of our parents. With what seriousness and devotion they forgot all worldly concerns then, and lived entirely in prayer! At dawn, each man in the house took a rooster, each woman a hen and recited the *kapores* (atonement) prayer. Then they swung the birds three times around their heads and tossed them away to be slaughtered and eaten. The bread for *Yom Kippur* was baked in the form of a ladder: step by step each Jew must draw closer to Heaven to find forgiveness and grace.

Another sacred obligation was the preparation of the *Yom Kippur* candle. Early in the morning of *Erev Yom Kippur* the old *gabete* Sarah appeared. (A *gabete* was an old woman who had voluntarily made it her life's task to do good works among the sick and poor, and for the recently deceased.) She brought a whole stack of *tchines*, little prayer books for women, in Yiddish. She also brought an enormous ball of wick thread and a large piece of wax. My mother would eat nothing until the candle was finished, so that her spirit would be softer and she would be more inclined to weep.

Sarah and my mother began the work by saying many of the prayers in the *tchines*, weeping intensely. Then Sarah put the ball of wick thread into her apron pocket and the two stood facing one another about three feet apart. They passed the thread from one to the other while my mother, in a tearful voice, spoke the names of all the members of the family who had died, mentioning their good deeds; for each one a thread was added to the wick, until it was good and thick. In the same way, all the living members of the family were remembered. If someone was very dangerously ill, it was the custom to measure the cem-

55

etery along its four boundaries with a thread and then to use this thread for the *Yom Kippur* candle.

That afternoon we ate lots of fruit, as the Law requires, so that we could recite one hundred blessings. Then we bathed and washed ourselves and put on white clothing, so as to appear before the Eternal Judge in purity and dignity. During the afternoon prayer people beat their breasts and wept, and the men hired the sexton to beat *malkes* (lashes) on their backs. I remember that they all came home with bloodshot eyes. We young people and children ate our evening meal in silence and dread. Then we all took off our shoes and the men drew a long white *kittel* over their clothes, tied with a silver cloth belt. (This white holiday robe would later serve as the Jew's shroud.) They put on silver cloth caps, tossed coats over their shoulders and, for the third time on that day, left for the synagogue.

Before he left the house my father blessed each child and grandchild, even the smallest, still in the cradle. His tender words mingled with his tears and the tears of the child whose head was bowed beneath his hands. All of the servants came and stood at the door, weeping and begging each other to *mauchel*—to forgive. Even my mother's voice trembled as she begged all her servants to forgive her in case she had slighted them or hurt their feelings in the course of the year. The souls of the grown-ups who went to *Kol Nidre* as well as those of the children who stayed at home—all were turned to Heaven.

After our parents had left for synagogue, we children gathered about our eldest sister, Chashe Feige, our protectress and teacher. She said the evening prayer. We stood beside her full of devout attention and did not budge. I heard her sob, and I would feel very anxious. At nine o'clock our sister told us to go to bed but we all felt so sad that we begged her to sit with us, and she stayed until we were asleep.

The next day it was dreary at home while the adults were in the synagogue. The shutters were closed, none of the rooms were set to rights, the clay pots still stood about with the stumps of last night's candles sputtering in them and filling the air with a heavy fragrance. It was noon before we children had any food. We ate cold *kapores* (the chicken from the day before) and white bread and tea, and then our friends arrived. Slowly our spirits lifted. At dusk the house was set to rights, many candles were lit, the samovar prepared, and wine and a braided *havdoleh* candle made ready. At seven o'clock the grown-ups returned exhausted from the synagogue. None touched any food or drink until they had washed and combed their hair, things forbidden in the morning.

After *havdoleh*, regardless of the fact that their stomachs had taken on neither food nor drink all day, the family piled into a mixture of sweet, sour, salty and bitter foods. All trace of tiredness disappeared. All faces glowed with inner peace and contentment. The *yomim nauro'im*, the days of solemnity, were over for a whole year.

We children also felt the difference between last night and this night. I was never too rambunctious or mischievous and I liked solitude, but the oppressive mood of *Erev Yom Kippur* and *Erev Tisho be-Av* tortured me quite badly.

At the head of the long table, leaning in a great easy chair, my father began singing the great, poetic prayers of the day softly to himself. My brothers-in-law and the other young men at the table joined him, and soon the synagogue cantor dropped in, and a number of other guests. Till midnight clear and joyful voices filled the house.

It occurred to no one to retire early after the exertions of the day, although you had to be in the synagogue again at daybreak, in order to confound the slanders of Satan. Otherwise he could turn to the Creator and say, "See, Lord, yesterday You forgave Your people their sins, and today nobody shows up. Your house is empty!" But Satan shall have no triumph over the Chosen People and so all the devout were in the synagogue very early in the morning (the service being referred to as "In God's Name").

They were there only a short time because only the everyday service was said and directly from there my father went to pick an *esrog*, a citron, and a *lulov*, a palm branch, and came home very happy if he had succeeded in finding an *esrog* completely without blemish, called a *mehuder*. In 1838 a fruit like that could cost five or six rubles since

57

it had to come from Corfu. Supply was limited and shipping difficult. Nevertheless every young man in our house received an *esrog* for himself.

One of these fragrant, magnificent fruits was wrapped very carefully in soft hemp and put into a silver dish, to be used in the course of the eight days of *Sukkos* (Tabernacles). The palm branch, myrtle, and willow branch, which belong with it in accordance with the Law, stood in a large earthen pitcher filled with water.

And the house was bright and cheerful again. We ate, drank, laughed, and chatted to our hearts' desire. I often heard it said that during the four days between *Yom Kippur* and *Sukkos*, the sins of the Jews aren't noticed and are not counted by God.

These four days were full of jokes and laughter. Many of these jokes were about the *zogerkes*. In the 1840s there were among the simple folk many women who did not know how to pray in Hebrew. Still, they felt a great need to pray on the Sabbath, and especially on the High Holy Days. And there were literate women who made a business of their learning, praying aloud for the others for a small fee. Such a woman was called a "zogerke" (literally, a "reciter"). In the smaller Jewish towns there might not be such a woman, and then a man (a "zoger") had to crawl into a barrel that was put right in the middle of the women's section. From the midst of this fortress, surrounded by women, he read out the prayers. As may be imagined, this custom often resulted in comical incidents. That barrel was an inexhaustible source of new jokes.

On *Yom Kippur* the *zogerke* was supposed to recite the prayers in a tearful voice, so as to bring the women's gallery to weeping and remorse. Now in our community there was a woman, the wife of the butcher, who was hard of hearing. She begged the *zogerke* to pray a little louder: she'd give her an extra large liver from the shop if she would do it for her. The *zogerke* answered in her weeping prayer voice, weaving her reply into the recitation: "The same with the liver, the same without the liver." A moment later the men were startled to hear the entire women's gallery sob aloud in full voice: "The same with the liver, the same without the liver."

A little while later one of the women was on her way home and met another woman just arriving at the synagogue.

"Where are they? What prayer are they up to?"

"Nu, the prayer about the liver."

"Liver? Last year we didn't say anything like that!"

"Today, *efsher* (maybe), because it's a leap year…"

SUKKOS

During the next three days, until *Sukkos*, we were free. We didn't have to study and, it seemed to me, even the young men neglected their daily prayers a bit. We had not been to *cheder* at all since *Rosh Hashanah* because vacation for Jewish children lasted until the month of *Cheshvan* (which began sometime in late September or October).

Right after breakfast the *sukkeh* (festival booth) was inspected. This was a roomy, long, high gazebo with large windows, which was not used at all during the rest of the year. It had to be washed and decorated and made comfortable, and the servant began this work immediately.

On the day of the eve of the festival all the carpets in the house were carried into the *sukkeh*, and the young people hung them on the walls under the direction of my father. Mirrors were brought, the furniture from the dining room, and even the chandelier. On the eve of the first day of the holiday everyone dressed festively. Mother and the young women lit the candles in the large, silver candelabra, and silently recited their devout prayers.

After that we all sat down very comfortably on the chairs about the table and admired the decorated *sukkeh*. The movable ceiling had been taken away and replaced with branches of fir trees; the blue night sky, glittering with silver stars, smiled in through the branches, casting a fairy-tale splendor.

Mother, festively dressed and wearing precious jewelry, sat among her married and unmarried daughters who were all richly adorned. Then the men came home from the synagogue and around the table we formed the exquisite picture of the Jewish patriarchal family of those days. In their long black satin caftans and wide satin belts, their costly tall sable hats and shining young faces they really looked better than the youth of today in evening jackets and white sashes with their blasé, bored expressions.

Father blessed us, all washed their hands, said the blessing, and took a piece of *barches* (white bread for Sabbath and holy days) dipped in honey. The evening meal began with pepperfish and ended with vegetables. Many, for whom the evening air of autumn was too cool, left the *sukkeh*; a few stayed on to chat.

On the following morning, the first day of the festival, there was an especially solemn service. It was an imposing sight to see the men stand in their places, row upon row, holding the slim palm branch in their right hand, and a fragrant, golden *esrog* in their left, to sing the Song of Praise, the *Hallel*, and then to watch the *hakofes*, the procession around the synagogue, led by the cantor.

Around one o'clock we all went back home. Many guests arrived and were offered wine and sweets. Everyone spent the afternoon as he wished; some slept, some went for walks, but no one forgot to be back in the synagogue for prayers by five o'clock. The second day proceeded almost exactly like the first.

On the middle four days of the holiday (*chol ha-mau'ed*), it is permitted to ride, to do business, and to shop, but the Jews of those days never did any of these things. Even the poorest artisans kept their shops closed, relaxing, eating and enjoying themselves.

On the fifth day of *chol ha-mau'ed*, *Hoshano Rabbo*, the night is spent once more in reading certain sections of *Mishna*.[1] There is a folk saying that on that evening headless shadows of those destined to die during the coming year would appear. On this night, Jews believed heaven opens up so that pious, God-fearing Jews can see all its glory. If at that moment you quickly call out "kol tov" (everything good), every wish will be fulfilled.

---

[1] Wengeroff is mistaken about which texts were studied at night on *Hoshano Rabbo*. *Mishna* was studied on *Erev Shvuos*, *Mishne Torah* (Deuteronomy) on *Hoshano Rabbo.*–ed.

On this night the *shammes*, the caretaker of the synagogue, pre-
pares *hoshanehs*, three little willow branches tied together into a little
bunch, and all hold this in their hands during the morning prayer.
This *Hoshano* prayer is said with great piety accompanied by copious
tears. At the end the leaves of the willow branches are beaten off.

The white bread is baked for this day in the shape of a bird. Folk
wisdom has it that on this day it is finally decided in Heaven who will
live or die during the year, and this bird flies up to Heaven and brings
back the decision on a scrap of paper.

The eighth day of *Sukkos* is called *Shmini Atzeres*. The morning
synagogue service begins very early to allow for the especially rich,
imaginative poem, the *Geshem* prayer, in which we implore the heavens to send down rain and which, while elevating the spirt of the worshippers, lengthens the service by more than an hour.

Shmini Atzeres lunch is the last meal in the *sukkeh*. By now, the
weather was changeable and sometimes very cold. Sometimes it even
snowed and we had to wear fur. Nevertheless, we persisted and took
all meals, even tea, in the *sukkeh* until the last day. Old and young, even
we children, observed the religious ordinances very strictly because
our parents understood how to maintain their wishes and their will in
the household.

Then, following the prescribed prayer closing the last meal in the
sukkeh, the furniture, piece by piece, was brought back into our living
quarters and the booth which just a short time before had been so
splendidly decorated now stood empty and forlorn, a symbol of all
this-worldly splendor.

The last day of *Sukkos* is called *Simches Torah* (The Rejoicing in
the Law), when Jews celebrate the Torah, the eternal and precious
treasure of the people. On this one day of the year there were no limits:
you could see drunken Jews in the streets, and things got a little wild
even in our house. My father and all of the guests considered it a *mitzveh* to get a little tipsy at the table, and my parents allowed the young
men to dance in a playful, high-spirited way. Father joined whole-
heartedly in the religious songs for the day.

Simches Torah had another special meaning for my father. As I have mentioned, his main occupation was the study of the Talmud, especially when he had suffered serious financial reverses. At such times he would turn his back on the world, flee into his study and live only *al ha-tauro ve-al ha-avaudo,* in study and prayer. When a Jew finished studying a tractate or, especially, the entire Talmud (*gantz shas*) he would make a *siyum,* a celebration of finishing. My father would defer his until *Simches Torah,* when the colorful activities continued until evening. After *mincheh* and then *havdoleh* we all sang *zmiraus* (religious songs). The samovar bubbled and steamed on the tea table until late at night.

Simches Tora ends the High Holy Days, although the day afterwards, called *Issru Chag,* is also treated as a holiday. The table remained set as for a holiday, the noonday meal was taken early and consisted of delicious cold leftovers from the day before—pepperfish, roast turkey and so forth. Only the borscht (a soup made from pickled red beets) was made fresh. And so, slowly, life returned to normal.

ALMS ON *ROSH CHODESH* (THE NEW MOON)

We had a special way of observing *Rosh Chodesh* in my parents' home. Each month, on the day before *Rosh Chodesh,* beggars—old, sick, half-naked men and women dressed in rags with distorted faces, young people, girls, and children—came to our house to get their *Rosh Chodesh* money. Many people fasted on this day as well as every Monday and Thursday, distributing alms among the poor.

On these days you could see the *gabetes* in action—those religious souls, good, selfless women, whose life work it was (and still is in Lithuania) to visit home after home in the poor districts of the town to reduce the want and misery there.

In pairs they hurried through the streets, begged food from the business people and shopkeepers and came to private homes to beg money or food, old clothes, and so forth. I have a lively memory of one *gabete* in particular who came to us often. She was an angel of great goodness and soul. Her name was Itkeh *die hefterkeh* (the embroiderer). She told my mother of all the misery and poverty in the city. She said that pearls and diamonds lay about the streets, but few bothered to pick them up. What she meant was that there were so many opportunities to do good among the poor, and so few people took the trouble, although these are the only jewels you can take along to the other world when you die.

My mother distributed a considerable sum on *Rosh Chodesh*. Old men and women got a coin of three Polish *groshen*, that is one and a half Russian *kopeks*. The younger the poor person the less, down to one *groshen*. Children were given only a *pruteh* (penny). This coin was a third of a Polish *groshen* and thus a sixth of a *kopek*, and was minted in Brest-Litovsk by the Jewish Town Council, with the permission of the Government.

I remember that this *pruteh* was given only to poor people. It was not valid tender in business. At first it was cast in lead with the Hebrew inscription "pruteh achas" (one *pruteh*). But it was misused, and so it was done away with. After that it was printed on parchment about three inches long and an inch and a half wide, with the same inscription. Soon this parchment money was done away with also, replaced by a medium-sized wooden button, with the word *pruteh* impressed in sealing wax in a little groove.

The following day, *Rosh Chodesh* itself, we considered a half-holiday. In synagogue half of the *Hallel* was said, at home there was good food at noon, and all day long the work of the hands was forbidden. *Rosh Chodesh* played an important role in Jewish life. It was customary to use it as the terminus for renting apartments and hiring servants, and important business of the household was scheduled for this day, especially the "setting of the geese": Thirty or forty geese were forced together into a small cage so that they could hardly move. They were given a great deal to eat but very little to drink, to fatten them. This was done to them for exactly twenty-one days so they would get very fat and their liver would get very large and then they were slaughtered. It was believed that if you varied this procedure by so much as a single day the whole effort would be in vain.

The geese were imprisoned on *Rosh Chodesh Kislev*. On the twenty-first day of *Kislev* the slaughterer came with his assistant, drew the great slaughtering knife from its leather shaft and made it incredibly sharp, tested its sharpness on his fingernail, and then together with the cook and the night watchman complete with lantern, he would enter the goose pen to carry out their death sentence. Of course before he did this he said the prescribed blessing. The work took an hour.

The slaughtered geese were dragged into the kitchen, where some poor women plucked them, singed them, cleaned them and salted them for the required full hour. Then cold water was poured over them three times and they were kosher. The noise in the kitchen and in the whole house was very great. It was important to hurry, because for *Chanukkah* much goose fat, goose liver, very good patés of liver, and especially the tasty *gribbenes* (cracklings) were required. The wonderful aroma of the stewed giblets filled the house.

There was a superstition or mystical tradition that the slaughterer must eat a limb, foot or head of the fowl he had slaughtered every day from *Rosh Chodesh Kislev* to *Rosh Chodesh Adar*—that is, for three months—or he would go lame. We always left him the left leg of every goose; however, since he couldn't eat all that, a soup was made out of the many little feet he had to eat.

There was also great significance in the rendering of the goose fat. This had to be done in total silence, either before break of day or late at night, to avoid the evil eye. Otherwise it would all run out of the pot. But if the rendering was done by one silent person, then, it was believed, the good spirit of the house would arrive in the shape of a dwarf and make the fat rise over the top of the pot; if you decanted it into another vessel, it would keep on growing—there would be more and more of it—until all the empty vessels, even the great water pot in the house, would be filled. After that the dwarf would disappear.

CHANUKKAH

By the Sabbath before *Chanukkah* the *menorah* (*Chanukkah* lamp) must be polished and ready, and we children attended the polishing, inspecting each little part with pleasure. Our *menorah* was made of silver filigree, shaped like a sofa. On the back sat an eagle, and above that a life-sized bird with a little crown upon its head. On either side of the sofa there were small silver cylinders for the candles. Upon the seat were eight miniature jugs filled with oil—in memory of the little jug of oil that was, so the story goes, found in the Temple in Jerusalem after the Maccabees had driven off our enemies. Because, miraculously, this little jug managed to supply enough oil to light the Temple lamp for eight whole days and nights, we Jews celebrate the Feast of the Maccabees every year to remind us of the miracle. It is primarily a festival of victory.

With high anticipation we awaited the first night of *Chanukkah*. While Father was at evening prayers that night, Mother filled the first little jug with oil and threaded wicks into the little cylinders. She stuck candles into the two side candelabras, and another candle into the crown of the little bird. We children stood about and followed every move with rapt devotion.

Then Father performed the ritual of kindling the first light in the *Chanukkah menorah:* He spoke a blessing, lit a thin wax candle, and used it to kindle the wick in the first little jug of oil. Now it was holiday time—while the oil in the jug burned, it was forbidden to do any work.

On the fifth night my mother invited all our friends and relatives. That was the night she gave us the *Chanukkah gelt* we had been waiting for—usually bright new copper coins. You stayed up later than usual that evening, and played cards longer, and a rich supper was served. The invitations read, "You are invited for *latkehs*." The main course of the meal was a kind of pancake made of buckwheat flour with goose fat and honey; but it can also be made of wheat flour, yeast, preserves and sugar. These *latkehs* are very tasty. There was a kind of punch concocted of beer, oil and a little sugar. Also narrow slices of black bread, toast sprinkled with sugar and ginger, roast goose with its side dishes including sauerkraut and pickles. At the end there was a rich dessert of sweets and fruit that left a deep dent in our cellar and pantry. Each guest was expected to taste, judge—and praise—the various dishes.

65

It was a day of rejoicing for us children. Even we little ones were allowed to play cards that night. Feeling like millionaires, we dug out all our copper coins and settled down around the table with our little cousins. Our parents, the grown-up sisters and brothers, and some friends who had dropped in formed a larger circle.

You could read the outcome of the card games in our faces; some lost all their *Chanukkah gelt* and worked hard to hold back the tears. The only hope was another evening of cards, when with better luck you might refill your pockets.

On such evenings my father skipped even learning Talmud and sat down to cards although, like my mother, he had no idea of the rules of any game.

Another popular game was *dreidel*, also known as *goor*. Dreidels were little pointed dice cast of lead, which could be spun on their point like a top. On each side there was a letter. If your *dreidel* came to rest on *nun*, you lost; *shin*, you left your stake in the pot; *heh*, you took half the pot; but if you got *gimel*, that was *goor*. Then you took the pot.

From my description, a young person today might get the impression that life in a Jewish house of the old days was unbearably strict. Not so. The Jews of that time enjoyed many pleasures, quiet enjoyments—but always in their own house and within the circle of the family. We didn't run around to ballrooms or journey to faraway spas. We lived quietly, well, and long. We gave to God what was His and took from life what gave us pleasure.

Life was full of deep solemnity and symbolism, much more so than social life and customs today. Of course, today's manners are also meant to bind people together and link individuals into higher forms of community. But such community seems undeniably pale in comparison to the strong social bonds prescribed by Jewish Law and achieved by the Jews of those days. They went surety—they were *orev*—one for another. They vouched for each other. Expressions like *kol Yisroel chaverim* (all Jews are friends) and *acheinu bnei Yisroel* (our Jewish brothers) really meant something!

This was the reason that Jewish free thinkers who openly transgressed a religious commandment were reproached by people. For example, on the Sabbath one was supposed to walk only a limited distance and not carry even a cane, an umbrella or a handkerchief unless there was an *eruv* (a symbolic marking of territory). If a free thinker was seen on the streets carrying such "burdens," he was met with hostile stares. He was offending the basic idea of the Law of Moses—the responsibility of the individual toward the community. After all, the entire people would have to atone for the sin of the individual.

FIRST CHANGES

נראה אם יפרחה הגפן פתה הסמדר הנצו הרמונים שם אתן אדדודי לי.

Tsirl Waletzky

LILIENTHAL AND THE BEGINNING OF ENLIGHTENMENT
[1838–1842]

I was fortunate to witness the liberal reforms of Czar Nicholas I which brought about the spiritual and even physical regeneration of Lithuanian Jewry. Yes, there were religious wars fought within the Jewish family, but we have made enormous progress, and one cannot but admire—and bless—the ideas that lay behind the legal reforms of that time. Just remember the mostly uncultivated, poverty-stricken Jews of the 1840s and compare them to the Lithuanian Jews of the 60s and 70s, numbering so many men of completely European culture, men whose great achievements in the most diverse fields of literature, science and art, were acknowledged with secular honors and titles.

In the late 1830s the bulk of students in Brest, as in all Lithuania, was made up of *yeshiva bochrim* (lads). While their religious and intellectual development was strictly regulated at great expense to the community, their physical needs were met more haphazardly, and they usually looked weak and impoverished. For their daily food, their clothes and their shelter, they were dependent upon the generosity of the townsfolk. At best, they were given a mid-day meal, but even that was not available every day. They slept on the hard wooden benches in the Houses of Study. And they got their always-out-of-season clothes from generous citizens. In this way they eked out a living until they were twenty when they married, the good talmudists among them sometimes quite well.

These *bochrim* were divided into three classes according to the level of their knowledge, and my parents always had one or another of these as our guest at the mid-day meal. The oldest was Shamele, a quiet, clever but clumsy blond youth with good-natured blue eyes, who always wore, summer and winter, the same long caftan with torn elbows. The second, Fishele, had black eyes and was always lively. The third and youngest was Motele, a quieter, more thoughtful young man.

Most of these young men came to study in Brest from the surrounding towns and villages. They tended to be naturally witty and

71

quiet, and they performed all kinds of services in the houses where they took their mid-day meal. Hence they were well situated during the period of spiritual upheaval associated with Lilienthal to sneak Enlightenment (that is, *apikursish* or heretical) books to the young people in the city. Often one or another of them crept into our yard at twilight, sneaking in like a cat, with a package of such intellectual contraband. He would head directly for the stairs leading to the study of my brothers-in-law, and then disappear in the early evening darkness. If the watchful eye of my mother had seen him, he would have been in trouble. At least for that day, he would have had to remain hungry.

Fishele gradually taught himself enough on his own to become a good teacher. He married a fine girl and, as an educated man, found himself well received in the upper levels of Jewish society. Shamele, on the other hand, as we heard later, did not limit his life to the large folios of the Talmud.

The Enlightenment movement would leave deep marks even in the orthodox circles among the poorer Jews. After just a single decade, one could see most children of the lower classes, even craftsmen, sitting in school, and European education became the common possession of the Jewish population. Shared education led to a melting together, an equalization of patricians and lower classes. The trained expert, the doctor, the lawyer, and so forth, now took the place of the traditional *meyuches* (aristocrat).

Talmudic education did not end; it was just evaluated differently. By the end of the 1860s, the young men whom I described above looked quite different. Their external appearance left little to be desired. They had learned to read and write Russian, and they had a sense of world history. But they also remained true to the old religion and had complete faith that a better time was approaching for God's people.

Out of this group came the small-town rabbis of Lithuania, the *dayanim* (judges) and *more horoes* (those versed in the law) who were called upon to decide issues of kosher and *treif* and ritual hygiene, the *magidim* (preachers), the *shochtim* (ritual slaughterers of both fowl and large animals), the *chazonim* (cantors), and even the *batlonim* (literally: lay-abouts)—poor talmudists of whatever age who were called upon to recite Psalms, hymns or sections of the Mishna at festive or sad occasions or, day and night, beside a corpse. A poor boy would often, after serving for several years as a senior *behelfer* in a *cheder*, become a *melammed* himself.

A small group remained apart from these functionaries. They were called *prushim* (separate ones)—young men and old who devoted themselves body and soul to the undisturbed study of Talmud. Separated from wife and child, removed from their home and the world, they spent their entire lives drawing fine talmudic distinctions, plumbing the depths, and discussing the various interpretations with others. These ascetics lived in the little town of Eishyshok in the province of Vilna, literally living on the charity of its townsfolk, and depending especially on the wonderful women who saw it as a sacred duty pleasing to God to send them food and drink. Such a woman might have barely fifty rubles to her name, and with this she ran a business and nourished her children and husband, while the latter dedicated his life to Talmud study. These days, only a very small portion of the Jewish people devotes itself to *talmud torah* (study of the Talmud) in this way.

One day my father returned from *mincheh* with wonderful news: a Doctor of Philosophy named Lilienthal had been commissioned by the Ministry of Education (under the cultivated and humane Minister Uvarov) to travel throughout Russia and to investigate the competence of the *melamdim*, in whose hands rested the early education of Jewish youth. My father, a strictly observant Jew, was not too upset about the impending reforms; he himself had long been dissatisfied with the poor methods of instruction in the Jewish schools of Brest, and had been wishing for many improvements. My two eldest brothers-in-law and the other young men of the town also received the news with great anticipation, although they dared talk about it only in whispers. As for the *melamdim* themselves—they were simply in despair.

73

When Dr. Lilienthal came to Brest my father decided to take his sons-in-law to pay the Doctor a visit. My mother objected but my father was brief and to the point: if he didn't take the young people to Dr. Lilienthal, they would find the way by themselves. I suspect that this was just an excuse. My father was very anxious to make the acquaintance of Dr. Lilienthal, to learn as soon as possible the precise details of the impending revolution in the system of education. But my mother's eyes were sharper. She saw more deeply, as was confirmed in the end.

It is impossible to describe the ecstasy of the young men over the prospect of visiting the interesting Dr. Lilienthal. My eldest brother-in-law was especially happy. In addition to outstanding talent and an unusual knowledge of the Talmud he was possessed of unflagging industry. At the age of fourteen he had almost the learning of a rabbi.

Dr. Lilienthal made it a point to gather many of Brest's young people around him every day, speaking to them of acquiring West European learning, offering useful bits of advice, sketching out their future as men of culture. He won the hearts of these impressionable young people who, while remaining true to their parents' religion in matters of observance, were branching off into new paths in all other respects, turning ever further from the cultural orientation of the older generation. This was typical of the Lilienthal epoch. Quietly the cultural revolution began among the Jews of Russia. The young people set about the intellectual work with great energy. It took very little time, and relatively little effort, to effect the reforms. A refreshing breeze swept through the Jewish society of the city of Brest, and all the other Russian Jewish towns.

My father spoke constantly of Lilienthal and of his great, important assignment. He was enthusiastic about the order and method that would be introduced for the first time into the education of young Jews, although he was worried by some of Dr. Lilienthal's impious talk and by the fact that certain sections of the Talmud would no longer be studied, so that law suits could not, in the future, be decided in accordance with talmudic jurisprudence.

My brothers-in-law were even more enthusiastic but they had to

74

watch themselves, so as not to wound my mother who worried darkly about all these changes. There were altogether about twenty young men in Brest who were great partisans of Lilienthal and zealously promoted Western culture. At first they had to announce quite limited goals—a person ought to be able to address an envelope in Russian—in keeping with the limited mentality of many people. Remember too that my brothers-in-law and their contemporaries had little fluency in European languages: a bit of reading and writing in Russian and Polish and somewhat greater proficiency in German. They had some inkling of the classical literature of these languages, and of some of the sciences. The merchant class at that time was using a mixture of German and Russian when necessary, while the proletariat used a babble of Lettish, German, or Polish when they traded with villagers in the markets. They could not read, write, or speak any European language (except for a very limited kind of Polish).

Imagine the following scene. The day after their visit with Dr. Lilienthal my brothers-in-law are sitting thoughtfully together in their study.

"We'll find the books," says the elder eagerly. "We've just got to be very careful. Sneak the work into our Talmud time. But don't let the parents catch on."

Phlegmatically the other replies, "Sure. You start and I'll go along."

Dr. Lilienthal had advocated they first study the Russian language, then natural science and German literature. My brothers-in-law got hold of the necessary texts and began to study, of course at the expense of their Talmud learning. A careful observer might often spot a volume of [Friedrich] Schiller[1] or [Heinrich] Zschokke[2] inside the Talmud folio; in Zschokke, Engelbert's idyllic way of life filled

---

[1]   Friedrich Schiller (1759–1805), influential German playwright, poet, and essayist.–ed.

[2]   Heinrich Zschokke (1771–1848), one of the most prolific and popular German writers of his day.–ed.

young Jews with enthusiasm. The Princess of Wolfenbüttel[1] aroused pity and sympathy, especially among Jewish women; the role model of all the younger men was Schiller's Marquis Posa.[2] There was a work-a-day Russian grammar to hand, and a volume of natural history.

One morning in the memorable summer of 1842 my brothers-in-law fetched their new books from their hiding place, never dreaming that they could be overheard, and laid them on their open Talmud. Together with their friend Reb Herschel, a *melammed* from Orlo and a brilliant man with great knowledge of Talmud in his own right, they began a loud debate about a sentence in Schiller's *Don Carlos*. As a precaution in case of interruption, they were reading and disputing in their accustomed Talmudic sing-song.

But my mother was watching them with a sharp and troubled eye. Ghosts had been haunting her since Dr. Lilienthal's visit. She was convinced that a foreign element had moved into her house and that it would make the study of God's word secondary. To reassure herself, she decided to go to the young people's study. At the bottom of the stairs she paused to listen and then went up joyfully, to the encouraging sounds of learning from above. How they were studying! But when she pressed her ear to the door and paid closer attention she was seized with horror. A terrible expression of anger and disappointment distorted her features. Instead of "omer Abbaye," all she could hear was "Marquis Posa" and "the Duke of Alba" and other sinful trash.

She opened the door with a trembling hand, and stood at the threshold so angry she couldn't utter a word. Three heads turned in surprise, and three young men were too stunned even to cry out. Their first move was to drop all the books under the table. They had no wish to spite my mother. It pained them that their "trash books" were causing so much unhappiness. But the charm of all this novelty—the attraction of these foreign languages and sciences, after the sameness of Talmud study—it was all so irresistible.

[handwritten margin note: going against Talmud]

---

[1]   The title character of an epistolary novel by Zschokke.–ed.

[2]   The central character in Schiller's play "Don Karlos, Infant von Spanien" (Don Carlos, Infant of Spain), 1787.–ed.

My mother was the first to pull herself together. "*Oy!*" she cried out. "In my own house to see the word of God mocked! In the same melody in which you learn Talmud you mock Him with your *apikoros* (heretic) books! And you, Reb Herschel—you need this? What are you going to do with it in Orlo? You want to become an *apikoros* too, like my young ones?"

She was so agitated that her legs shook under her. The young men remained silent, their heads turned to the window. My mother received no answer, her fears could not be contradicted, and she silently left the room.

A short time later she surprised my eldest brother-in-law alone at the new learning. It was an early morning that same summer. The mountain near our house still stood in fog. I happened to be in the yard, saw my mother come out of the house and leave by the main gate, and followed her. She took a few steps along the lattice-work fence of the flower garden and stopped.

"Who's standing there?" she said, as if to herself—or was it to me? She took a few more steps and cried out in a loud voice, "Yes, yes, I think it's David! What's he doing there?"

She hurried to the corner of the garden, where a large poplar tree stood. No mistake—it was David. My brother-in-law was wearing only a thin robe, the ends of his belt tossed lightly over one another—not tied, as required, into a firm knot. His chest was bare, his hair uncombed, one earlock caught all the way behind his ear, the other moving along his cheek like a little snake; his black velvet yarmulke bore traces of a down bed pillow; his naked feet were thrust into slippers. The morning fog lay upon the cold, wet, trembling figure whose right hand, undaunted, kept working away pieces of the poplar bark and digging little insects out from under, dropping them—not without disgust—into a little box with a glass lid.

It must have been a funny sight. My mother called out half astonished, half amused, "What are you doing there?"

"Nothing," he answered laconically, without interrupting his work.

"What's in the little box on the ground?"

77

"Nothing!" repeated the natural scientist caught in the act.

"Why are you here so early?" inquired my mother.

"Early! It's not early at all!"

But it was no good, for Mother leaned over the fence and spied, not without anger, a book as well as the little box. Now she understood that both served the same purpose, and with a despairing sigh she silently cursed Dr. Lilienthal. She stood transfixed for a while, staring at the things before her. Then she turned into the garden. The half-naked researcher divined her purpose and skedaddled, leaving all the booty behind. He lost one slipper in his flight, and held the rest of what he was wearing clutched to him with both hands.

Quickly my mother went over to the poplar to look into the box, and to her indescribable amazement found there only an ordinary housefly, a beetle, a ladybug, an ant, a worm, and many other insects stuck on pins. She couldn't believe her eyes.

She shrugged as if to say, "Why does a human being need such vermin?"

What startled her even more was the book. Next to some explanatory paragraphs she found illustrations of several insects, including as luck would have it a portrait of a "domestic insect" (that is, a cockroach) lounging at its ease. She shuddered with disgust. She could understand why the young would want to study Russian and German. The pleasures of literature were familiar to her, and she was well-read in Hebrew. But that anyone—let alone her own sons-in-law!—should take an interest in the manner of locomotion of an ant, or how many feet a beetle had or what kind of eyes were given to a worm—well she just couldn't understand that at all.

She gathered up the trophies of the morning and returned to the house by the same path along which the fleeing hero had stumbled a few minutes earlier, dropping a slipper as a token of his defeat. She picked up the slipper too, brought everything into the dining room, and put it all on the window sill. My father was up by this time and had a good laugh.

Our house was not the only one to witness scenes like that. All the young men's friends were enduring similar difficulties and unpleasantness, and worse. My brother-in-law David eventually had enough of this persecution. One day when he was called to lunch he reported that he was sick, and on that same evening without a word to anyone, even his wife, he traveled home to his father, a rabbi in the little Polish town of Semjatitcz. He stayed there for a while, and my parents and my sister were glad he was far away from the growing Lilienthal movement of Lithuania. Later on it required considerable effort to persuade him to come back to Brest.

These three young people, my brothers-in-law and their teacher, were probably the first in Brest to reach for the apple of knowledge that Lilienthal held out. To avoid scenes, they found a quiet little spot between two hills and away from our home, where they met with a like-minded group to debate literary questions and to decide burning cultural issues. But for all his exertions, my eldest brother-in-law never could find the spot on the apple where he could get a good bite. His "Asiatic" education resisted every assault from Europe, and he could have done much better for himself and for society with his Talmud learning. My younger brother-in-law enjoyed the apple, and in a short time became what was by the standards of that day an educated man. Reb Herschel the *melammed* grabbed for it with his plebeian hands and took a great bite. Soon the "Orler" was transformed into an interesting, cultured Mr. Hermann Blumberg. In short, each youth of Brest enjoyed the apple of knowledge to a greater or lesser extent, but all tasted of it. The seed that Lilienthal sowed in Brest bore fruit in accordance with the soil upon which it chanced to fall. These young people were pioneers, although they themselves were condemned to cultural sterility. Though not a single outstanding personality emerged from among this early group in Brest, they smoothed the way for the next generation that would have an easier time getting an education, and would have much less prejudice to overcome.

Dr. Lilienthal's great success was made possible by the intellectual background of Russian Jews. Boys (though not girls) were trained to study from their youngest days. The young scholar devoted his entire day to the study of Talmud, with nothing else to distract him. Since he knew nothing of the myriad entertainments available today, he spent all his time within the circle of his own family and was devoted to it.

The young man of those days became attached to tradition at a very early age and found great beauty in religion. He experienced the pressures of growing up on the school bench without revolutions or love affairs to distract him from the contemplative life. Even after he was married and had children, he did not have to engage in business since the parents took it upon themselves as a sacred duty to support him so that he could study Talmud.

This was what led to the system of marriage in which parents chose the mates for their children. The bride should be pretty, clever, and well mannered, but above all she had to be a *bas tovim*, the daughter of a learned and religious man. I can vouch for the fact that where the parents' choice was made without the pernicious influence of the god Mammon, it seldom went awry. I remember that there were many very happy marriages in those days. The high moral character of the young couple hallowed their union and safeguarded their faithfulness to each other. They did not become disappointed or tired of each other, and did not chase after novelty. And in the dreary autumn days, in the cold, short, lonely days of winter, in old age when the fire had long burned out, the truly divine spark of love still glowed and could sustain the shivering soul.

The Enlightenment shattered the sacredness of this marital life and destroyed many dear treasures. Unfortunately, the dazzling brilliance of European culture burst upon our amazed young people without a mediating dawn. Fully grown men who, up until that moment, had led an almost ascetic life were blinded by the new ways.

THE CZAR'S DECREE

A splendid sight: Czar Nicholas I surrounded by his glittering entourage, his tall figure, in shining good health, towering over all about him. His military parade uniform was a tightly fitting jacket with bright red appliqué and cuffs, many star-shaped medals on his vest, massive epaulets, wide blue diagonal sash, sword and dagger at his side, a three-cornered hat across his head topped with a mighty white plume. His military bearing and his face with its regular features, clean-shaven double-chin, full blond whiskers and flashing gray eyes, all expressed the greatest self-assurance.

To his right stood Crown Prince Alexander, who at that time, in the year 1835, was still a young man. His build was tall and massive. In contrast with his father's light blond hair, Alexander's was raven black. He had a narrow black mustache and black eyes. His whole being seemed to radiate mildness and friendliness, without a trace of his royal father's self-confidence.

To this day I remember well how the Crown Prince had at that time already won the hearts of all the people. This sympathy he justified in 1861 when, as Alexander II, he freed the serfs.

Surrounded by many generals, adjutants, and engineers, the Princes stood on the Mountain of the Tartars. A flat green lawn lay like a velvet carpet before their feet. The dark blue dome of the heavens rose above. The sun was reflected in the medals and gold-embroidered uniforms of the officials. This entire gleaming show seemed to us children like a mirage as we stood beside our childhood home, about a hundred *faden* (seven hundred feet) away.

The Czar pointed with his right hand in various directions. There was a lively debate among the gentlemen, which led the masses of people surrounding them to assume that a very important question was being discussed. Sometimes a general, then an adjutant was sent down from the mountain to look at our house and inspect it, measure the green meadow that surrounded our house and garden, and then report back to the top of the mountain. The gaping multitude was exhausted with a thousand surmises, gave each movement of the Czar's hand a thousand interpretations, all but the right one.

At last the word came that he had designated the entire area of the Old City of Brest as the site of a fortress of the first class. The property owners of Brest were informed through an *ukase* (edict) from the Czar that their homes would be appraised by a commission named specially for this purpose. The Government would pay reparations and in addi-

81

ukase = edict

tion an area was set aside four and a quarter *versts* (that is 1½ to 2 English miles)[1] away, for resettlement.

For my parents this project was a catastrophe. Not only our splendid house but also our big brick factory was to be torn down. The factory produced large sums of income every summer, for my father had accepted an order for millions of bricks for the fortress projects that had already begun and were in the process of being built. It was very hard for my father to master his fright, but he and the others trusted the government's assurances of reimbursement.

Then the devil sent one of his messengers of Hell—an apostate Jew and shady lawyer named David Rosenbaum whom people eventually called David the Black One. At that time the prevailing language in Lithuania was still Polish, but this man knew Russian well enough to appear in court and write petitions in that language. He gained the confidence of both the property owners and the Commission, and all the owners hurried to put their property into his hands. But soon he had alienated both sides and, to get revenge, he sent reports to higher officials saying that the Commission was issuing falsely inflated assessments. I'm sure that there was no truth in his denunciation, but the interests of my unfortunate parents were hit heavily by his act of revenge.

My father had never used this lawyer in the first place and so, to get even, the man made my father one of the victims of his tale-bearing. Soon the government put a halt to all of the assessments and then ordered every property owner to demolish his home at his own expense. There would be a fine if the order were not carried out quickly enough. We had hardly any time to find a new place to live in the New City.

Of course there could no longer be any question of building anything new, and the rich were as helpless as the poor. Prices rose three-

---

[1] This equivalency is Wengeroff's. Sergei G. Pushkarev, *Dictionary of Russian Historical Terms from the Eleventh Century to 1917* (New Haven: Yale University Press, 1970), gives several possible definitions of a *verst*, which would yield distances of 2.6—over 4 miles.–ed.

fold, but people with cash hurried and paid anyway. Even so, only about a quarter of the large population found places. The large mass of the people remained virtually homeless. We children were excited about the upcoming move, while at the same time I was upset that soon I would have to leave my playmates in the *cheder* and in the suburb of Zamuchawicz that I knew so well. Our lives would be radically different. In the end, it took no less than fifteen years to settle all the claims. That was time enough to drive many property owners from their homes, rob them, and plunge them into the deepest misery. Many became beggars and many emigrated. I see heartbreaking scenes of those sad days before my eyes. They still make me shudder.

On one autumn day of that terrible year—1839[1]—the cloudy sky hung like molten lead over the earth and over the souls of the citizens of Brest. The north wind blew cold and whirled street dust and yellow fallen leaves into the eyes of pedestrians. I was just on my way home with my mother, and our way to the suburb of Zamuchawicz led past the poor, small houses of the neighborhood.

We heard a mixture of Yiddish and Russian—arguing in Russian, scolding in Yiddish, and much weeping. Leading me by the hand, my mother stepped closer. A wrenching tragedy played out before our eyes. The deadline for moving out had passed but these sorry people had not yet found any alternative shelter, and thought that they could stay in their old home for the time being. But they were wrong. The police sent an officer with orders to press them to move, and to expel them bodily if necessary.

This harsh order was just being executed as we stepped into the little house. The woman of the house, a sickly, thin woman, her face contorted, packed all she had into an old green-painted wardrobe. Her very old husband carried the smallest child in his arms. Beside him stood two more children, a boy of about nine and a girl of about six, whose hands and naked feet were frozen blue. They trembled, for their thin bodies were covered only with rags. On the table there was

---

[1] This is the date given in the second edition. The first edition (p. 151) gives 1836.–ed.

half a loaf of bread. A few pieces of wood smoked in the stove with their meager meal cooking upon it.

The family was just about to sit down to eat when the messenger from Hell arrived and declared that there was no room for them here anymore, not even this one day could they dare to remain. Without time for their meal, they rushed to pack and grab what they could. Even in the poorest household, there are so many things that have some value so long as they stay put. But once you move this worn-out stuff it falls apart and breaks. Anyway, where should these people bring their poor possessions if they had no shelter to go to?

They hardly had enough to rent a small place to sleep. Sighing and screaming, complaining and cursing, the woman filled half of her wardrobe with her things and then took the little one from the arm of her husband. Now the old man began to pack his treasures: the large and small folios of his Talmud, and his prayer books, which at that time every Jew, however poor, possessed.

This man was a home owner. Soon the *Chanukkah* lamp, his wife's four brass Sabbath candlesticks, the hanging candelabrum, their Sabbath clothes, his long caftan, silk belt and *shtreimel*, and all of the rest of their household goods—the water barrel, the worm-eaten dining table, wooden benches, a few wooden poles and so on—everything was thrown on the floor. The people kept tripping over one or another of their possessions. It was terrible.

My mother stood in the doorway with me and tried to offer them words of courage and trust in God, while also trying to calm the policemen, who actually left soon after. My mother reminded the people that they had forgotten the pictures hanging on the wall. There was a picture of Moses with his Sacred Tablets on Mount Sinai; Jacob with his twelve sons, the twelve tribes of the Jewish people; and a picture of the menorah, the seven-armed candelabrum, which stood in the Temple in Jerusalem. *Mizrach* (East) was printed on this one, for a Jew always stands facing east in prayer. With pictures like this, a Jew of that day tried to preserve his tradition and the memory of the splendor of the past for those who would come after.

The owner raised his eyes to the pictures and wanted to take them

84

down, but his wife screamed in a voice clogged with tears, "Let them stay here, these pictures. What are we going to do with them in the *komerne* (rented lodgings)? It's over with us. I'm no longer a housewife, you're no longer a homeowner. We don't have a corner to ourselves. Let these pictures go to the devil too, just like everything else we have. Oh, God why did you allow me to live to see this destruction, this *churben*?"

The old man continued packing and when he had finished his sad work he brought out a farmer's cart and loaded up his possessions. The green-painted wardrobe, which had the most important household goods in it; the long wooden poles and the bedding, into which the three children, trembling with cold, were wrapped; a ragged, padded blanket was thrown over all of it. The man, as the strong one, still had the courage to look around in the devastated rooms but found nothing more worth taking.

Then with great courage and presence of mind, he lifted the windows, doors and shutters off their hinges, and put them on the wagon. "I'll still get some money for those," he said. Deserted stood the house without doors, without windows, like a widow, more desolate even than after a fire. The clouds peered in and the autumn wind raced howling through the dead rooms; and slowly, over the unpaved country road, the broken, despairing inhabitants led their vehicle which sank up to its wheels in mud, into a hopeless future in the New City.

My mother called out "Go with God" to them as they left on their way, and the housewife called back, "Be well." The man wept; the children accompanied this scene with loud yells and screams. Nobody thought of trying to calm them, because the grief of this moment shut off all senses. I also felt that a terrible fate was being played out here, and tear upon tear streamed from my eyes.

At home my mother reported what we had just seen, and heavy gloom descended on us all. Soon, perhaps tomorrow, this fate might befall us too. My married sisters knew that from now on they would not be able to live with their parents, that Father would lose his entire wealth with the land. They had to think about setting up homes of their own, a task they were unaccustomed to, even though they already had several little children.

THE MOVE TO THE NEW CITY

The Government treated my father with comparative leniency, but the officials could not allow us to live in the Old City forever. One morning my father came from the New City and said that for the time being he had found us an apartment to rent.

I listened with great interest. Despite the sad moves of our neighbors I still felt a certain pleasurable excitement at the thought of the great impending changes. Where the grown-ups thought with a shudder of all of the work and all the discomfort of a move, for children there was a special charm and pleasure in moving into a new place. The grown-ups might flee from empty rooms, but every child finds great fun jumping around in them and listening to her voice echo.

Mother went with her older daughters to look at the place. She had little choice but to like it. Soon the packing and gathering up began. A lot of our expensive furniture had to be sold because it couldn't fit into the small rooms in the New City. The move was to take place on a Tuesday. My married sisters would move with their families first.

As the appointed day arrived, we had our breakfast all together at the family table of our parents for the last time. Everyone was silent, overcome by feelings that were hard to express in words. This sorrow was very deep. The new situation was harder to bear than fire damage, for fire is the power of the elements, coming from the same Hand that we worship even when it is destructive. But to leave your house and grounds in the best condition, to move from what is comfortable and familiar into the unknown, into a dark future, that is the torture of all tortures.

I admit that I had been excited at the thought of moving to a new place. But now we were all silent.

After breakfast the wagons were loaded with my sisters' furniture. My older sister, Chenyeh Malkeh Günzburg, was led to the street very carefully, since she had just recently given birth to a little daughter. The little delicate creature was bundled into pillows and blankets and brought to the wagon, where the two older children were already sitting. As if it were yesterday, I see the picture before me, how the old nursemaid Rashke went through the empty rooms to lift the baby from her cradle and bring her to my sister in the wagon. Many hot tears poured down her wrinkled cheeks.

This day brought an end to the patriarchal life in the house of my beloved parents. One member of the household after another pulled away. Quite different times began. Never again did we children come under our father's unlimited power.

UPROOTING THE OLD CEMETERY

Not only were people required to move to the New City. The centuries-old cemetery whose earth held thousands of human bones was to be demolished. Despite appeals and prayers led by Rabbi L. Katzenellenbogen, the government remained adamant.

A day was set for the re-burial. It was on a Monday as I recall. The entire Jewish community—young and old, men and women, rich and poor—fasted and then went to the old cemetery. Psalms and prayers were read, the dead were begged for forgiveness as is usually done at a burial, and then the sad work began. One of the most terrible curses among the Jews is, "May the earth cast out your bones." And so we saw the terrible curse fulfilled on these bones.

A few days before, sacks made of gray linen had been prepared to hold the remains of the dead. These little sacks sufficed to tuck away an entire human being who had been so proud in life, so self-confident, so insatiable, so full of untiring wishes and demands. Everything turned into just a little pile of dust, hardly a burden for a single hand.

The whole community took part in this, put the contents of these dug-up graves into the little sacks, tied them with a little thread and piled them on a wagon standing ready. There was no distinction made of rank and position in society. None of this was considered—all were equal. The entire mass of the people was deeply moved as they did this

87

work. Here was not a single family grieving over a member, but an entire population grieving for its desecrated dead.

Finally all of the graves were empty and the wagons were covered with black cloth. The cantor said a prayer and *kaddish,* and the great procession began to move. Many followed the procession, a long way from the Old City to the New City, barefoot. There had never been such a funeral.

The Government had sent a military guard of honor, partly perhaps also because among the disinterred corpses there were many victims of a great epidemic. The soldiers marched along shouldering their weapons, close to the wagons. The citizens followed in deep silence.

There was a new cemetery near the village of Bereswke, a distance of six *versts* (just over 3½ miles) from the Old City, and there the little sacks of bones of those who had no gravestones were put into mass graves. The others were buried in individual graves with the old stones set in place. On these one can read the Hebrew inscriptions to this day, dating back several centuries.

It was already beginning to get dark when the mass funeral in the new cemetery was over. People scattered without a sound. That evening our house was filled with sorrow and great mourning. My parents silently turned inward. No one spoke. Everyone was preoccupied with thoughts of death and the transitory nature of earthly life.

It may be that this heavy day paralyzed my once resilient father. He never really recovered from the heavy blow that tore him from his own threshold. After fifteen years of difficult litigation, he received a considerable sum from the Government for his real estate, but he was an old man by then, estranged from business. He had become sedentary, a scholar whose activity was fruitful only in his study before the folios of the Talmud.

New orders still came in, from the great construction of the fort. But it was as though Father had been torn from the earth in which he was rooted. No further fruits would ripen.

Life in my parents' home took on a completely different shape.

Our old home had been elegantly furnished—from the formal rooms to the carriage house. Here the little rooms seemed poor. Of course it was the same mahogany furniture decorated in gold bronze that filled these small rooms, but oh, in what condition! Faded, shabby, many sets were missing pieces, many a table limped on one leg. The backs of the chairs no longer offered solid support, gold was chipped from the frames of the great mirrors.

On the other hand, this period was one of the richest in content for my father, illuminating the noblest traits of his character. More than in earlier days, he had the opportunity now to help and advise those closest to him, and to earn love and admiration in Jewish society by his great talmudic learning, and his knowledge in other spheres of Jewish literature. Once he had liquidated his business, he devoted himself fully to the Talmud and lived *al ha-tauro ve-al ha-avaudo,* for study and for prayer.

In the small apartment many books were added to Father's library. There, in the early Forties, he wrote the two works that I have already mentioned. He continued to rise at four o'clock, summer and winter, and sing his morning prayers. I awoke to the sound of these melodies and remained in a deep, religious dreamy state until the break of day. Father still had the time and desire to take an interest in the affairs of the community and, with his loving fatherly eyes and wise words, to oversee the behavior and manners of his children.

Of course much had changed in the new circumstances, but not our behavior or our self-assurance. We had lost our wealth. Many of the costly things disappeared from our house. But our home remained, as before, a gathering place for intelligent company. Every distinguished visitor to the city of Brest came first to us, sure of a hearty welcome. Our dress was simple, but none of the children envied their friends their expensive clothing. Life in the house rolled along in a regular, comfortable way.

SABBATH IN THE NEW CITY [1847]

Friday had a different feel because already before the break of day the kitchen was filled with preparations for the Sabbath. Wonderful large breads and many kinds of cake were baked, and my mother took a piece of the raw dough, said a silent prayer, and threw it in the fire.

Happily I helped the cook and got the first sweet to eat. At that time I was already fourteen. Everyone in the house got up early. We ate fresh white bread with butter and coffee, and I wrote a list of everything I had to buy for the Sabbath. Taking my hand basket and napkin, I went to the market. First I bought a fish, the fundamental ingredient of a real Sabbath. My father laid great store by a good fish. I bought the very freshest pike, which is especially favored by us Jews. Then I went to the fruit stalls, and then quickly home, where I found my mother reading the Torah portion for that Sabbath.

When I appeared she put the Bible aside and checked my purchases. My father came from his study, examined the fish, was generally satisfied, reminded me to add a lot of pepper because it improved the appetite. After I had given the fish to the cook to clean, I tied on a large apron and quickly went to wash my father's handkerchiefs, collar, and muslin sleeves, which had to be dry and ironed before the evening.

Then it was the turn of the fish. My father loved to watch this procedure and smiled as he praised my skill, tasted the sauce, and again reminded me to add more pepper. After much tasting and trying the fish was finished. I put it on a dish over a pot of hot water to keep the sauce from drying out. Again the vegetables were tasted and the spices corrected and then I cleared the space by the stove for the cook. I made tea for my parents and siblings. On Friday we had tea earlier than usual and drank it in haste. Then I went through all the rooms to put final touches on the cleaning, moving one and then another piece of furniture, removing dust.

In the meantime the laundry had dried and I began to iron. Then I distributed the clean linen to my parents and siblings. We put on Sabbath clothes. In the winter mine consisted of a blue wool dress, my favorite color; and in the summer, a stiffly ironed cotton dress. My youth made up for the lack of velvet and silk that we could no longer afford.

Now my parents went to the synagogue in their Sabbath clothes. Of course my mother first covered the table with a white tablecloth, covered two Sabbath loaves at the head of the table with a prettily embroidered cloth, and lit the candles with their blessing, thus fulfilling two of the commandments required of every Jewish woman. She thanked God that she had been privileged to light her rooms for the Sabbath.

While she was in the synagogue, we three girls had the duty of lighting two more candles each on Friday evening in the chandelier in the dining room. In the other rooms there were also candles lit in the wall sconces and soon everything glowed in the light of all the candles. We girls, in fresh Sabbath toilette, in the cleaned rooms, felt as the Chasidim say, that "Heaven grants a *neshomeh yeseireh* (a second soul) on the Sabbath." This was the only time in the week when we could sing, without being disturbed, our Russian, Polish, German, and Jewish songs in full voice. Sometimes we danced together with neighbor children. And we didn't forget to pray either. In the meantime the servants set the table for the evening meal.

At Father's place I set the large silver cup and the carafe of wine. When he came in and called out, "Good Sabbath!" in his strong voice, the warmth of Sabbath came with him. He spread out his hands and we children—the oldest first—received the blessing. Father's face shone in happy Sabbath peace. His laughing features were quieted by the peace of his soul; the sorrow and worries that had so tortured him in the time just past were driven away, forgotten, by him and by his house.

Father prayed over our heads, bowed in love and respect; often he pressed and stroked our heads but there was never any kiss or similar endearment, because that would have been considered frivolous in the views of that day. After we received Father's blessing, he and the other gentlemen present sang "*Sholem Aleichem*, may you have peace," the verses with which every Jew receives the angels of Sabbath peace.

91

Then there followed the Song of Praise of the Housewife, *Eishes Chayil*, the hero woman, taken from the Proverbs of King Solomon; praising the woman who arises when it is still dark to prepare food for her husband and children and servants. The work of her hands, the red woven sashes, are praised in the gates of her city. She is a crown for her husband. Beauty and grace are idle trifles and transitory; praise is due only to a God-fearing woman.

The men sang as they walked up and down the room, in a very beautiful way. I was a teenager then and when I heard these songs, although I only half understood them, I would feel great pride, and determined in my heart that I would become worthy of such praise myself. My father made *kiddush*, drank more than half of the contents of the cup and gave it to Mother, who touched it with her lips and passed it around to us children.

Then without saying a word, we all washed our hands, and said the blessing while we dried them, very quietly no matter how many were present. We children often were tempted to whisper or to giggle, but a severe look from Father quieted all mischief. Father said a blessing over the two breads, also called *lechem mishneh*, cut one of them into two parts, ate one bite, and until he had finished this bite, said not a word....

The next morning my father woke up at four o'clock as usual. As it was Sabbath, he could not kindle any lights, so he would call the servant to fetch the Christian night watchman to bring light into the house. Michalka, the experienced night watchman, lit the candles in Father's study and in the kitchen for the servant. Father sang his morning prayers, turned some pages in the great Talmud folio, and drank his tea, which had been prepared the day before and kept hot on the great kitchen stove in some hot sand. The samovar was never set in my parents' house on the Sabbath, nor was coffee or other food cooked or warmed.

Now my father, in darkest night, and in the winter in the deepest snow, paying no attention to snow and frost, went to the *Chevreh-Tehillim Beis-HaMidrash*, the house of prayer and study of a society dedicated to reading all the Psalms from beginning to end every week.

Every day some of them were sung in chorus with one member of the community beginning the first sentence in the chapter and the community following. My father belonged to this organization but participated in the singing only on Saturday. The members were mostly artisans, for whom it was impossible all week to give themselves this pleasure of the soul in the early morning hour. But on this day of rest every Jew, having been asleep since nine o'clock in the evening, was physically and spiritually strong enough by four in the morning to go and meet his comrades in the bright, warm, roomy house of prayer. There was no fixed tune for these Psalms; but each Jew understood the words completely and saw his own experience in them. He would sing the texts with a melody of his own that rose from his innermost soul.

After morning prayers, about eleven o'clock, everyone went home to enjoy the wonderful midday meal: everyone loved the *shalet*[1] and *kugel* that the Sabbath angel had been cooking since yesterday. It was about this meal that Heinrich Heine once wrote: "The Greek gods on Olympus ate ambrosia only because they didn't know anything about *shalet*!" After honey cake and sweets, the servant brought in cold salt fish, hard-boiled eggs with onion salad, goose liver, goose fat, radishes, calves' feet with eggs and garlic, and spicy herbs. Then the *shalet* was served. After twenty hours of standing in the oven, it was tasty. (Jewish stomachs in those days were very strong. The greasier the *kugel*, the more the diners liked it.) There were *zmiraus* (religious songs) at the table and, of course, we were pious and could not pass up the "mitzveh" to sleep on the Sabbath. The children could play outside or in, depending on the season.

After the late afternoon prayers, there was a third meal, "Sholosh Suda," served at home in the half dark. By religious law, both fish and meat had to be eaten, and even the children tore into it with a fero-

---

[1] *Shalet* is the term used in western Yiddish for the dish known in the East as *tcholent* and in Hebrew as *hamin*. It consisted of a starch such as potatoes or barley slow cooked with vegetables and fatty pieces of meat in a covered pot in a sealed oven from before the Sabbath until lunch time.–ed.

cious appetite. Again there were beautiful hymns. Again the men went to the synagogue, returning in the dark, when my father made *hav-doleh* (the ritual prayer to mark the end of the holy day) over a cup of wine.

There were more *zmiraus*, for the evening was considered a half holy day and no work was done. There was yet another meal, the so-called "Melaveh Malkeh," named for the departing Sabbath Queen. Since the fire couldn't be lit until it was truly dark, the red beet and fowl borscht wasn't ready until about eleven o'clock and it was then that everyone (except we youngest children) had to come to the table and thus end the Sabbath holiday.

The *Gzeyreh* [1845] *The Harsh Edict*

In the old days, clothes were not determined by passing "fashion." Rather, custom determined how we dressed, and our costume distinguished each group, each class of people one from the other.[1] People didn't want to be like everyone else in the great stew of humankind, and one's clothes reflected stability, tradition, and honor.

With all this in mind, you can understand what effect it had on the Jews when, in 1845, the Russian government ordered them to give up their old costumes and put on modern dress. For the great mass of the people it was a catastrophe. They were embittered. Only their help-lessness, the fear typical of *golus*, kept this bitterness from escalating into a wild rage. If the Jews of that time had been strong, organized, powerful, then this change of costume would have led to insurrection and revolution. As things were, there was only painful resignation. Our traditional costume was mourned like a beloved departed person, and those able to see deeply could understand that adjusting to modern dress was only the first step on the way to deep forms of assimilation affecting not only our way of life, but our cultural views and the traditional teachings and customs of our faith.

---

[1] For a detailed description of Jewish dress style, see the Appendix.

94

The *ukase* was called "the *gzeyreh*" (the harsh edict)—not one of the many *gzeyros* that overcame the Jewish people, but simply "the *gzeyreh*." Many felt that under these circumstances *yehoreg ve-al yaa- vor*—a Jew had to sacrifice himself to sanctify the Name of the Lord. But the Russian government cared little for Jewish Law, for the anguished debates in the communities, for the mourning and grieving and complaints of the pious. It simply set a deadline by which all Jews in Russia, men and women, must appear only in European costume. The government orders applied only to street clothes and did not affect how people dressed at home, and many Jews kept their accus- tomed dress there. When it was dark out, you also might see Jews hur- rying about dressed as in the old days. The government seemed not to object. After all, what with the poor illumination of those days in the small cities, in the evening and at night clothes couldn't really be seen clearly. And to no one's surprise, there were exceptions to the general rules. For a certain fee, you could buy two years of permission to retain the old costume.

The changes in the costumes of the women were as radical as those of the men. (I am old-fashioned, and I believe that the change was not necessarily for the better.) Poor women clung to their cos- tume with extraordinary love, and even in the greatest poverty, when all sorts of things were restricted, they refused to change.

The new law often had tragicomic results. Sometimes, I am still tempted to laugh when I remember, but my laughter is mingled with deep pain and rage over the humiliation of human beings. One Friday morning in the summer of 1845, for example, I was in the Brest city marketplace where many Jewish women had gathered to shop for the approaching Sabbath. Suddenly there was a great tumult, and every- one began running in different directions. I hurried over to see what was causing all the uproar. From the middle of the crowd I could hear laughter and wailing. I saw a Jewish woman with her head literally bare, since her hair had been cut off in accordance with talmudic law. This unhappy sacrifice stood horrified first of all because standing with her head totally bare under the open sky was a sin. But she was also deeply shamed before the staring crowd. In a voice choked with

95

tears she pleaded for mercy from the policeman who had grabbed the headdress off her head and was holding it up, shaking it like a trophy, making the crowd laugh. With one hand she tried to pull the corner of her apron up to cover her bare head, while the other hand dug in her pocket to produce her cap, which conformed to the new Russian ordinance. The unhappy woman kept crying in the most pitiable tone, "*Panotzik!* (My lord!) *Panotzik!* Here! Here I have it! Here it is! Here is the *lappen* (rag; bit of cloth) in my pocket." Finally she had set the cap onto her naked head, which made her look very ugly. The constable calmed down and went away.

Soon he had another victim. This time it was a Jew who came to the market in a long-skirted caftan. The policeman mocked him and, calling a second policeman over for support, cut the long skirts of the caftan into the shape of a jacket with a huge pair of shears that he carried at all times. Not enough that this exposed the Jew's underpants. Now the policeman tore off the man's hat and cut off his *peyes* so close to the ear that the poor man screamed in pain. Then he let him go. The people in the market accompanied this "corrected" Jew with loud jeers and insults.

"Executions" of this sort could also occur on the highway. If a policeman came across an old-fashioned-looking Jew but had no shears with him, he would perform his duty anyway. He would lay the Jew on his side on the ground, stretch the *peye* over one stone close to his cheek, and rub it with a second stone until it was torn through. The Jew suffered horribly.

Such goings-on seem incredible today, but these surface tragedies were only a small foretaste of the great, deep changes in preparation at that time.

CHAVEH'S WEDDING [1848]

I was fifteen years old when my sister, two years older than I, was engaged. Our parents and those of the bridegroom conferred with one another through a *shadchen*, a marriage broker, and discussed how much dowry, clothing and jewelry should be given by each side to the young couple. My sister did not get to see her bridegroom, the companion of her life, at this time at all. She had no chance to assure herself that she could love him, and that he lived up to the image of her intended that a young girl secretly builds up in her mind.

Our parents just informed her that a certain Mr. F. from the city of Z[aslov] was interested in her hand. And since he was from a good home, rich, not ugly, and an independent businessman, although already divorced, our parents felt that this was a suitable match and gave their agreement. Now my sister was to do the same.

As for Chaveh, she made no objection and simply agreed to whatever our parents decided. It was a matter of course that she would be content with their choice. It was customary to marry off your daughters in this way, and then the daughters were happy in their marriage. The girls of that time knew that the man destined for them by their parents was also destined for them by God. One submitted to married life with patience and devotion.

In those days marriage was considered a holy bond that only death could sever, not simply an arrangement based on goodwill. There was rarely any friction between the couple. For the most part they lived a happy, contented life into high old age. And this in fact was the fate that God had prepared for my sister.

So my sister became a bride. She received beautiful diamonds from her bridegroom and frequent letters that she answered immediately. These letters displayed a certain sympathy, attachment, and love—but no romance. The writer would simply report that he or she longed for the other, was very happy, and looked forward with all his or her heart to the reply. And in this way five months passed. One morning, as my mother sat with all of us at the breakfast table, she said to Chaveh, "I hope that your wedding will take place in three months' time." Chaveh turned pale, and Mother began to calm her with affectionate words. She smiled, and yet quite seriously she said, "It's time. You're eighteen."

Chaveh got up and went to her room, where she began to cry very hard. You can guess what kinds of feelings were in that stream of tears, but our mother attached no importance to that. Even my sister prob-

97

ably couldn't justify these tears to herself. Perhaps her pride was hurt. She didn't even know her bridegroom personally. She wasn't to see him until the wedding.

The preparations began. First the wardrobe. Material— cloth, linen and so forth—was brought from the stores. But Chaveh seemed to pay very little attention. She became thoughtful, quiet, withdrawn. My mother and older sisters organized the sewing, while the bride began to write more frequently to her bridegroom, probably to restore her shaken calm. And his replies were very pleasant.

At the engagement, our parents and those of the bridegroom had set a Thursday in September of the year 1848 for the date of the wedding. (It fell on a *Rosh Chodesh*—the first day of a new month.) I was old enough to wear a long dress to this wedding. I would be the oldest maiden in the house, myself a candidate for marriage. I was very busy with household duties and in preparations for the wedding. Often I spent the entire day in the kitchen, baking, roasting, and cooking. But I loved this, while my sister preferred reading and sewing. My older sisters took care of procuring the household items and clothing for the bride. A soft lilac silk dress trimmed with white lace would be her wedding dress, and there would be a myrtle wreath and a long veil. This dress was very modern, very up-to-date.

On the Saturday before the set date all our girlfriends and acquaintances came, and we celebrated and danced till we were tired. (There were no boys, so we girls danced with each other. Our religious upbringing forbade dancing with actual men.) My father and the other men enjoyed watching us in the beautiful and graceful solo *kazatskeh*, in the fashionable *gallapade* (danced round and round the salon in pairs with a halt in each of the four corners), in the cheerful circle *beygeleh* dance, and then in the *chosidl* (little chasid) dance accompanied by fanfares and tambourines. Finally, the *contredanse*, which required grace and expertise. The waltz was not particularly popular.

The days between Saturday and Thursday were restless and filled with work. Every evening the musicians came to play a good evening for the bride, a *dobry vecher*, and every morning we heard a good-morning serenade, *dobry den'*. We girls did a cheerful dance to this music. Chaveh had hoped that her bridegroom would arrive at least two days before the wedding, and was more cheerful during those last days. But when Wednesday of the last week arrived and her hope was not fulfilled, she became ill-tempered and often cried in secret. You could see her impatience in everything she did.

The preparations for the wedding continued. Thursday dawned with splendid weather and sunshine but no bridegroom. Finally, at eleven, the courier arrived with the good news that the bridegroom and his entourage were at the last post station and were on their way. Quickly we got dressed and prepared breakfast. I had to help, and so was only half finished with my toilette. But the bride refused to get dressed until at least she had talked to her bridegroom. Today that sounds quite rational and reasonable, but a strict look from her mother and a word from her sisters was enough to make her give up this demand.

Soon Chaveh returned, dressed as a bride. She had hardly looked in the mirror, and we could see the storm raging inside her. Custom was still a powerful force in those days, and so she submitted. By now it was noon. The invitations to the wedding had gone out to friends and acquaintances on the same morning, and some of the guests had arrived.

Chaveh was not actually a beauty, but she was tall and carried her head proudly. She had a high forehead and intelligent eyes. The seriousness of this hour illumined her with a romantic glow, and her features showed mildness, submission and devotion—all of which we had been missing in her lately. Meanwhile, my father had gone to greet the bridegroom at his lodgings and could assure my sister that the young man was a nice person. Then there was music that moved everyone to tears, as is customary on such occasions.

Father and Mother led the bride into the wedding room to the sweet, exalted music, and seated her in the armchair in the middle of the room on a beautiful carpet. They were both crying. As Chaveh let go of their arms she sat thoughtfully, closed within herself. Nervous expectation, joyful excitement, the thought that her entire future was being decided—all this raged within her. O, the life of a woman! How full of meaning that expression is!

My father withdrew, but Mother and all of us, wearing our best clothes and all our jewelry, remained near her. And then, a few moments later, the servant in the hall announced that the bridegroom had driven up.

My mother rose. Uneasy but proud, she glanced at my sister who sat pale and staring at nothing. Mother whispered a few words of loving encouragement and went to receive her guests. Father had gone out to the hall to meet them. He embraced the groom and kissed him on both cheeks, and led him to Mother, who waited in the reception room. She, of course, was forbidden by custom to express her pleasure and satisfaction by a kiss or a handshake. But her eyes and a hurried phrase or two indicated that she was satisfied.

The bridegroom seemed to pay little attention to the embrace of my father or the friendly words of my mother. He looked across the heads of everyone surrounding him into the second parlor, where the star of all his future life was shining toward him.

Led by my father, all the members of the wedding came into the parlor. My sister rose. In calm dignity she faced her bridegroom and fixed her eyes upon him so steadfastly that, as I think, he lowered his gaze before hers. His nature was gentle, mild and peaceable; hers knew little sentimentality but was healthy, cool, bright as a winter's day. Her presence had an electrifying effect upon him; he could hardly master his emotions, and mumbled a few disconnected words to which Chaveh made a measured reply. Not even at this solemn moment were they permitted to shake hands.

The bridal couple were permitted to go into the next room, at first with both sets of parents. Finally they were left alone for a while so that they could, at last, talk without witnesses.

If ever the dictum, "*Veni vidi vici*—I came, I saw, I conquered" applied, this was the time! Hardly half an hour had passed when the young couple returned to the wedding parlor glowing with joy.

Breakfast was set out and enjoyed in the happiest humor. Many more of the invited guests were arriving, and since it was autumn and the days short, we had to hurry. It was past three o'clock. There was dancing in the parlor; the bride was drawn into it along with everyone else. For a while the bridegroom was allowed to remain and watch the dancing, but not for long! My mother was milder in such matters than my father. She withdrew into a corner of the room and invited her future son-in-law to take a seat beside her. After an hour of such entertainment, she reminded him that it was time to go. He withdrew with a low, smiling bow to the bride.

The *bedecken* (veiling) began. The music became soft and quiet, the bride's wreath was taken from her head, and all her hair unbraided by her friends and laid about her neck and shoulders. There was a sudden sadness in the mood of all the women in the room. A *badchen* or *marshalik*, a master of ceremonies, reminded the bride that this was a decisive day for her, marking a new stage in her life. She was to see it as a Day of Atonement and pray to God for forgiveness for all her sins. The parents of the time thought that they bore responsibility for every action of their unmarried children. After marriage the children took this responsibility upon themselves. My sister needed no reminding. Her tears flowed copiously.

After this speech the bridegroom returned in the company of his parents and the rest of the wedding guests, led by the Rabbi. He took the veil from a platter of hops and flowers and placed it on the head of the bride. The company scattered flowers and hops over her and uttered their good wishes. Another half hour passed in good cheer and music while the heavy bridal gown was replaced by a lighter dress and the veil was arranged and adjusted again.

Then we all went to synagogue—not in carriages this time, but on foot through the often very dirty streets. The marriage of two people is a public act, and must take place in the presence of the entire public. If anyone should recognize either of the young people as an already married person, here would be his chance to prevent bigamy!

After the *bedecken* the groom had been led with martial music to the door of the synagogue, where he was placed under the canopy. Now the band came to meet the bride and escort her too. She was led by her attendants to the left side of the groom. The music stopped.

The *shammes* filled a cup with wine, and an esteemed member of the community was given the honor of pronouncing a blessing over it. At the appointed place in the benediction he paused. The *shammes* handed the wedding ring to the groom, who held it high and said, *"Harey at mekudeshes li betabas zu ke-das Moshe ve-Yisrael."* [1] He put the ring on the bride's right forefinger. Then, accompanied by a cup of wine, the *sheva brochos* (seven blessings) were pronounced, praising all the noblest of human emotions: love, friendship, brotherhood, the faithfulness of married couples.

Then the *ksubeh* (marriage contract) was read aloud—a document in which the husband promises his intended to be hers, to feed her, to dress her as befits her station and to protect her. The document was handed to the bride while she was standing under her wedding canopy. The benediction over the wine was completed and bride and groom both drank, and then the glass was placed on the ground where the groom smashed it with his foot.

The company shouted *"Mazel tov!"* And then arm in arm the married couple walked home, accompanied by deafening fanfares and the entire crowd. The old women danced in a circle directly in front of them, for it is a great *mitzveh* to amuse the bride and groom (*mesame'ach chosen ve-kalo*). They danced all the way to our house.

Now the music was still. It was of the utmost importance to see whether, and partly to see to it that, the bride crossed the threshold first. There is an old superstition that whichever partner crosses the threshold first will have the upper hand forever after. All the women took off their jewelry and placed it in a jumble on the sill for the newly married pair to step over. We observed these customs quietly and with good humor. Among common people it often came to blows, with the bride's people on her side and the groom's on his fighting for position.

---

[1] "Thou art hereby consecrated unto me with this ring according to the laws of Moses and of Israel."

Imagine all this if the weather turned out to be rainy! All the women's finery would have been ruined and it would have all been the bride's fault, for it was her sweet tooth and her licking of stewpots that brought rain on her wedding day.

The wedding crowd brought the bridal couple to their room, where they were given tea, bouillon and sweets to break their fast, for they had eaten nothing all day. This first bouillon was called "the golden soup." Only the close friends and attendants of the bride were allowed in the room with the couple. The others went away, to return two hours later for supper, the so-called *chuppeh-vechere* (wedding-canopy evening).

At this meal all sorts of frivolous conversation was the order of the day. There was a luxurious feast climaxed with much drinking, and after it was over the company remained at the table to hear a talmudic discourse (a *drosheh*) from the groom. Then the "*drosheh* presents" (i.e., the wedding gifts) were offered to the bride and groom. The same *badchen* who had spoken to the bride so seriously before the ceremony now entertained the guests with improvised bits of doggerel and anecdotes, treating each guest in accordance to the size of his gift. The *badchen* stood on a chair as one gift after another was handed to him, and he praised its value in exaggerated terms and in a kind of sing-song. The already somewhat tipsy company laughed hysterically. He addressed some jokes directly to the bridal couple. Very late at night the meal was officially ended by the Grace after Meals, concluding with a repetition of the seven wedding blessings and another sip of wine for the bride and groom.

Next came the "kosher dance." The veiled bride was placed in the midst of her attendants, one of whom handed a corner of a silk handkerchief to the bride and the opposite corner to one of the gentlemen. Holding the handkerchief they danced a turn or two, and then the *badchen* called out, "All right, you've danced!"

The bride went back and sat among her attendants. In the same way she "danced" with every gentleman present, all this time veiled. When it was almost light everyone sought some corner and the entire company nodded off in blessed slumber.

The next morning the day began late. The bride remained in her room until my mother and elder sisters brought her a simple woman called a "gollerke," armed with a huge pair of shears. At my mother's command she took possession of the head of my poor sister, leaned it against her breast, and beneath her murderous shears one strand after another of the beautiful hair fell from my sister's head, as Jewish custom demands. In less than ten minutes the sheep was shorn. She was left only a little bit of hair over her forehead so she could brush it back. No trace of her own hair must show. Then she got a tight-fitting silk cap with a wide silken band over the forehead the same color as her hair. (In homes like ours the old Jewish customs, which had gradually attained the status of laws, were observed as strictly as possible.) A pretty, coquettish little cap was set on the bride's head, which made her look quite a bit older.

We sisters of the bride covered her face with a cloth of white silk and led her into the salon, where the gentlemen of the house and many guests were already assembled. Whoever wanted to see her face for the first time under the cap had to give a gift to charity. Even the bridegroom and the parents on both sides had to do this. Then various opinions were expressed about her changed appearance, and soon there was a cheerful argument in progress.

My sister and her husband lived with us, supported by our parents. His parents gave the bride a number of very beautiful presents but then they left, traveling back to their home in Zaslov, and one more young pair lived the old life.

Chaveh was the last of the sisters engaged and married this way. My own engagement only two years later was already very different. By that time, the reform under the government of Nicholas I had greatly influenced the Jewish way of life.

THE HASKALAH
IN OUR HOME AND BEYOND

Tsirl Waletzky

SECOND PERIOD OF THE ENLIGHTENMENT

In 1846 the Czar ordered that no Jew could live within fifty *versts* of the Russian border. This meant the ruin of thousands of families. Sir Moses Montefiore, the English philanthropist, took it upon himself to travel to Russia and was successful in having the Draconian order reversed, at least for the moment. This was not the first time that Montefiore had protected his coreligionists. All the Jews of Europe still remember in great detail his memorable trip to Egypt, where he blocked the blood vendetta, saved the threatened community and restored Jewish honor throughout the world.

[handwritten margin note: Montefiore saves Jewish communities]

Montefiore and his wife were received everywhere in Russia with great honor. In each large city, Montefiore was received by a high official who then accompanied him to his next stop. In this the officials were acting on government orders, and it was all they could do to hide their annoyance. This gave the Jews at least as much pleasure as the old couple's actual humanitarian efforts on their behalf.

The couple was well received even at the Court of the Czar, where the courtiers paid homage to Sir Montefiore, "the English Sheriff." Czar Nicholas gave him an audience, was very gracious, and promised Montefiore to be more considerate with his coreligionists. But at the end the Czar remarked: "If only more of the Jews in my country were like you, Sir." He advised Sir Moses to become more closely acquainted with the Jews of Lithuania and of Poland.

On their way back from this visit, Sir Moses Montefiore and his wife were received with great honor by the Jews. Every city of any size prepared a reception for them. The rabbi and the leaders of the community, accompanied by prominent delegates from other cities, went quite a long distance on foot to meet the guests and welcome them. Unfortunately, they could not speak with them directly because Sir Moses Montefiore and Lady Judith spoke only English. Dr. Loewe served as interpreter.

The Montefiores were most interested in the life of the Jews and made themselves familiar with every detail, both in economic and in cultural matters. Neither the Montefiores nor Dr. Louis Loewe, Sir Moses' companion and secretary, concealed the fact that they were pained by the appearance and manners of the Jews. Dr. Loewe said over and over that the acceptance of Western European culture and education was an absolute *sine qua non* for Russian Jews. In the days of the Messiah, when Jews would be restored to their land, they must not be found inferior to other peoples. Jewish youth must educate themselves, so as to be prepared for citizenship and freedom when it finally came.

The exalted couple did not come near our city, of course, but a group was sent to Vilna under the leadership of Rabbi Jacob Meir Padover to convey the best wishes and thanks to Montefiore. My father would have been the first on this deputation, but unfortunately an illness kept him at home. In spirit he followed every step of the prominent travelers; he got detailed reports almost every day. Our house rejoiced over each report! I can still see the wonderful glow of happiness in my father's eyes whenever he could discuss each individual event with his table companions—us, his children.

It was during the stay in Vilna that Louis Loewe proved to the great congregation in *shaul*, by a talk rich with arguments and citations from the Talmud, that Jewish tradition does not exclude a study of science and of foreign languages. His words had a tremendous effect, for Loewe was a highly educated man in the European sense of the word, as well as a good Talmudist, and therefore able to legitimize the new values. Jews everywhere adored, indeed they almost deified, Montefiore, a generous and brave philanthropist, and this same feeling was extended also to his companion Loewe. Anyone privileged to be the constant companion of Montefiore must obviously speak from pure ideals and be motivated solely by the desire to ennoble the Jewish people and make them secure.

In times like those, it was easy to understand why Moses Mendelssohn had become a guide for the perplexed. His German translation of the Bible, and his philosophical works, had brought Jewish youth closer to the German spirit and the German language. Up until this time they knew the Bible only as a religious book, but now they saw new points of view. People began to see this Book of Books with worldly eyes. What had been untouchable could now be studied critically. This was a revolution for young minds.

Mendelssohn

Such young rebels had been referred to at the end of the 1830s as *apikorsim* (heretics); now they were called "Berliners," and the dead Moses Mendelssohn (whom they called "the Dessauer," after the city of his birth) was hated by the older generation even more than the living Lilienthal. The German-Russian works, the *treif* little books, were barely tolerated by the old people; they had to be cleared away and hidden like other workday materials before the beginning of the Sabbath. But there was enormous pressure for Enlightenment among the youth and such rules did not survive for long. No matter how angry and upset the parents, eventually they had to give in.

The enlightened ideas of "Berlinism" found their most fertile ground, of course, in Lithuania, which borders on Kurland and its German culture. The first Jewish scholar in Russia, L[eon] Mandelstam, came from this region. He had become an enthusiastic Mendelssohnian by the time he was seventeen, and in 1844 he translated the Bible into Russian. Because it was then forbidden to write about sacred things in Russian, Mandelstam's translation of the Bible could, at first, appear only in other countries, and was published in Russia only in 1869. After Lilienthal went to America, Mandelstam was given the position of Learned Jew in the Russian Ministry of Folk Education. He had the task of putting into motion the plan worked out by the Minister of Culture Uvarov and by Lilienthal, for the reform of education and the administration of the newly founded schools. An entire generation of *yeshiva bochrim* began to learn the Russian language with the aid of Mandelstam's dictionaries.

The young people's piety was greatly shaken by their new knowledge of the works of other nations. Received tradition and observance of the old laws and customs began gradually to disappear from Jewish life. As had been predicted, the word of God lost its pride of place and the Hebrew language was neglected.

Aside from my two brothers-in-law, already mentioned, there were two other members of my family who were carried along by the new ideas. One was my older brother, Ephraim Epstein, the other the husband of my sister Kathy, Abraham Sack. Both were talented, industrious young men, eager for knowledge, members of the élite of the city of Brest, where the circle of the enlightened was already quite large. They spent their boyhood years over the Talmud folios, but by now the *melammed* had given way to a teacher. The study of Talmud filled only some of their hours, not the entire day and night as in the days of my older brothers-in-law.

The two young men did continue their studies under the guidance of my father and a *melammed* for the first few years of their marriages. But Lilienthal's movement was penetrating even more widely into various levels of society. The young people in Brest took every opportunity to study foreign books. They organized meetings to read German classics, scientific works, and, in particular, the ancient Greeks. Gradually they admitted even women to these meetings. All the parents disapproved because many a Jewish custom was broken on these occasions. Often the meetings took place on Saturday, a desecration of the Sabbath.

Arguments and ill will entered family life and the battle between young and old could play out over apparently trivial details. We young people did not realize what the old people knew: that even the smallest change in external behavior would carry with it an inner revolution of the personality. I have to smile when I remember how offended my parents were by my sisters' attempts to break away from old-fashioned clothing. In the 1840s a strange new fashion—the crinoline—appeared. Of course, we imitated this monstrosity in a very primitive way: we sewed a wide hem on a cotton frock and threaded a cane hoop through it. There was a second hoop about a quarter meter higher.

After great effort, my sister Kathy was joyfully in possession of such a construction. One morning we were sitting happily in the dining room. Suddenly a barrel appeared in the room, and in the middle stood Kathy. My mother's eyes widened. "What kind of a barrel are you wearing?" Immediately she ordered that the puffy thing was to disappear. My sister, who was very sensitive, began to cry violently. She remained standing there for a while without moving, until Mother cried out, "Shall I help you undress?" That was enough. Weeping, Kathy ran to her room where my mother followed her, took possession of the fatal garment, tore out the hoops, folded them like a snake, and brought them to the kitchen. A good fire was burning in the hearth to boil a pot of water. The flames grabbed eagerly at the new fashion and in our home, at least, the crinoline had a positive effect: the water came to a boil faster.

My sister Chaveh fared no better. She had made herself a *manishka* in accordance with the fashion of the day—a kind of *jabot* of white muslin, in which she appeared one Friday night at the dinner table. My parents were indignant. My father said angrily, "You look like a *goy* (gentile)! How can a Jewish daughter wear a dress that is transparent over the breast?" My sister dared to say that she meant well, she just thought that this new fashion suited her face. But there was no discussion; the *jabot* was not permitted at the table, and for this Sabbath the peaceful atmosphere in our home was destroyed.

In those days the word of the parents still had power. Let me illustrate this with a story that, if not earthshaking, does contain a piece of Jewish social history. Sabbath afternoon, after the obligatory Sabbath nap and the *oneg shabbes*, most Jews went for a stroll on the boulevard and enjoyed the evening twilight. The men, of course, walked strictly separated from the women. As the Bible says, if you go to the right, I will go to the left.[1] God knows for how many centuries this custom had been observed among the Jews.

Now, it happened that my brother-in-law, Abraham Sack, wished to visit his mother with his wife. And so the young man, powerfully motivated by the spirit of the time, dared the unheard-of. In revolutionary fashion, he proposed to pay this visit *together* with his wife. Of course his *Sturm und Drang* was not quite audacious enough to take him through the busiest streets. Well, all right. They left the house together, passing the windows of our dining room, where, it so happened, my father was drinking his afternoon tea. Seeing the two sinners, he was seized with rage, rapped on the window panes, and called to my sister in a commanding tone, "You go back, *now*! Your husband can go alone. For a Jewish woman, for my daughter, it is not fitting to walk

---

[1]   An ironic reference to Genesis 13:9.–ed.

together with her husband, especially in bright daylight." My brother-in-law was, of course, very upset, but dared not object openly and went on alone. And my sister, who had come back into the house, followed her husband only once she could assume that he had reached his goal.

But my father's authoritative position gradually eroded. After difficult inner warfare he was forced to recognize in the end that the fence about the Jewish religion had been broken. He was inconsolable that his most precious jewel, the religion that he had protected and defended through all the storms of life, was now ridiculed, that the Sabbath and Holy Day had lost their sanctity and had become work days. Warnings and protests were without effect against the spirit of the time. Was it any wonder that eventually the old and the young couldn't tolerate living together?

Neither my brother nor my brother-in-law Sack could remain in the house. They were driven out into the wide, wide world. Neither had ever seen a city larger than Brest, but each hoped to prosper in foreign lands. Although they took little baggage, they took with them the honest willingness to work, light hearts, strong self-confidence, good resolutions, and an unshakable faith in humanity and in the future. Furnished with these special necessities of travel they tore themselves away, not without pain and battle from their wives and children, and followed their dark urgings.

Sack never lost, even in later life, either the power of his modern convictions or his knowledge of the old Jewish culture. Throughout his life he remained a fighter for the Enlightenment. He remained untiring in his desire for the new era with all its cultural richness. There was an elevated tone in his house, which his outward success never coarsened. His noble character, his love of human beings, the joy he took in his work, his readiness to sacrifice, marked him as very special. Alexander III awarded him the title of *Excellence* when he was named Director of the St. Petersburg Discount Bank. Even in his will he left the beautiful instructions that his wife, my sister Kathy, was to give from her goods to the poor, the struggling, the despairing. Many a noble deed came from her quiet room and her generosity was well known to artists and scholars everywhere.

112

[Abraham Sack's siblings reflected the rapid transition from old to new ways.] Abraham's older sister was raised in the old ways. She was obedient and self-abnegating before her demanding mother, and when she married, she was tender to her stepchildren. For the older ones recognition of the value of the *Haskalah* had to be painfully won; but for his younger brothers it was Bible and Talmud that were merely an adjunct to the new curriculum. They turned their greatest energy to the study of foreign languages.

Similar, and yet different, was the life of my brother Ephraim. I can't close this chapter without speaking with deep feeling of his changing fortunes, his wanderings. My brother Ephraim was more like my mother than my father. My father was tough and strong, my mother was soft and dreamy. Ephraim clung to her with all his soul. He was the only son in the house, the bearer of the name, the *kaddish*. Little wonder that he was the favorite of father and mother and all of us sisters. My serious-minded father introduced him so early to the sacred domain of the Bible that before he was ten years old he knew much of the Five Books by heart.

By age eleven, Ephraim was at home with the thoughts of the Prophets. He found spiritual nourishment in their power, their melancholy, their depth, their vast religious world. His greatest pleasure was the privilege of reading the portion of the Prophets aloud before the congregation in the *shaul*. All the romanticism and the dreamy transport of boyhood was expressed in his wonderful voice, and all listened to him with great devotion. My father was full of pride, certain of an heir who would be a dedicated Jew.

When Ephraim was twelve years old, the world of Talmud opened to him. In addition, however, he also learned the Russian and German languages and sang the songs of these foreign people with great joy. He was by no means one to sit around indoors. The seriousness of his studies never replaced his glee in being young. Among his friends he was one of the funniest, his games full of inventive ideas tumbling over one another. He could cheer up the saddest person. Often we sisters would laugh with him, half amused and half annoyed.

We called him the "head turner." Really, he could turn anybody's head.

And so he grew up. His conception of Judaism became freer, for no young mind could remain aloof from the spirit of the Lilienthal epoch, but the power of his deep faith was unshaken.

Then an event changed his life: our parents pressed him to marry, and they chose our cousin. He didn't love her, she didn't love him, but our parents' will prevailed. Grandfather did not wish to see the property dissipated, and so regardless of his own wish, Ephraim had to marry the girl. After the birth of his first child, with the agreement of his wife, he went to North America. But it was the unhappiness of his life that had driven him from home—that and the discord between him and his parents. The Enlightenment had driven a deep gulf between father and son.

His exodus to America represented an escape from slavery. There, in a free country, he wished to begin a new life: to work, to study, to try again with all his power, and his richness of soul, to reach new goals. The passage was terrible. Nine weeks in a sailing ship, almost four weeks of these through storms and icy cold. He found himself in a strange land, lonely and forsaken, his money spent. Since he had never learned a trade, he couldn't live by the work of his hands. He tried business, he tried factory work, but this was no life for an intellectually inspired man.

Then a star of hope arose in his night—Lilienthal! The same Lilienthal who had aroused the longing for culture in the youth of Brest now lived in New York. Ephraim went to him. He told him his story of suffering. But he received a cold reception, which completely confused the soft nature of this young recruit in the battle of life. The power of one hard word! One good word instead, and how different my brother's life could have been.

He turned again to hard labor. After all, work on the land had been held up to the young "fighters" as the highest ideal. He went to a farm owned by a Christian who took him in hospitably. Soon he was able to buy a little farm of his own about twelve miles from New York. And here, in a new circle of friends, he adjusted completely to his new

Pauline Wengeroff's brother, Ephraim Epstein

circumstances. He went to church, he listened to the sermons, especially those of one minister who spoke of sin and punishment, repentance and absolution. Since he had removed himself from all Jewish companionship, these sermons were his only spiritual recreation.

Then he was reunited with a companion of his youth from Brest, who had landed in America after many wanderings and earned his living by crafting wind instruments. This friend had left Judaism, and found ways to influence Ephraim to be baptized.

Results soon followed: Ephraim aroused attention, and his great knowledge of Biblical and Talmudic literature was put to use. He gave up his farm, became a theologian, and wandered as a preacher from

115

city to city. He even completed studies at a Christian seminary with great success, sending for his wife and child from Russia.

But although they came, and there was superficial peace in their home, there was no companionship. In the life of sensitive people, much is bent that can never be straightened again. Many a gap can never be filled. His new friends pressed my brother to dedicate his life to a mission to the Jews. He agreed on condition that he might study medicine first, and after three more years he was a doctor. He was called to the Balkan peninsula and lived there for several years, but his missionary work was unsuccessful. He was denied the means for a missionary school, whereupon he abandoned this activity, and from then on was simply a physician, finding a large clientele among Jews, Turks, Bulgars and Greeks. Early in the 1860s he received news that Grandfather had died, and he and his wife had inherited several thousand rubles.

His family life was no happier in Turkey than in America. His inheritance came at the right time to fulfill his unquenchable longing to see his mother and siblings again. The siblings, perhaps, could forgive, but our mother knew no forgiveness. There was a painful, heartbreaking meeting in a German city, where our old mother fell at her son's feet and swore that she would not rise until he had returned to the faith of his fathers, and would never, during her lifetime, return to America. My brother promised. He remained in Germany, living as a strictly observant Jew. A son's love for his mother had won out. He remained with his mother and father in Germany for a short time, and they were very happy, having attained the aim of their life—their son belonged to them once more. It was as though, in their old age, they had been gladdened with yet another child. And before they left for home, our parents also resolved another very difficult task. They arranged a Jewish divorce to end my brother's long-broken marriage. His wife kept one child—the other one had died.

My brother went to Vienna to deepen his medical skills, and while he was there our aged mother left this earth. Now Ephraim was free to think of a return to America. In the meantime, the Austro-Italian war had broken out, and my brother served during the sea battle off Lissa as a medical officer under Admiral Tegetthoff. He celebrated this battle in an epic poem in the English language. Tegetthoff accepted his dedication of this poem gratefully, and the Kaiser rewarded the rhyming doctor with an honorarium of 600 *florins.*

Now my brother returned to America, where he served at various universities as a professor of languages. But soon he took up the practice of medicine again in Chicago. There, to this day, he is co-editor of the *American Journal of Clinical Medicine.* He remarried in Cincinnati. Seven children were born to this marriage. And despite his eighty-one years, he is active and energetic, and his fellow citizens hold him in high honor.

ROMANCE

Tsirl Waletzky

MY ENGAGEMENT

Ratomke Station near Minsk, July 20, 1898. Written under the oak on the little bench in the woods. Memories of my engagement in the year 1849.

50 Years later

It so happened today that I came upon the strong box in which I keep my correspondence with my husband during the year of our engagement. I opened it and turned the yellowed pages, deep in thought, and before I knew it I was surrounded by the entire happy past. I forgot my surroundings and read. Gradually I felt the crust of ice that life has built about my heart melt away. My youth arose within me, and with it all the feelings I once experienced, so fresh, so lively, as if it were all just yesterday. I forgot the present, all the worries, all the suffering through which I have lived in these forty-seven years. Once again I was sixteen-year-old Peshinke in her cozy home surrounded by parents and siblings. One picture after another rose fully formed in my memory. The last months of an existence without worry; school, eager studies, then the sudden unexpected awakening of an unfamiliar feeling that came into my life—young love, dreams, hope, longing, engagement, wedding. They would not let me go, all of these dear memories. The wish arose in me to set down all I have experienced for my children, as a remembrance of their mother.

After the marriage of my older sister Chaveh F., I had more than ever to do in the household. In addition, I studied a great deal and became more and more diligent. An inner voice told me that I didn't have much more time in my father's house. Along with a few other girls I attended a private school where we were taught Russian and German. Our teacher was an elderly gentleman named David Podrevski. His crooked mouth sometimes made it hard for him to speak or to pronounce the difficult Russian words; at times we could hardly understand him. Of the two languages he was actually fluent only in German. His knowledge of Russian was very tenuous. Two rubles a month for three hours a day of instruction—that was his honorarium.

I took great joy in books. In those days there was no children's

121

library at our disposal, so I read everything that came into my hands. Fairy tales, all sorts of tales in Yiddish, the *Gdules Yosef* ("The Greatness of Joseph"), *Tzenture Venture* (adventure stories), and the *Bobe-Mayses* (*Bovo Buch*).[1] My spirit was most impressed with the rich fantasy of the Oriental tales of *A Thousand and One Nights*. This kind of literature contented me until I was eleven. Later *Robinson Crusoe* became my favorite book, and even later Zschokke and Schiller, whose first volume of poems we girls sang and learned by heart.

Friedrich Schiller played an important role among the Jews, both in their life and in their literature. His poetry blew like a breath of spring into the depressed, dark atmosphere of the ghetto. Jews admired the splendor and beauty that suddenly appeared before them. He was the poet Jewish young people read when they first became interested in non-Jewish literature. They grew enthusiastic about his poems and improved their German through them. The boys memorized him just as much as the girls, and soon the works of Schiller constituted a *sine qua non* in the program of study of an educated Jew. They studied Talmud and Schiller, and they studied Schiller using the talmudic method. Every important sentence was studied and examined, analyzed, and debated out loud. Questions and possible answers were suggested and the discussion continued until a satisfactory solution had been found and the deep meaning that was said to lie behind the words was revealed. At that time the best Jewish poets were translating world literature into Hebrew. Everyone tried his hand at Schiller. His intellectual character, his seriousness, pathos and idealism were all popular; he framed history within a moral context.

In school I came across my first Russian book, a collection of the poems of Griboedov and Zhukovskii. Many poems in this collection

---

[1]   The biblical Joseph story was often treated by popular writers. The *Gdules Yosef* mentioned here was possibly the Yiddish dramatic treatment by Eliezer Paver (1801). On the various Yiddish books mentioned here, including *Robinson Crusoe* and the nineteenth-century popularization of the Arthurian romance, the *Bovo Buch*, into the often reprinted *Bobe-Mayse*, see Israel Zinberg, *A History of Jewish Literature* XI (Cincinnati and New York: 1978), p. 150f.–ed.

moved me to tears. There was also a story in prose about the life of a settler named Vadim and his friend Gostomisl. I read this tale of Russia's ancient heroes over and over. And to this day, sixty-five years later, I know the whole story by heart.

One beautiful spring morning, some months after my sister Chaveh's marriage, I was sitting on the balcony of our house doing my homework. Both my parents came out to join me. Mother pulled me to my feet and turned me around slowly, smiling and looking me up and down, all the time exchanging significant looks with Father until I turned crimson. I could not imagine what it all meant, and I didn't dare ask. At last she noticed my embarrassment and stroked my cheek very gently. Then off they both went, deep in conversation.

I sat where I was and tried to figure it out. I turned the matter this way and that, but could make absolutely no sense of it. Finally I concluded that it must be about the blue summer dress I was wearing, Mother's favorite. Father made it a point that we were to be well dressed at all times; she must have been showing off the frock to please him. This is how innocent we were in those days, at a time when our parents were already busy with our wedding plans.

From that morning on, the whole family behaved in a new way toward me. Repeatedly I would catch people staring. Several days passed before anybody thought to tell me that Father had responded in the affirmative to a proposal for my hand in marriage.

A rabbi, a teacher of Talmud, had written seeking a bride for his pupil. In accordance with patriarchal custom, my future husband's parents had sent their adult son's teacher out into the world to find him a wife, and everywhere he went the marriage brokers pointed out pretty girls from good families. He had been to several other towns without finding the girl he was looking for and now he was coming to Brest to meet me, a daughter of Yehuda ha-Levi Epstein. His employers were wealthy people who always chose brides for their sons from among Jewish families of distinction. The wealthy Jews of that time always sought out a *bas tovim*, the daughter of a man learned in Talmud, for their son, just as they would spare no expense to marry their daughter to a young Talmud scholar.

arranged marriages

123

Our house was in an uproar. Everyone knew about the expected guest and about his errand. I alone dared not think about it.

My older sisters and their husbands formed a family council. My eldest brother-in-law undertook the role of go-between in the negotiations with the representative of my future in-laws. The family council invited the representative to tea. Nobody seemed to think it necessary to tell me about it.

On the appointed day, only oblique references were dropped at the lunch table. My parents seemed particularly cheerful, while on the other hand my own heart began to fill with foreboding and with an excitement I could hardly master. I had all I could do not to burst into tears at the table.

As soon as the meal was over I went out alone, to sort out my thoughts and try to come to terms with these staggering new emotions. Rejecting my sister's advice to put on a party dress, I kept on my little blue dress with the black silk apron. "He" would see me as I was every day, as my family saw me, as I saw myself.

When I returned to the house toward evening the stranger had already arrived. I was told that he would not have time to stay for supper, but that he did have to have a look at me. Father had sent word that I was to bring a light to his study.

I put two candles in the candelabrum and lit them. The short walk to Father's study seemed endless that day. My thoughts were racing, while a storm in my chest was doing its best to shut off my heart. Outwardly I was calm.

I knocked at the door softly, opened it, and waited—on the threshold of the study and, as it seemed to me, of my whole future life. The candles I was carrying blinded my eyes. I raised them aloft and stood there, illuminated, waiting.

From the sofa in the far corner of the room I heard my father's voice in conversation with the strange gentleman. Still holding the candles up over my head, I walked toward his voice.

The stranger rose.

"This is my Pessele," said Father.

Large, intelligent eyes gave me a look so deep and probing that I

124

knew at once that the rabbi had found what he was looking for. I flushed, unable to speak. In my shyness and confusion I kept holding the candles high over my head until Father called my attention to them. Then I set them down, glanced once more in the gentleman's direction and quietly left the study.

All my loved ones assembled in the dining room pelted me with questions till I begged them earnestly not to speak of the whole matter, which only made them laugh and tease me without mercy.

An hour later Rabbi Brim took his leave of my parents. That same evening he set off for his home in Konotop, 800 Russian *versts* away. Soon he wrote my father that all had been arranged in accordance with his wishes: The rabbi, Mr. Wengeroff, and his son would be leaving within the next few days on their long journey to us. We were to come to meet them in the little town of Kartuskaya Beryosa, fifteen miles from our home. If we liked one another, the engagement would be solemnized then and there.

I was a very young girl, with little notion of the feelings of love between men and women. Now suddenly, as though torn from a deep slumber, I was assaulted by all sorts of astonishing thoughts and feelings. I would sit by myself at dusk, daydreaming about *him*—the companion of all my future life. About our life together. Those were tranquil dreams, full of light, full of the confidence that only good things lay ahead.

I was never alone, for the image of my intended was always with me. Sometimes he was blond and blue-eyed. Other times his hair was black, and then deep eyes, warm and dark and full of love, gazed into mine. Then I would blush. But although they embarrassed me, I loved those daydreams, loved them beyond anything in the world.

Sometimes, as I sat there lost in thought, the girls at work in the garden would sing me songs of gentle teasing and flattery. My favorite was the one about the beautiful descendant of rabbis.

> *Fair, I'm so fair,*
> *Fair is my name,*
> *You know I came*
> *From rabbis.*

I sit on the roof,
Sweating in the sun,
With blue socks on,
I'm worth thousands.

Coffee in the mugs,
Mead in the kegs
A thousand dollars
In my bags.

Magnificent preparations were made for my engagement. I received very beautiful presents. It was decided that my youngest married sister and her husband, my older brother Ephraim, my sister Kathy, and my older brother-in-law, Samuel Feigish [1] would accompany my parents and me to Kartuskaya Beryosa. The Wengeroffs' journey from Konotop took them fourteen days. As soon as they had arrived they notified us by special express courier and we set off, arriving in the little town the very next evening.

It was June 15, 1849. That date is engraved upon my heart. I shall never forget it.

At our inn they told us that the Wengeroffs were staying at the town's other inn, just across a narrow alley from ours. Our host assured us that we could easily peek from our windows into theirs, especially from the windows of the room he had prepared for me. I went straight upstairs to put my things away. I was very tired, but all the same I kept lifting a corner of the muslin curtain to steal a glance at the window opposite, and a soft voice whispered in my heart that the same maneuver was going forward across the alley. In the end I succumbed to fatigue and fell fast asleep.

Loud voices roused me early the next morning. I could not help overhearing a debate next door in my parents' room between my mother and my brother-in-law. They were arguing about details in the financial clauses of the engagement contract. Dowry, presents, jewelry.

---

[1]   See note 13 to the Family Tree.–ed.

It was Father's voice that cut them off at last: "If the young man's Talmud learning is good, the rest will fall into place."

Then he prepared to examine his future son-in-law in Talmud, the examination that would decide my entire future life. The depth of his knowledge of Talmud determined what kind of family a young man could hope to marry into. This was the only available criterion, since Talmud was the only intellectual nourishment and at the same time the only refining influence accessible to a young Jew. His understanding of Talmud was decisive.

My father crossed over to the Wengeroffs' inn.

He returned to us at last in the most joyous frame of mind, full of praise for the young man, full of enthusiasm over his knowledge of Talmud. He was also quite taken with the elder Wengeroff, and in short wished to delay the matter no further and was determined to solemnize the engagement that very day. We two, I and my intended, were to become acquainted before the ceremony. He had invited father and son to call upon us.

When I arrived in the dining room my family was already assembled. A few minutes later a handsome elderly man entered the room unannounced, accompanied by a young man of powerful build.

We all rose and went up to them. I was so excited I could hardly stand on my feet. Seated once again, I struggled for the self-control to carry on a proper conversation with the father of my intended. But soon we all had so much to say to each other that the talk became general.

Our family spoke the so-called "Russian-German," while the two Wengeroffs used a kind of Lithuanian-Yiddish dialect, but not very skillfully. Eventually it turned out that they were actually much more fluent in Russian, and with relief we all switched to that language. Soon our little circle seemed as intimate as though we had known each other for years.

Gradually, the young people were drifting into an adjoining room. My intended joined them after a bit, and then Kathy suggested to me that we follow. Here etiquette was cast aside and we sat wherever we liked, so that it seemed natural for me to sit next to my fiancé.

After another little while, however, the room seemed to clear as one by one the others disappeared, leaving the two of us alone.

I was furious. Unable to utter a word, I fell into an embarrassed silence.

But then he began to speak. Trembling with emotion, he spoke to me of his feelings. He spoke of love, of devotion, of his hope for everlasting bliss. And his eyes spoke for him more eloquently than his words.

Two young people not even engaged must not spend too much time alone together. Soon there was a soft knock at the door, and Kathy came to fetch us. Everyone was waiting in the main room to celebrate our betrothal. Following an ancient custom that is observed among religious Jews to this day, the *tno'im* (pre-nuptial agreement) were drafted. This document stated precisely how much my bridegroom and I were bringing into the marriage, when the wedding would take place, and so forth. The *tno'im* were read aloud, and then a plate was smashed as a reminder of the fragility of human existence. And as a warning.

General congratulations, general enjoyment of wine and sweets, merry and cheerful activity all round. We enjoyed a jolly lunch together; my bridegroom never left my side.

In the afternoon we were all invited to the Wengeroffs, where time passed pleasantly over a bubbling samovar, a rich spread of delicacies, and comfortable talk. My father expressed the wish that his future son-in-law become proficient in German, which he considered socially indispensable in our country, and both father and son agreed that this was reasonable.

Soon the young people executed the same little maneuver as before. Finding the quarters too close and the business talk of their elders boring, they disappeared one by one into my bridegroom's nearby room. Now the question arose whether it was proper for me to join them there. Mother said it would be immodest. But my older brother-in-law stood up for me, and in the end she permitted him to escort me.

When I appeared on his arm at Chonon's door, my bridegroom went nearly mad for joy. With every passing hour our happiness and

128

our liking, attachment and sympathy for one another seemed to grow. We drank deeply from the well of happiness.

It was getting late—in the opinion of our elders. My mother came and whispered to me that it was improper to spend so much time in the room of my fiancé. I sensed a trace of disapproval in her tone. So we went home. Behind us in the dark little street I could hear the footsteps of young Wengeroff giving us escort, but, afraid of annoying my mother, I didn't dare turn around.

That is how strictly our mothers watched over us. It was not that they didn't trust us. It was simply their sacred traditional task to guard us with tenderness and solicitude in our inexperience. Mothers of today, reading these lines, may well wish that they were back in those days.

Next morning I awoke in a glow. No need on that day to persuade me to wear my very best! We were upset for a while when it was announced that we were all starting for home that very afternoon. But then, seeing our sad faces, our parents took pity upon my fiancé and me and agreed to put off the departure until the following morning.

We shouted for joy. They left us young ones to our own devices, and first of all we went for a joyride through the countryside in almost unrestrained merriment, had several adventures involving various peasants, and returned to our families in the greatest good humor. We spent the rest of the day in tomfoolery, drinking tea, nibbling pastries. We formed a choir and sang our Polish-Yiddish songs, my fiancé sang us his Russian ones and so the time passed until evening. Finally overcome by fatigue, we parted soon after supper.

But that night I could not get to sleep. All sorts of audacious thoughts and images passed through my mind and kept me wide awake. I had never felt like this before. I had had no inkling that anybody could feel like this. My heart filled with the bliss of it.

My readers will have noticed the great upheaval that had taken place in Jewish family life in the short time since my sister Chaveh's engagement. She had her first glimpse of her bridegroom a few moments before her marriage ceremony. She did try to resist putting on her wedding gown until she had at least spoken with him, but one stern look from Mother was sufficient to tame her. And even once the bridal couple stood face to face at last, they were forbidden to exchange so much as a handshake.

By contrast, I was permitted to go into my fiancé's room accompanied only by my siblings, and to make an excursion into the countryside in a group consisting entirely of young people. The seclusion of Jewish family life was beginning to break up. Imperceptibly, foreign elements were beginning to creep in. Scarcely one generation after mine, all the age-old Jewish customs would be no more than fading legends!

The next day I rose very early. Drearily I began to make my travel preparations. Our carriage was at the door. My parents and siblings were ready.

The Wengeroffs came over to have breakfast with us. I glanced at my fiancé, and found traces of tears upon his cheek. We had so much left to say to one another. Neither of us spoke.

At the breakfast table only the older people said anything at all, while we young ones sat in an uneasy silence. Then, after the meal, when we rose to say good-bye, I lost control altogether. I embraced my intended—this was completely unheard-of at that time—and burst into violent tears. Our parents were so moved by this that they permitted us to walk ahead together for quite a distance, with everyone else following in the two carriages.

Our parting was delayed one more time by my sudden discovery that I was missing my magnificent new watch and chain. We went back to look for them, we actually found them, and everyone agreed that this was a very good omen for us. But then at last we had to return to our families and get into separate carriages. One last look, and the vehicles set off in opposite directions. As the distance between us grew more and more rapidly, I sank back into a corner, steeped in grief and indescribable pain. It seemed to me that all that was precious and beautiful in life was vanishing behind us.

After a while Kathy tried to bring me out of it, and I was shocked to realize that by my behavior I had been proclaiming, for all to see,

130

an emotion that I had meant to harbor as the closest secret of my heart. I was embarrassed and ashamed of my weakness. But gradually I grew calmer and consoled myself with thoughts of our next reunion. My parents promised that we would meet once more before the wedding. And so, little by little, the pain of parting abated and we arrived at home fresh and in good spirits.

Relatives and friends began arriving to congratulate me and to see my beautiful presents: a long string of pearls, long diamond earrings, the watch and chain. Over and over I had to assure everybody that I was feeling "thank God very happy."

Engagement gifts were decreed by custom, not by personal preference, and some were so indispensable that even the poorest bride and bridegroom had to have them. Every bridegroom must be given a *talles* (prayer shawl) and a *kittel*. The latter was a long white garment he would wear on *Yom Kippur* while he was young; at his *Pesach seder* table when he was the father of grown children; and, finally, in his grave. If the bride was poor, a collection would be taken up for her so that she could give him the *talles* and a skullcap of silver thread, and also a watch with a black silk cord that she had braided herself. Chaveh had decorated hers with great artistry in colorful glass beads.

If the bride was wealthy, her bridegroom would receive a *shtreimel* (a Sabbath hat made of precious furs) and a silver snuff box. When it came to wedding presents, her in-laws gave the bride her prayer book, called *Korben Mincheh*. And even if her dowry amounted to as little as one hundred rubles, a wealthy girl always received a *kanek*, a choker of black velvet set with rows of genuine seed pearls. The pearls *had* to be genuine, but their size depended upon the relative wealth of her in-laws. There might be silver ducats suspended from the *kanek* or, among the truly rich, several golden coins worth fifteen rubles each or larger coins bearing the engraved profiles of three kings with a value of thirty rubles each. These coins were called "show pieces." Among other gifts, there were two veils of delicate white netting for her head, and if there was very great wealth also some diamonds, usually set as earrings, some ropes of pearls, and a golden chain. The chain, which became popular in the 1840s, was often worn in the street sewn onto the bodice of a coat in intricate patterns. Also in the Forties, a gift watch for the bride became popular. All these wedding gifts were presented to the couple on their wedding day by the two sets of parents. They were brought into the bride's home about noon by a man called the *badchen*, accompanied by a band playing cheerful music.

The present generation's sensibilities may scorn such minutely regulated arrangements, but their purpose was to forestall misunderstandings between the two families and to prevent quarrels and feuds.

I returned to everyday life. Embarrassed to be treated as a bride, I begged my family not even to mention my fiancé. I refused to be "special" in any way, and made a particular point of fulfilling all my household duties exactly as before. At that time I was actually the one who managed the household, since Kathy was not interested in it and our mother had taken to spending her days chiefly in prayer and in reading Psalms and other sacred texts such as *Menoires Ha-Mo'er* and *Nachlas Zvi*. [1]

At the same time I applied myself with great diligence to my lessons with Mr. Podrevski. I had made up my mind to master both grammars, the Russian by Vostokov and the German by von Heyse, before my wedding day. All work was easy for me now—there was such joy, freshness, love of life in me, such happiness, that it spread through the whole family. Gladness and delight reigned in our house.

Three weeks had gone by since my engagement, when one day Father returned from town beaming and handed me a sealed envelope addressed to me.

"Here's a letter for you, it must be from your bridegroom."

It was the first letter I had ever received in my life. My hands trembled as I opened it. Here is what it said:

---

[1] The references are to a Yiddish translation of Isaac Aboab, *Menorat ha-Maor* (fourteenth century) and Zvi Hirsch Chotsh's Yiddish translation of excerpts from the kabbalistic classic, the Zohar.–ed.

Much beloved and precious Peshinke, you should live and be healthy, only soul of mine!

Now we are in Slutzk. By now surely you are back home, and I am already a distance of 275 versts from you. Only yesterday I was beside you, and I heard your dear, sweet speech! Oh, how happy I was. But now I see only that after the two hours my father wants to spend here I will have to travel on—with every minute, every second, to go farther and farther away from you, my precious Pessunyu. My precious, only soul Pessunyu, you can imagine how I felt when I sat down in my carriage to begin the journey, and two seconds later I could no longer see you! How it was for me after that, I could describe in pages and pages, but I am afraid that maybe this would disquiet you. Only you can understand, angel mine, the only thing that will be my consolation, I will read your handwriting so precious to me, in which I will read of your feelings toward me. Oh, then I will be newborn! After that it will be all the same to me how I make the time pass that separates us from one another. I will obey any command of yours; it will be my joy, just so I receive your sweet letters with your words in them!

In the middle of the journey we had one other delay. Two stations after leaving Berese. We stayed there six hours, from ten in the morning until four in the evening, and all that time I was cheerful, thinking how much farther from you I would have been already if we had spent all that time traveling instead.

I hope that you will give me the pleasure of gladdening me with your letters, I'll stop begging for that now.

Be healthy and cheerful, and God grant that we see each other soon, my precious Pessunyu.

Chonon Wengeroff

P.S. Precious! If you could write the envelope to my name, I beg you very much to do that. Forgive me that I write so poorly, but I had to write in pencil.

I beg you to ask all the others to forgive me that I have not written to them also; we are hurrying so. Once again remain in good health, as is wished for you by your

Loving
Chonon.
July 8, 1849. 10 o'clock in the morning.
I am writing the address to your name. My father told me to do that.

133

As I read his heart's outpouring of endearments, my confusion was boundless. My parents asked me what was in the letter, but I could not tell them. I begged them with tears in my eyes to allow me to grant his wish to write to him often. They agreed, which was astonishing in light of the Orthodox orientation of the time. It shows the kind of people they were: so great was their joy that their Pessele had received a letter addressed to her by name, that they gave their permission. I was careful to ask them to add a few words to each letter that I wrote, for it would have seemed frivolous to carry on an unsupervised correspondence with my intended.

I have preserved every one of the letters of my bridegroom. They are my dearest treasure and to this day, fifty-nine years later, they are all in my possession. Sometimes I turn the yellowed pages, conjure up that beautiful time and bask again in the joy of long ago.

At that time, a great worry dampened my joy. My youngest sister Helene suddenly fell ill with a dangerous nerve fever. The doctors had given up on her when suddenly she got better, and God gave us back our precious little sister. This is how it happened. My little sister was lying pale as a corpse, unconscious, when the doctors tried one last remedy: She was put in a cold bath for ten minutes and then back into a pre-warmed bed. But in all the excitement of heating up the bed a hot water bottle had been left in it, and the child was lying directly on this very hot bottle. A deep burn wound was created, which proved lucky for her. The doctors were sure that without this wound she would have died. This is a good example of the medical science of that day. It used to be a very popular method in cases of serious illness to create a pustulating wound, using a hair rope. This, it was believed, would "suck" the disease out of the body. Slowly but steadily she recovered, though she was kept in bed for several months more. Together with my younger sister, I had to play the role of nurse because the suffering child found it more pleasant to have relatives around her than a strange nurse. I was near her day and night. I slept in a bed next to hers and, since she couldn't feed herself, I fed her. It was a bad time for me. Only the letters of my fiancé bucked up my willpower and gave me fresh strength.

But there was a trial ahead specifically for me, as well. I heard *sub rosa*, as it were, that my parents were no longer pleased by my frequent exchange of letters with my fiancé. In their opinion the whole thing, that is to say my entire position as fiancé, was not at all certain. My pain was boundless. I wept whole days and nights. I tried to ascertain the reason for their disapproval, but for a long time I couldn't find out anything. At last, my younger brother-in-law took pity on me and told me that my fiancé had been denounced to my parents as a bundle of all bad character traits. I suffered indescribably. My father was full of sorrow. The mood in the house was very depressed. Finally, my father wrote to Homel, a little town near Konotop, where we had a relative, Reb Isaac Epstein, and begged him to look into the matter thoroughly.

Soon he answered that there was no basis for the slander. The family Wengeroff, my relative wrote, was an honorable one and the young man a good human being and a good Talmudist. This news quieted the storm in our house, the dark clouds scattered, and bright skies shone once again over my life, filled with jubilation. My passionate yearning grew in power, our correspondence in frequency. My siblings teased me and laughed whenever a letter came, but they rejoiced with me.

Life at home returned to normal. Winter was near an end; spring announced its arrival very early that year. My sister was recovering and could leave her bed.

Now our mother began the great preparations for my trousseau. Linen, silk, lace and woollen stuff was bought. There were discussions, choosing, buying, all in haste. I was often consulted, but I expressed my opinion shyly and with blushes. The underwear was made outside the house, but the dresses were sewn at home, not by seamstresses but by journeymen tailors. They were all young fellows who, as coincidence would have it, also belonged to the synagogue choir. As they worked they often liked to sing, usually religious songs from *Purim* plays, Achashveros plays, or a Joseph play. This latter was their favorite, and they repeated it many times. They distributed the parts among themselves and sang like this:

135

JACOB: I am the tree of the whole world and here are my branches *(with his hand pointing to his children)*. Therefore, I beg the *oylom* (the public) to be quiet a little.

It's two years since I left the house and not, *chas veshulem* (God forbid), for a *parnuseh* (livelihood) but because of the *tzores* (sorrows) that befell me.

La, la, la, la, la, la, la, la, la, la, la, la.

My son Simon, my son Simon, you are my best son, you are my favorite son. Tell me the truth, tell me the truth. Where is he, where is he, my son Yosefel?

THE SONS: Father, dear sweet father, we don't know where he is.

JACOB: My son Ruben, my son Ruben, you are my best son, you are my dearest son. Everyone will praise you. Tell me the truth, tell me the truth. Where is he, where is he, my son Yosefel?

THE SONS: Father, dear sweet father, we can't show you our *ponim* (face). We sold him to the *Midyonim* (Midianites).

JACOB: If you want to give me my life, bring him to me soon.

(Joseph is brought in. Jacob falls into a joyful ecstasy.)

JOSEPH SINGS: I have many sheep and much cattle. I have a wife with two children. One is called Menasse, the other is called Ephraim, and they have made me a big man in the land *Mitzraim* (Egypt).

La, la, la, la, la, la, la, la, la, la, la, la.

They also liked to sing a cheerful little song about a tailor.

I sit, one leg tossed over the other
And sing a little song sweet as sugar.
To be a shneider *(tailor) is good in this world.*
Wherever he goes, he earns money.
If the yolden *(light-headed youths) found this out*
They'd all want to be shneiders.

Sometimes they sang songs about me and my fiancé. Some of these songs are still fresh in my memory.

Kallehle *(little bride)*, kallehle, *cry, cry, cry.*
Your chossen *(bridegroom) will send you a plate of* chrein *(horse-
    radish)*
And your tears will pour all the way down to your toes.

I'm sitting on a rock
Crying and crying.
All the girls are becoming kallehs
But nebech *(alas), not I.*

And then there was:

A boy takes a girl by the hand and believes that the world is his. He
gives her coarse wool to spin into fine silk.

THE GIRL: *I will spin coarse wool for you into fine silk, and you will*
    make a ladder for me all the way up to Heaven.

THE BOY: *I will make you a ladder all the way to Heaven, and you*
    must count the stars for me that are in Heaven.

THE GIRL: *I will count the stars in Heaven for you. and you will*
    empty the sea for me with a little pitcher.

THE BOY: *I will empty the sea for you with a little pitcher, and you*
    must catch the little fish in the sea for me.

THE GIRL: *I will catch the little fish in the sea for you, and you shall*
    cook the little fish for me without fire, in some water.

THE BOY: *I will cook the little fish for you without fire in some water,*
    and you shall have seven children from me and remain a
    young woman.

The maid Mariasheh also teased me with a song whenever she saw me
running about the house joyful and happy, or sitting in a corner
absorbed in my dreams.

CHORUS: Oy vay, *how can you live!*
        You give koved *(honor) to your* shver *(father-in-law)*
        and shviger *(mother-in-law).*

If I get up late,
My beize *(angry)* shviger *says*
I lie like a nveileh *(foul corpse)*
Half the day in bed.

CHORUS

If I go gich *(fast),*
She says I'm wearing out my shoes.
If I go pameilach *(slowly),*
She says I'm too happy.

CHORUS

If I bake greiseh challehs (large Sabbath loaves),
My beize shviger *says*
That I'm driving her be-dalles *(into poverty).*

CHORUS

If I bake small challehs,
My beize shviger *says*
That I'm dragging dalles *onto her.*

CHORUS

If I go nicely dressed,
My beize shviger *says*
That I'm making her gemein *(poor).*

CHORUS

If I get dressed mi'es *(ugly),*
My beize shviger *says*
I'm causing her a busheh *(embarrassment).*

CHORUS

and then there was:

Dearest daughter, daughter mine,
I will teach you how to be with a shviger.

If your shviger *is out of the house,*
Don't give money to the poor.

When your shviger *comes from* shul *(synagogue),*
Meet her halfway, carry a chair to her.

When your shviger *goes to the table,*
Give her the best piece of fish.

Closer and closer came the time to leave the home of my parents, and this dimmed my joy. Before the departure for Konotop, I was to go to Warsaw to say goodbye to relatives, especially to Grandfather, and to receive his blessing for my marriage.

This was early August, 1849. At that time, the Polish-Russian border was near the little town of Terespol, four Russian *versts* from Brest. I undertook this journey with my father. But before we got to the border he was forced to leave me, and I had to manage all the formalities of the border crossing myself. This was my first independent step. I must confess my courage was not very great, and when I entered the office where I had to show my passport, I felt very uneasy. Tears came to my eyes and I would have liked to sob like a little child. I was ashamed of this weakness and tried to control myself. They had me sign a document in this office, another independent deed.

Finally, I was on the other side of the border. Here I was met by our friend, Reb Yossele, who took me to his family in the little town. The next day my father, whom I was expecting with great longing, arrived, and we traveled together to Warsaw.

We stayed there eight days. Grandfather received me with special consideration. My aunts and uncles treated me the whole time with great tenderness. I got very pretty wedding presents from everyone and a piece of silver from Grandfather and—the blessing.

It was a moment I cannot forget. Grandfather stood in the middle of the parlor. My heart pounding, I approached him and bent my head in humble submission. He laid his hands on my head and pronounced the blessing in a loud, trembling voice. A joyful stillness filled the room. Only the aunts sobbed quietly. My mood was so solemn, so sad. I felt for the first time truly what a serious change my life was to undergo. With a heavy heart I said goodbye to my dear, revered grandfather, because the thought would not leave me that I was seeing him for the last time in my life. Thoughtful and much more serious, I returned home.

The trousseau was complete. My mother packed all the beautiful new things with love and care into a massive, metal-lined trunk. In addition to underwear, I was given the following things:

> A wedding dress made of heavy gray silk in alternating bands of antique moiré and satin, trimmed with lace made of flocked silk.

> A dress of *muslin de laine*, checked dark blue and white, ankle length, very simple fashion, a yoke at the top, a belt in the middle, long Grecian sleeves.

> A dress of dark blue satin, trimmed in front with dark blue velvet, long narrow sleeves with velvet cuffs.

> A black taffeta dress, called a *mantine,* without any trim.

> A dress of green wool with black trim in beautiful patterns.

> Further, two dressing gowns, one in light blue muslin with simple white lace, another one of terry cloth, very loose, called a *rubashka,* a little shirt.

> Further, three coats, one a *mandaronka*—that's how the raincoat of that day was called—of dark blue material; one *ziganka* of gray silk; with a plain square piece at the neck and gathered cuffs, trimmed with red silk ribbon and gray tassels. And an *algierka,* a long coat with Grecian sleeves, empire, made of black silk. In front at the breast there were two silk ropes, ending in large tassels that were tossed back over the shoulders.

> Further, two day caps, one of blonde lace with a blue ribbon for holidays; the other, everyday one, simpler. And with that, six morning caps in coquettish shapes.

> Further, a pair of pink gloves with white tulle lace for the wedding.

Everything was ready. Now the preparations were begun for the long trip. I was left to myself, and had time to say goodbye to everything I loved.

These were difficult days for me. A mixture of feelings and desires was at war within me. Sometimes the thought of my reunion with my deeply beloved gave me such shining joy that everyone who passed me had to smile, that's how happy I looked. But then again tears would fill my eyes, and I would sob quietly in some corner, overcome by the pain of parting. But soon I would be laughing again, with ecstasy and joy.

The last Sunday before our departure I had to pay farewell calls on relatives, friends and acquaintances. I performed this duty accompanied by an elderly woman named Reizeleh, who was known all over town as a *sarverke* (waitress).[1] She served as honor escort for all the Jewish brides in Brest.

At noon on the day before the last day we were all sitting together at the mid-day meal, when my older sister became aware how pale I looked, and then the others noticed it too. Father asked me with tender concern what was worrying me.

I was tortured by a dream I'd had: I was all alone in one of the narrow little streets I used to pass every day as a little girl with the *behelfer* on the way to school. Suddenly an enormous black ox bounded toward me in wild leaps. I trembled with fright. The ox with his giant horns kept coming nearer. I tried to hide, but couldn't find any corner. I ran to the left, to the right, but the black brute followed me everywhere.

Finally, exhausted with fear, I surrendered to my fate. Suddenly a little man appeared in the semi-darkness of the narrow little street, wearing a belted black silk caftan and a high sable hat. His face was all wrinkled. It bore the features of my grandfather. An unusually long gray beard surrounded his face and hung all the way down to his knees.

The little man took me by the hand and, casting sidelong glances at the brute, said, "Come with me. Don't be afraid."

---

[1] A *sarverkeh* was a woman who served in all the better Jewish homes during the holidays and prepared sweets, jams, and preserves.

Trusting and thankful I went with him. After a while he stopped, let go of my hand, showed me the way and suddenly disappeared from sight. And the brute wasn't there either.

Trembling all over I awoke, but could not rid myself of the heavy impression of the dream.

Everyone listened to me with great attention. My father was the most moved of all. As soon as I had finished my story, he quickly got up from the table and went to his study, where he leafed through a large book.

Finally he came back, beaming joyfully, and said, "Be calm, my daughter. You will have very noisy children."

I blushed, embarrassed, and dared not look at anyone. My family laughed and teased me and tried to get me to look up, but I sat that way till the end of the meal.

Our departure was fixed for the next day. Our carriage stood before the door. It was a *fügon*, a long vehicle covered in leather with little curtained windows, with three post horses in harness. The excitement in the house reached a climax. People were running to and fro. Many things were quickly gathered and packed into the carriage. There was still a great deal to do in this last hour before our departure.

The carriage was heavily loaded inside and out, since we were going to be *en route* for fourteen days. We took along great supplies of baked goods, smoked fish, salted foods, and a whole case of cognac, rum, liquor, wine, tea and sugar, to last all of us. These provisions were packed into a large, square chest lined in fur and bound with strips of tin, called a *pogrebez*. Five comfortable seats were arranged for the travelers.

I could not tear myself away from the house.

Finally Father called out in a tone of command, "Enough, enough!" Decisively, he helped me into the carriage first. Then followed my mother, my younger sister whom I loved deeply, and our eight-year-old brother. Then a short command in real Russian, "*Pashel* (Let's go)!" and the carriage set off. Among the tears, well-wishes and blessings of those left behind, we drove away.

I was sobbing like a little child. The carriage went faster and faster. Through my tears I watched all the old familiar streets disappear. Houses where I had been in and out for years to visit dear friends, people whom until today I had seen daily. My favorite places moved past me, then behind me, and disappeared never to return. Gone the beautiful time of carefree, happy, earliest youth.

It was the year 1850, the 5th of August.

MY WEDDING IN KONOTOP

We traveled day and night, interrupting our journey only for a Sabbath rest from Friday noon until Saturday evening. After seven days, when we had covered half the distance of our journey, the carriage gave out. We were forced to camp in an open field. A carpet was spread and our provisions fetched, and soon the samovar was bubbling and humming. We all sat around it and forgot our unpleasant situation in the murmur of the samovar and cozy conversation.

The day of the wedding kept coming closer, and we were still far from our goal. Father sent a dispatch rider to Konotop asking for an eight-day postponement of the wedding. In Konotop they were in despair and held a grudge against my parents for a long time, because the enormous store of fowl and other foodstuffs was bound to spoil in this hot season of the year.

It was another full six days before we arrived at the penultimate station, Baturim, the historic residence of the *hetman* (Ukrainian chieftain), Mazepa. Here a messenger brought us the news that my father-in-law, accompanied by several gentlemen, was waiting for us at the next station. My heart began to pound stormily, but I kept a stubborn silence, fearing that any word out of my mouth would be followed by a stream of tears. I was close to the goal of my most beautiful dreams. In an hour, my longing would become reality. I hardly dared think of the kind of happiness to which not every girl could aspire.

We girls saw to our toilette. I chose a dress that was very becoming and examined myself in the mirror, which showed me the reflection of my own happiness. Then we got into the carriage and quickly drove on. Along the way we met a carriage coming toward us, and even from a distance we recognized my father-in-law and Mr. Brim. Half an hour later we arrived at the last station before Konotop. We were very close to our goal.

And then we drove into Konotop. The suburbs were not very promising—lots of little huts with straw roofs. My sister was almost horrified by the village character of this little town, but it was all the same to me. What did I care about the town? Only the image of my betrothed hovered before me, like the pillar of fire before the Israelites in the desert at night, banishing all sad thoughts.

We drove through a long, uneven street, the same straw-covered huts on our right and left. Finally we arrived in a broad square where the first large elegant stone house stood, with a green tin roof. This was the goal of our journey, the house of the Wengeroff family. Accompanied by a curious crowd, our carriage drove through the entrance and halted before a large balcony completely crammed with people.

My future grandmother-in-law came forward to receive me, kissed me and gave me a piece of "sweet bread." She impressed me as serious and worthy of respect. On the other hand the "aunt," the step-mother of my bridegroom, won my trust and affection right away. And her embrace seemed more hearty, intimate and tender. The other people who were introduced to me at that time were the wife of my bridegroom's elder brother and his younger sister. I already knew so much that was good and lovely about her, that I embraced her like a long familiar friend.

But over all their heads, I searched for my dearest, my nearest, for whom I had longed this whole year so passionately. But he was nowhere to be seen. Accompanied by them all, I went through the entrance hall into the salon. And here my bridegroom received me, beaming with happiness. Our reunion was silent. Truly, no words were needed. Our eyes said what no poet has ever found words to express.

Evening came, countless lights burned, and the house and the

144

people looked very festive. Tea was served. The older sister-in-law never left my mother's side, the younger never left mine. My bridegroom, in order not to transgress good manners, was forced to keep my father company and stay among the gentlemen. However, he made bold from time to time to sit down beside me and whisper a few dear words to me.

Soon we were invited to dance and both of us, my sister and I, must take part although we weren't particularly in the mood. We danced a polka mazurka with figures, which was very well received. Altogether, on this evening we were the center of the cheerful wedding company.

After the dance we were invited to table. My bridegroom sat with the older gentlemen again at the other end of the table, and again we could communicate only with our eyes. After the evening meal, half asleep with exhaustion, I separated from my bridegroom and all present, and remained alone in our lodging with my sister. We exchanged all sorts of remarks and observations about the company we had just left.

Suddenly, the door opened and a very comical apparition entered the room: A small, squat person with a very blunt, typically Russian nose, small lively eyes, a wide sunburned face, dressed in the local costume of Russia Minor. On her head she wore a turban made of a colorful woolen cloth onto which bright red artificial roses and even brighter green leaves were fastened, covering much of her face. In front and behind, her entire body was covered with two colorful aprons beneath which she wore a white, much longer shirt with plump, colorfully embroidered sleeves. On her neck she had a mass of corals, colorful beads, and brass coins. She wore large rings in her ears, but no shoes or stockings, and her naked feet left much to be desired in the cleanliness department. She was the servant bringing us fresh water and inquiring after our wishes. We were seeing this peculiar costume for the first time. At first we were speechless with surprise and broke into loud laughter. We laughed for a long time after the girl had left, and chatted happily. Before we fell asleep, my sister Cecilie hugged me hard and cried out, "You're happy and will be very happy, sister!" I, too, believed in my happiness. My heart was full, pounding

145

like a storm. I could have embraced all of humanity in that hour. Over-whelmed with joy, cradled in sweet dreams, I fell asleep.

When I woke up the next morning, Father was visiting the *mechu-tonim* (in-laws). Mother and my sister were ready to go out, and from the house there had been several inquiries for me. I dressed quickly, and when I had finished my toilette my mother herself brought me the *ziganka* (overcoat) and we left our quarters. We were expected for breakfast at the Wengeroffs'.

In the informal, intimate and hearty atmosphere there, my shy-ness disappeared. We young people were allowed to withdraw into another room. No need to tell us twice! We were frolicsome and unre-strained. My mother-in-law and future sister-in-law studied my trousseau piece by piece, with expertise and deep interest. My mother earned much approval. They were astonished by one item of lingerie, the petticoat, for when I came to Konotop no woman was wearing this. Actually, even my sister Chaveh's trousseau had included no pet-ticoats. In the short time since my sister's wedding, many a new cus-tom had been introduced at our house.

Jewish women in Konotop wore no petticoats, but wore their dresses directly over their shirt. Wearing a petticoat was considered "Christian." Only in the winter did the women wear thick flannel pet-ticoats and very thick, high men's boots. Of course, it goes without saying that in a very short time all of Konotop knew about this piece of my trousseau; and not long after, other women in Konotop fol-lowed my example. Anyway, the Jewish women in Konotop found it easy to adopt a new piece of clothing into their toilette. Culturally, and even more so socially, Konotop stood far behind Brest. No one here knew much about fashion. My things were admired. I myself was wondered at whenever I walked through the street, and in a short time I set the fashion in all of Konotop.

On the day before the wedding other guests were expected from St. Petersburg, a brother and brother-in-law of my future mother-in-law. They arrived during the midday meal, two good-looking, elegant gentlemen. They wore short, light-colored silk summer suits, a sort of travel costume, and wide-brimmed white straw hats, which they took

146

off as they entered the dining room so that they remained sitting bare-headed, while the other gentlemen wore little black velvet caps. My father-in-law was somewhat offended. This free, unrestrained behavior of his guests disturbed him the more because the presence of my dear father radiated a deeply religious atmosphere. But the young men noticed their error quickly and sought to fit in. So they put on their hats for the blessing after the meal and mumbled tensely, which seemed very funny to us.

After the midday meal I left the company. In accordance with old custom I must undergo a ritual cleansing. This ceremony was an unspeakable torture for me; my delicate feelings were tested sorely. The religious formalities of the *mikveh* (ritual bath) seemed to have no end. I was washed, my nails were carefully cleaned, and at the end, in accordance with the regulations, I had to submerge completely three times in the pool. Silently I submitted to the commands of the old women who were treating me like a sacrificial lamb. How glad I was to be allowed to leave them at last.

old Customs

In the evening there was dancing again, and now not just girls but also some of the young men took part. Of course, this was against the custom. But the older people were gathered in a distant room and the young took advantage of this opportunity. On this evening, the eve of my wedding, we separated early. But for a long time I could not fall asleep and said farewell with melancholy to my maidenly dreams.

MY WEDDING DAY

I awoke with the thought that this was the most significant day of my life. We all made a most careful toilette on that day. I put on the heavy gray silk dress and the myrtle wreath with the long white veil. White gloves, a fan, and a delicate lace handkerchief completed my outfit. They put a cape around my shoulders and we got into the carriage that brought us, along with a gaping escort of the curious, to the Wengeroff house. The sisters-in-law welcomed us at the entrance, and in the parlor were the in-laws and many strange ladies and gentlemen. It was some time before my bridegroom arrived surrounded by many gentlemen. He hardly dared to look at me, for according to custom, bride and groom are to remain separated during the last hours before the nuptials.

Without any ceremony, I was led into the wedding chamber. There wasn't even an armchair for me, such as was customary among my people. I had to think back to the wedding of my sister, with what solemnity everything had been done then, how moved we siblings were when Father and Mother led the bride into the room to the sound of sweet music, and seated her in an armchair in the middle of the room on a beautiful carpet.

I became downright angry when I found out that the whole ceremony was to take place in a barn, in accordance with local custom. My mother and sister and I could hardly grasp such a thing. But it was unthinkable to demur, of course, and so we simply had to submit to the situation. People tried to comfort us by assuring us that weddings were always celebrated in this manner in Konotop, no matter what gorgeous rooms might be available for the purpose.

In the barn we took our places on chairs while the crowd settled on plain benches. A shrill, discordant music struck up, and into the barn there danced an old woman, gyrating in wild circles. She held a cake high above her head and delivered herself of these words: "Zivie Kumanov, Zivie Kumanov, Zivie Kumanov!" As she sang she kept egging on the musicians.

My sister and I had never seen the like and were overcome by uncontrollable fits of giggles. One sister-in-law noticed this and hastened to explain the scene to us. It seemed that in accordance with the custom of the place every friend of the house would send the hostess a cake. The name of the baker was announced in this peculiar manner. This did nothing to make the scene any less hilarious to us and we struggled not to giggle. The same ceremony was repeated several times, accompanied by the calling out of the names of different friends.

At three o'clock in the afternoon the ceremonies in the barn were at an end and I withdrew to say the afternoon prayer and change my dress. My mother went with me. In a voice full of emotion she spoke to me of the seriousness of the wedding day, which for the bride represents a second Day of Atonement, on which she must pray to God for forgiveness of all her past sins. Tears poured from my eyes. I clutched my prayer book and prayed. My sacred conversation with the Lord lasted a good hour, and I returned to the barn with tear-stained cheeks.

The maidens present approached me, took off my bridal wreath and let down my hair, which had been done up in many little braids so that the entire female company could take part in the loosening of the hair of the bride. They spread it on my shoulders and on the back of my neck. I sobbed with emotion. Then the bridegroom appeared surrounded by the other men. He took a white silk scarf from a platter of hop flowers and, under the direction of the rabbi, placed it on my head. At the same time the whole company scattered hops over me, just as had been done for my sister Chaveh. My bridegroom was led to the synagogue, I was led there by my parents, and the actual wedding ritual was performed there. Afterwards, on the arm of my new husband, I walked back to the house to the strains of merry music. I really needed his arm, since I still had that silk scarf on my head and over my eyes.

Back home we went into the guest room, where at last I was allowed to take off the silk scarf for a moment and look into my husband's eyes. We were served tea, which we took with true delight. In accordance with Jewish custom we had been fasting all day.

During supper, served in the barn to the entire town, I sat at the ladies' table and my husband at the gentlemen's. The *sheva broches* (seven blessings) that the rabbi recited at the wedding were repeated, a ceremony that must be observed for seven days. *Mesame'ach chossen ve-kaloh* (entertaining a bridegroom and bride) is one of the greatest and most important *mitzvehs*. Accordingly, our wedding feast stretched into the middle of the night.

Next morning, a woman arrived carrying an enormous pair of shears, and under the direction of my mother she cut off all my hair. She left me a bit over my forehead as a kind of memento, but even that was covered by the wig. Now this wig in itself represented enormous

149

progress, of course. All my sister had been allowed was a cap surrounded by a ribbon dyed the color of her hair.

The operation was over. I glanced into the mirror, and stared back in horror. My husband comforted me at once and assured me that I looked every bit as nice as before. So in time I calmed down. A little cap was perched on top of the artfully constructed wig. Then they led me into the parlor, wearing a pretty silk dress, supported on one side by my mother and on the other side by my mother-in-law. Everybody liked my looks and many a remark made me blush deeply. My husband never left my side.

I had been guarded night and day for the past four weeks—called the copper, brass, silver and gold weeks—since it is during these weeks that a girl, according to a Jewish superstition of those days, is particularly susceptible to falling under the spell of demons. A bride is *never* left alone during those weeks, especially during the last one, until she is led to the wedding canopy. After the ceremony the demons lose their power. I had begun to see these demons lying in wait for me; free now of their lurking presence, I rejoiced in my liberation.

Several days went by in happy celebration. I felt at home in my new circumstances and stopped thinking of the separation from my parents with quite so much fear. *Rosh Hashanah* was fast approaching and my parents wanted to leave. But the Wengeroffs would not hear of it. So my people accepted their sincere invitation to remain for the holiday, and we were able to observe it together. But after the High Holy Days they began their journey to Brest, and we took our leave of one another for several years.

An eighteen-year-old bride, I had moved to a strange country, among strangers with their strange ways, with a husband whom I loved passionately but who was really still a stranger to me. This was how the parents of that time married off their unprepared, almost unsuspecting, children. And although they loved their children dearly, parents felt no doubts or worries. They trusted in the help of God and gave their children over to their fate.

Thus began my orderly Jewish married life.

MARRIED LIFE

Tsirl Waletzky

FOUR YEARS IN THE HOUSE OF MY IN-LAWS

Konotop, which was to be my second home, was a small town of some ten thousand inhabitants. It looked very much like a village. Most of the population was Christian—shopkeepers, officials, farmers. The small Jewish population consisted mainly of grain merchants and tavern keepers. My father-in-law was the wealthiest man in the town. He was the *otkupshchik* of Konotop: he had the Government monopoly on brandy and hard liquor so long as he sent his monthly payments into the Treasury.

Every city had such a concessionaire. These leases were very lucrative for the government, yielding hundreds of millions of rubles annually, a sum that was said to go exclusively to the Army. But in normal business times the concessionaires also made a good income out of it. They were extended considerable privileges, were under the government's protection, and led an elegant, well-to-do life. At their frequent large parties there was good food and drink. The most beautiful horses and the most elegant carriages in the city all belonged to them, and they lived in their surroundings like local independent lords. As I have said, my father-in-law had such a brandy concession.

Only the upper layers of society enjoyed wine and beer in those times. The people drank hard liquor. Of course, the upper class did not scorn hard liquor either, and they liked to enjoy a little glass to encourage their appetites. A workman would drink quite large doses to "renew his strength" during breaks in his work. However, the biggest buyers of hard spirits were the farmers on the land, who drank to anesthetize themselves. The pub was a farmer's club; every day after work the farmer went there, drank his vodka, sang some sad or funny songs, and often, when he was very drunk, danced.

Liquor was more costly in the cities than in the country and there was a great deal of smuggling. A *rogatka* (toll booth) stood at the entrance to every town, with a *strazhnik*—a guard with the large brass emblem of the concession on his breast and a thin iron rod in his hand. He guarded the city line, poking his rod into every wagon that passed him, and woe betide the farmer or the merchant in whose wagon something was found! The unhappy one was dragged to the authorities. a protocol was taken down of the facts of the case, and those who were caught smuggling were labelled as criminals and fined very heavily.

The concessionaire counted on such happy incidents: this money paid some of his expenses for personnel, especially the many mounted and pedestrian overseers. Even so, there was much smuggling. Whole shipments, up to twenty or thirty barrels, made detours into the cities through canyons, through woods, in the dark, on stormy winter nights. Not infrequently battles broke out between the armed guards at the town line and the armed smugglers, leaving many dead and wounded. Seized wagons were brought in triumph into the government building, where the trial would be held. No exceptions: everyone who crossed the town line must submit to inspection.

Most of the Jews in Konotop were Chasidim, a sect that is so often misunderstood and whose teachings are so often slandered. Chasidism originated about a hundred and fifty years ago in Volhyn, in reaction to the dominant talmudic scholarship of Lithuania. It was at one and the same time an expression of the rising mysticism of the age and of the battle between romanticism and cool rationalism. True piety is to be found not in quibbling sophistry nor in hair-splitting interpretations of the words of the Bible, not in constant brooding over the Talmud, not in lifeless disputes over words. Heart and emotion ought to be our means to serve God. Enthusiasm, ecstasy, and sincerity must remove a person from all that is material and lift him to spiritual heights. Worship is to be joyful, jubilant.

There are only a few who can reach inspiration through total enthusiasm and higher illumination. Such a person is a *zaddik*, a *Rebbe* who is to be believed and trusted unconditionally. There must be beauty everywhere. The beauty of the *Rebbe* is expressed in all his movements and rouses great enthusiasm in his followers. Chasidim make pilgrimages to the *Rebbe* whenever they can, not only to learn Torah and to pray, but also to live in his pious presence and enjoy his beauty. The *Rebbe* partakes of God, and his adherents in turn partake of the *Rebbe*. With some, it is the custom to grab passionately for the

154

remains of his food and follow his slightest movement with ecstasy. They watch him dance and they dance with him.

And since the *Rebbe* is the embodiment of all nobility in the soul, and God is revealed in him in the purest form, does it not go without saying that the life of the *Rebbe* should be preserved from all material worry? Everyone, even the poorest Chasid, took it as his highest duty to contribute the so-called *pidyonim* (literally, redemptions) for the support of the *Rebbe* [in return for his blessing].

The Chasidim lead a strange life. They honor their body because it, too, is a vessel of the Lord. They are concerned to appear before God in a state of purest cleanliness. They wash often, they bathe several times a day, especially in flowing water. Winter or summer, these are sacred practices. Despite all this, we must remark that the Chasidim of Lithuania are much more sober and temperate and more understanding of practical life than those of Poland. They are thoughtful merchants, good family men, and faithful husbands. The ecstasy that removes them from practical life is expressed in prayer and especially in those holy hours when once a year they travel to their *Rebbe* to celebrate *Rosh Hashonoh*.

It is said that to understand the intricate ways of the Kabbalah, study the deep meaning and relationships among the strange customs of the Chasidim. Thus I remember that before the great, awesome Day of Atonement, on which the Almighty makes His decisions regarding life and death, great wax tapers were made in chasidic as well as in *misnagdic* houses. The wick, folded seven times, was laid into the wax after the name of every living and every dead member of the family had been constructed from it. The difference between the living and the dead is merely superficial.

The *Misnagdim* are great enemies of the Chasidim. In Lithuania there is little difference between Chasidim and *Misnagdim* and they seldom come in conflict, since they have much in common, especially their great respect for the Talmud. However the Polish Chasidim more or less ignore the Talmud, deriving wisdom and ecstasy from their own holy books.

We see this animosity in a *misnagdic* song about the Chasidim:

155

Who is going into shul?
Our holy little Jews.
Who is going into the tavern?
Our little Kotsker *Chasidim.*[1]

The Wengeroffs were Chasidim, but Lithuanian Chasidim. I, the daughter of a *Misnaged*, saw and heard much that was new here, and gradually had to get accustomed to much that was strange.

My in-laws were very hospitable and many people came to their house. But this social intercourse was very different from what I had been accustomed to at home. Since there were no distinguished Jewish families in Konotop, a very friendly, lively social life developed with non-Jews. Young officers, as well as land owners with their wives and siblings, liked to visit my in-laws. Among them were many who later on would be famous in Russia: Dragomirov (who was later Governor General of Kiev and a teacher of Alexander III), Ponamariev, Mescentsov, and others who later became well known as authors or military men.

With this social life, some "Christian" ways had crept into the home of my in-laws, creating a mixture of true Jewish religion with non-Jewish customs. Gradually I began to adjust to this new life, and became very close to my in-laws and to my husband's siblings, who all tried to help me over the pain of separation from my own people. I was like a daughter in the house.

I also undertook much of the work in the household. For example, it was soon my job to pour tea in the morning and evening, and that took two hours each time. This duty was exhausting, especially in the middle of the summer during the great heat. When I was finished with this work I was dripping wet. Here at the bubbling samovar my father-in-law, who was usually a silent and somewhat morose man, had very pleasant conversations with me and always asked after my health.

---

[1] Followers of Menahem Mendel of Kotsk (1787–1859), one of the outstanding leaders of the Chasidic movement.–ed.

THE MIDWIFE

Two people were the most active: my father-in-law and his mother. At the time when I joined the household my grandmother-in-law was still a beautiful woman. She was of medium build and had beautiful eyes, a slightly downturned nose in an oval face, and brilliant white teeth in a small mouth that seldom smiled. On her chin, strangely enough, there grew a beard, which she had to have removed every week.

Despite her advanced age she ran a large household and was a model hostess, a superb cook and pastry chef. She baked everything from the simplest black bread to the tastiest delicacies. Her special art form was putting up fruit of all kinds: she managed to preserve not only the natural flavor of each fruit, but even its very shape and color. Her knishes were very popular, stuffed with goose liver or with sour cabbage steamed in goose fat.

But her masterpiece surely was her honey cake: Scald white honey. With a wooden spoon stir in a bit of finely sifted ginger and some rye flour. Allow to cool. Knead in some good, large hazelnuts. Knead small portions of the dough in both hands and rub, knead, pull and squeeze until quite pliable and easily detached from the palms. When she had done this to each portion of the dough, she baked all the loaves in a great casserole in the oven.

In addition to her cooking she had a great many other things to do, for all day long people came seeking her advice; she was midwife and confidante to rich and poor. I can see her returning from the synagogue surrounded by a crowd of her "clients." One might be looking for advice about finding a job, another concerned about the marriage of a daughter, a third complaining of a pain in his chest; a woman would be begging her to come to a daughter-in-law who had gone into labor; and so forth. Most of these she dispatched with an understanding word as she walked along. The others, whose need was more pressing, came right on into the house with her.

When she got home she looked about the household, had a bite to eat, stopped into the office to catch up with business matters, and then tossed her coat about her shoulders and hurried to the woman in childbed.

157

From her large store of cures and recipes she tendered medical aid to Jew and Christian alike. I still remember a few of her prescriptions: Chest pains and cough, boil up oatmeal, cream, butter and rock candy into a thick draught, take daily for an entire month; this extraordinarily nourishing drink strengthened people very quickly and eased the coughing. Then the convalescent must drink sweet cream that had been shaken in a bottle until small chunks of butter began to form on the surface. Carried out conscientiously, the cure usually worked.

For rheumatism, circulatory obstruction and headaches, drink daily for six weeks one large cup of sarsaparilla. For blood rushing to the head and for dizziness, let one dishful of blood. For painful feet, bathe in the liquor of boiled poplar leaves.

Often she also suggested baths prepared by boiling up hay—in particular, old dried-up bits of hay collected from the barn floor. These baths were among her recommendations as well for weak and sickly small children.

As a general remedy for all sorts of complaints, she applied a plaster of Spanish fly to the affected area until a blister had formed, which she opened with a pair of shears and kept open for some time with a special salve. For scrofulous children she suggested baths prepared with malt or with the bark of young oak trees. To relieve belly ache in two- and three-year-olds, she applied a mustard plaster.

A desperate remedy in cases of throat infection and swollen glands in very small children was massage through the mouth with her index finger, which she had first dipped in very hot water. Naturally these children made a terrific racket. I can see the old woman now, clicking her tongue and smacking her lips to try to distract them.

If all her remedies failed she had one heroic method in reserve, and I once witnessed this horrifying procedure with a child of my own.

It happened this way: Following the death of my firstborn son, I gave birth to a little girl who began to sicken in her first year of life while still at my breast. The little one weakened, grew pale and lost weight. One by one the old woman tried all her remedies; still the baby languished.

Then with deep solemnity, she said to me that there was one more thing we might try. But what she had in mind was a very dreadful remedy; it was quite possible that the child would perish in the course of it. It seemed to us that our child was lost in any case. We decided to take this desperate chance.

An ox was brought and slaughtered in the courtyard. Immediately, before the carcass had been skinned, it was slit open. The stomach was lifted out and wrapped in blankets, laid in a manger, and rushed into the sickroom.

There the old woman cut it open with an enormous kitchen knife. This done, she plunged in her hands, pushed the vaporous mash to either side, and set the half-dead baby right into the middle of it. While one hand cradled the tiny head, the other kept basting the thin little body with steaming pulp.

After just a few minutes of this, some color began to return to the tiny cheeks. The drooping eyes opened wide, and the weak little voice called out, "Mamme! Mamme!"

Grandmother lifted the baby out, bathed her and laid her in her cradle. There she slept quietly for about half an hour and then woke up hungry.

From that time on her health and appetite improved steadily. My daughter is fifty-five now, and I can vouch for this: she still has a great appetite.

You can speak of this grandmother in the terms you would use of a sought-after physician: she had a large practice. It goes without saying that her night's sleep was often interrupted. Her room had a large medicine cupboard, and a side window upon which it was permitted to knock at any hour of the night if there was need. Just rap gently and murmur softly, "Beilenyu!"[1]

In a moment she was awake, in ten minutes she was dressed to go out. Wearing great warm boots, a warm dress and a long fur coat, on her head a warm black sateen bonnet, she would gather up some medicines and drive off.

---

[1]   Diminutive of the name Bella (Beyleh)–ed.

Sometimes on these errands she encountered poverty so great that there were not even diapers for the newborn. Without hesitation she would reach down to tear the hem off her shirt and wrap the infant in that. She would make a fire in the stove, brew the tea, bathe the child, cover the mother with her own warm coat, and never leave her side until the pain had eased. From these errands she always returned in a fine mood ready to tell us all about her adventures.

It was the custom to make the midwife a present of a white shirt. My grandmother-in-law possessed a great store of such shirts, being of course far too sensitive to refuse the gift. These shirts lay folded in readiness against the day when some needy girl in the town got engaged, or when the old woman called upon a family so poor that there was not even underwear.

What a wonderful woman she was! Following one of her "all-night adventures" she would often go straight to her day's work. Without so much as a catnap she would see to the household and devote the rest of her day to the business.

Even on ordinary days she rose at five, recited several Psalms with great devotion, and then would take a cup of tea. At seven she would confer with the cook and leave for the synagogue.

Her personal needs were few. She ate very little and very simply, although for guests she always set an ample and varied table, as was the rule in every well-conducted rich Jewish household.

The entire population of Konotop, Christian and Jew, revered her. Her every wish was sacred, her word law, especially with her husband and with us children. She had that power, but she didn't make you feel it. There was no egoism or vainglory in her, no stubbornness—just deep seriousness, devout modesty and sincere submission to the will of God.

No need to stress here that she kept the promise she had made my mother-in-law upon her deathbed—to raise her three orphans and to see to their education, in Talmud as well as in secular subjects.

Her husband, a diminutive man with twinkling, good-natured eyes, was completely devoted to her. He recognized her absolute superiority and deferred to her in everything. It is true that he too was active in the business, but final decisions were hers.

About this couple a family secret was told to me: Many years earlier the husband had been put in prison as the result of a denunciation. Deeply shaken, the wife braved every danger to bring him comfort and strength, repeatedly visiting him in prison disguised as a soldier. Discovery would certainly have meant her death, but she persisted.

This woman was no exception, no isolated phenomenon. There lived among the Jews a great many women like that, and they can be spoken of as a type. I see the development of Jewish women as a long unbroken chain joined link to link, not as something coincidental, sudden, or new in Jewish life.

When I look at the young Jewish women of Russia today, crowding the university lecture halls and clinics, smoothing the way for the equality of women in society and in science, there arises in my mind the memory of that matron of Konotop. The sphere granted to her was so small. And yet within its limits, what a wide domain she was able to create for her generous activity!

Cheerfully my grandmother-in-law bore all her burdens, and remained healthy and strong into extreme old age. Her entire effort and thought was for her son, my father-in-law, the center of her worries and her hopes. It's true she had a daughter too, but she had very little interest in her. Her entire mother's heart belonged to the son, the bright star in her difficult life.

I had very little opportunity to get to know my father-in-law better because he was often away on business. And when he did come home, he was also completely occupied with business. He was an intelligent man with great talmudic knowledge, tactful to everyone, pleasant to his wife and a most patient husband. His wife, an intelligent but very domineering woman, was convinced that she knew it all, and the honor that everyone in the household gave to her and the measureless adoration of her husband supported her in this self-confidence. She knew some Hebrew, which made her even prouder, the more so since education, not only in Konotop but in all of Russia Minor, was seldom seen among women of that time.

She rose very late. When she appeared in the dining room, either my elder sister-in-law or I took care to prepare her breakfast very care-

161

fully. And her criticism began at that moment. She criticized all day long: the housemaids, the serving-man, all got their share in the course of breakfast. After breakfast she sat down on a veranda where like a princess she could oversee her entire domain. Everyone in the house, men and women, male and female servants, trembled at her voice.

In addition to a brother-in-law, his wife, and my sister-in-law Kuntzeh, an exceptionally good and beautiful woman, the other members of the household were the very young siblings of my husband, still children.

It was an elegant Jewish house, and here I had the opportunity to practice and develop further everything I had learned in my parents' home—hospitality, care of the poor, study, piety, honor to parents. These virtues we Jews expect will make us happy; they are practiced with great eagerness. I felt special respect and admiration for my in-laws because they took orphans, and children of their poor relatives, into the house and raised them in a suitable way, married them off, and helped them to start businesses.

The Sabbath was observed and held sacred here also, but it was not characterized by the same festive beauty as in the home of my parents. Friday night seemed to me very prosaic. It disturbed my piety to hear conversations about business at the Sabbath table. My father-in-law chatted with his father about horses he had bought, their good and bad attributes, their illnesses. The young people, my husband among them, often fell asleep out of boredom at the table, until my mother-in-law laughed and teased them awake in time for the blessing after the meal. Nobody here thought of *zmiraus*, the holy Sabbath songs. Sabbath regulations were observed as prescribed, but circumvented when necessary in a shrewd way. If a business letter came on the Sabbath, a *shabbes goy* (a gentile who helped on the Sabbath) opened it, and then one just read it perfectly calmly.

How different it had been in the house of my parents. There the Sabbath was really holy, and my father on that day had seemed like a venerable rabbi. There was nothing of the businessman about him then. Neither Friday night nor all day Saturday was there a single word

162

about business matters. Even letters that arrived on that day were laid aside and not opened until the evening. In the Wengeroff household things were more prosaic. The still, clear, pious enthusiasm, the rapture that reigned on the festivals in my childhood home, was missing here entirely.

In other respects, the way the house was arranged reminded me of the home of my parents. There were large rooms here also, valuable furniture, beautiful silver, carriages, horses, servants, frequent guests. I read a great deal in Konotop, especially in Russian. The German books, like Schiller, Zschokke, Kotzebue,[1] and Bulwer,[2] which I had brought with me from Brest, I had read. Now it was the turn of the Russian books in the library of the Wengeroffs. I read the journals *Moscow News,* the *Northern Bee* (*Severnaia Pehela*), and so forth and taught my husband, who was very eager to learn, the German language.

His main study he devoted to the Talmud. Every Monday and Thursday he spent the night with his *rebbe*, bent over the great folios. They did not leave the study until daybreak. Often he sat there with his *melammed* for hours on a low stool, wrapped in a big blanket, ashes on his head, and "performed" the *golus*—that is, he lamented the yoke of the exile. This is an old custom, observed today by perhaps one Jew in a thousand.

Since our engagement, my husband was filled more and more with a mystical religious mood. He buried himself in the holy secrets of the Kabbalah and gradually this study aroused the romantic youth to a burning desire to go to Lubavitch, the seat of the head of the Lithuanian Chasidim. There he hoped to receive from the *Rebbe* a satisfying answer to all the questions and riddles that plagued him. There he meant to confess the sins of his youth and beg for atonement.

---

[1]   August von Kotzebue (1761–1819), prolific poet, novelist, and playwright.

[2]   Edward Bulwer-Lytton (1803–1873), influential English novelist and poet. Presumably Wengeroff read his works in German translation.

Only two years before, my husband had been interested in free ideas that actually had led to some unpleasantness with my parents. Now, after such a short time, he swung over to the opposite side, lost in a mystical, ecstatic frame of mind.

One morning, it was Purim, I was busy in the household. My husband came to me in the kitchen and told me, beaming with joy and excitement, that his father had given permission for him and his older brother, accompanied by their *rebbe*, to travel to Lubavitch. As a daughter of *Misnagdim*, I didn't understand the scope and seriousness of this event. I asked my husband uncertainly whether he was serious. His answer was a short but very firm "Yes." The preparations were made and soon a carriage with three strong horses stood ready for the departure.

THE CHANGE

I don't know what happened at the *Rebbe*'s, for my husband never spoke of this sad experience. I only know that a youth full of hope and enthusiasm left his family to make this pilgrimage to the *Rebbe* as if he were going to a holy man who alone possessed the power to lift the veil from great secrets, and that he came back sobered up. The blue flower that he, like so many others, went to find, was not there in the sunshine at the rim of a clean, refreshing spring. It was withered and very different from what he had pictured in his dreams.

Not despair, but a quiet sorrow descended upon him. The magic was gone, and with it the interest and application he had brought to religious practices and duties. He began to let go all that had been precious to him, so close that it had seemed to be in his very blood. This did not become apparent all at once, but only gradually, so softly that it was hardly noticeable at first. My husband still said his prayers, he continued to study with the *rebbe*, and even the nightly sitting and working over the folios did not end. But the loving heart of a woman who knows how to listen and is aware of the slightest movement cannot be deceived. This was no longer the lively interest of the seeker and student, not the deep passionate prayer rising to ecstasy in which a human being feels close to God and can converse with Him. Now, it was just a dead fulfillment of duty.

Young and inexperienced as my husband was, he did not understand how to find the middle way, so that the descent from ecstatic religious rapture all the way down to the total banality of everyday was just the distance of a single step for him. He took this step and turned into the opposite path, which many Jews had already entered. My deeply religious nature grasped this at once. My heart became very heavy with the premonition of all the battles I would face in the years to come.

Fulfillment of religious duties without religious conviction became a burden to my husband in the long run, and gradually he began to neglect them. Soon his parents noticed this; tension arose between them and their son. First my husband had his beard shaved off. His parents reproached him angrily about this and other observances he had been neglecting, which they had not mentioned before. It was also my first conflict with him. I begged him not to be vain, to let his beard grow back. He was offended, wouldn't hear of it, reminded me of his rights as lord and master, demanded obedience from me, demanded my submission to his will. That was a very sharp stab into my tender heart. The blue sky of my marital happiness was overcast.

Around this time I became a mother. The wish of my parents and in-laws was fulfilled, God gave me a son, the first male grandchild and great-grandchild. There was great rejoicing. That was a very difficult time, but love and care helped me through it. There were special methods in the ghetto to ease childbirth. The first condition: no one except the midwife and the oldest woman in the house must be apprised of the onset. If the impending confinement became known, it would be longer and dangerous. The woman in labor was led around the table nine times. Then she must cross the threshold of her room back and forth three times. All locks on all closets, on all wardrobes, on all commodes and doors—even the padlocks in the dining room—were unlocked. All buttons on the underwear of the woman in labor were unbuttoned, all knots untied. Then, in the naive symbolism of the people, the child would have an easier time being "untied" as well.

Of course during the first week after my delivery I was very carefully nursed. The first day I got only gruel, tea and toasted white bread. On the second day, there was a specific diet for the new mother. Early in the morning I had tea with the best cream, and two hours later *trianke*—an oatmeal gruel for people who had complaints of the chest. The old woman always handed it to me with these words: "This plate of soup, my child, will strengthen your insides and your breasts and heal them." After two more hours, I had to eat a fat chicken soup with a little chicken in it, and then again a *trianke*. But this was a different one, cooked honey that had stood open in a warm place for several days and was covered with an infusion of herbs such as nutmeg, cinnamon, cloves, figs, and carob beans. You'd drink a glass of this nectar and you slept very well, but you woke up with a great thirst that in turn called for tea. Of course there was also buttered toast, and two hours after that, stewed plums with almond cake, and in the afternoon again chicken soup with chicken.

This gluttony went on for eight days. In special cases it was continued for four weeks. The old women were firmly convinced that until a large pot full of chicken bones had been collected, that is until the new mother had consumed a certain number of chickens, she was still a maternity case.

As was customary, during the first week of my son's life more than ten boys, with a *behelfer*, came into my room every evening to say the first part of the *krias shema* (Deut. 6:4–9; part of the evening service), which religious Jews believed kept the evil powers away from the newborn. Every day after this recitation the children were given raisins, nuts, apples and cake, and the *behelfer* got some money at the end of the week.

For the same purpose of protecting the newborn, there were kabbalistic prayers called *shemaus* ([divine] names) hung on the wall over the head of the new mother and on the door, and laid between the pillows of the child. On the last night before the *bris* (circumcision), the child was protected with special care. This was his *vachnacht* (night of watching). On the eve of the ritual, the *mohel* (circumcisor) brought the knife in a sheath and often a work of Kabbalah, and the midwife laid both under the pillows of the newborn. Now, if the child happened to cry out at that time, the midwife would say knowingly, "He can tell what's coming." But if he smiled in his sleep, she said that the *malach,* the good angel, was playing with him.

On the eve of the circumcision of my son, we served a meal to the poor, as was customary among eminent Jews before a *bris* and before a wedding. The *shammes* (synagogue beadle) was sent into the poor district to invite the poor families. Even the beggars were invited to the *vachnacht.* The guests sat at rows of long tables set up in a large room in the host's home. First the men were served and then, separately, the women. In the course of time the menu had become fixed: at each place there was a *bulkeh,* a white roll. Beside it the glass of brandy and a piece of honey cake. Then there was fish or herring, roast and groats. There were large pitchers of beer on the tables and everyone could drink as he wished.

The host and hostess and their children served the guests. Before a wedding, the bride and groom also visited the poor and were offered *mazel tov* (congratulations). The poor generally behaved properly and the meal took its course in accordance with religious prescription, beginning with hand washing and concluding with *mezumon* (recitation of the Grace after Meals in the form required when more than three people—in our case, more than 200—had partaken of the meal). Then the men left, uttering their blessings and thanks. Then it was the turn of the women, and before they left everyone received a gift of money.

For our family celebration we had dear guests from abroad: The father of my mother-in-law, Abraham Zelig Selensky, and his wife from Poltava. He was an intelligent, distinguished, religious and very old man who was very popular in Poltava. One of the old school, he was not prevented by business from studying the Talmud with great diligence and application. He fulfilled all religious obligations very strictly. His four sons received a European education, but they understood how to grasp the new and work it in without neglecting the old ways. The eldest was especially knowledgeable in foreign languages; the second was a painter at Court, the third a lawyer, and the youngest a famous Talmudist. This Talmudist was so religious that he could not bring himself to have his long beard trimmed. He wore it always half hidden in a neck scarf to avoid ridicule.

But I wanted to speak of the *bris*. Early in the morning the midwife made her preparations for the bath; the bath preceding the *bris* is an especially solemn ceremony. The child is bathed very early. The water must not be very warm so as not to make the child too hot, for then he would bleed after the operation. There were always many old women present at the bath because it was considered a meritorious deed to pour two handfuls of water over the child, at the same time slipping a silver coin into the bath water for the midwife.

In the room where the *bris* would take place, two long candles in tall candlesticks were lit at ten o'clock. On a special table the utensils of the *bris* were laid in readiness. A bottle of wine; a cup large enough to hold the contents of one and a half eggshells; a plate full of sand; a tin of a powder made of moldy wood. Around ten o'clock the first guests came. The *mohel* ordered that the child be wrapped, and in wealthy homes the most precious linen was used for the diapers. A cap was put on the child's head. He was put on a silken cushion and covered with a little blanket of similar fine silk.

There was a very special method for the diaper change before the *bris*. One diaper was laid in a triangular shape. The hands of the little child were put on either side of his body and each one wrapped with a corner of the diaper. And then the fine little shirt embroidered with lace was turned up into a wide hem, and he was wrapped in a big second diaper, around which a very long, wide swaddling band was tied so tightly that he looked like a mummy. Only his little feet remained free so that he wouldn't be too hot, because of course if overheated, there was the danger of bleeding.

With great melancholy I looked at my child, who was about to make the sacrifice for his people. I pressed him to my pounding heart, but soon the midwife took him away and handed him to the eldest and most respected woman standing beside the bed. She rocked him a few times in her arms and handed him to the woman standing next to her, who also rocked him and then passed him along. And so the child went from arm to arm until finally he was handed to the godmother. She went all the way to the threshold of the room in which the act would be performed. As soon as the assembled men saw the child, they called out *"Baruch ha-bo—Blessed be he who comes."*

The *kvater* (godfather) took the child and handed it to the *sandik*, who, wrapped in a great *tallis* (prayer shawl), had sat down in a large armchair. His feet were on a foot stool. And then the *mohel* pronounced a very moving prayer. He begged Elijah, the guardian angel of the *bris*, the miracle-working protector of the Jews in all dangers, for his help. And then the actual circumcision took place. The child screamed once, and while the *mohel* spoke the blessing over the wine and named him, his soft whimpering was still heard, quieted only when the *mohel* dripped a few drops of wine from his little finger onto the baby's lips.

It is often the custom during the various stages of the circumcision, the blessing over the wine, the naming of the child and the final prayer, that various men are honored by being allowed to hold the child. During each of these parts of the circumcision, a different gentleman was given the honor of holding our child. The ceremony ends when the godfather hands the child back to the godmother. Then the mother, glowing with happiness, receives her child back into her arms and the little fellow is allowed to relax at his mother's breast. He has been accepted into the company of Israel and is a true descendant of the patriarch Abraham. The guests remain for a long time at a festive meal, for this *sudeh* is considered a particularly sacred meal.

Once the circumcision is happily over, and I actually don't remember any sad incident in connection with it, the might of the evil spirits is broken. My child's wound healed in three days, and this happy healing was celebrated again with a festive meal. Soon my motherly care was able to dedicate itself completely to my child.

It was taken as a matter of course in those days that every mother would nurse her child herself. Before the mother offered the breast to the child, she expressed a few drops to one side, because agitation, grief, worry might have poisoned the first few drops. The degenerate custom of bottle feeding had not penetrated into the ghetto. If a mother did not have enough milk, then she stuck a pacifier into the child's mouth. She took white bread or, if not available, black bread with a piece of sugar, chewed the whole thoroughly, wrapped it in a little rag and tied it with a thread. And that was the pacifier.

There were very strange methods to quiet screaming children. A child might be bathed and, after being dried, put on a large pillow, usually by an old and experienced nursemaid. Then his body would be rubbed thoroughly with Oil of Provence. The left foot was pressed together with the right hand over the stomach of the child, so that the elbow and knee were side by side. Then the same maneuver was performed with the left hand and the right foot. Then the little legs were stretched and the arms put tight next to the body, and the child was then lifted up and rocked for a moment head down, then put on his stomach and his back and feet gently rubbed. And no matter how loud the child had been screaming before, this would quiet him.

There was an even more drastic method. If even wild rocking of the cradle, which was usually swinging from ropes attached to the head and foot end, was in vain, then the nursemaid would carry the child into the kitchen, rock him on her hands, and then lift him over the stove into the chimney, murmuring some unintelligible words. And really the child became quiet, provided that the nursemaid had not forgotten to put pepper and salt in two little bags beforehand or, in the worst case, into her hand, and walk around the child several times with this salt and pepper in her hands. Sometimes this circling of the child sufficed by itself to quiet him. But certainly it was a remedy against the evil eye, which was to be feared if strangers looked at a sleeping child.

Another sure remedy consisted in the mother going down on one knee; the child was pushed back and forth between her legs. Unfortunately, there were many children whose restlessness was the beginning of an illness. If a child did not progress, if he remained thin and weak, then the old experienced women diagnosed *rippkuchen*: the ribs of the child had begun to rot. I think it must have been an illness like the one that nowadays we call the English Disease. Of course, these children cried a lot and to get to the bottom of this disquiet, the wise women knew a strong method. They laid the child on the bed and took a rolling pin around which in those days washing used to be wrapped, put it on the child's ribs, and rubbed a thick board over the wrapped rolling pin, beating the rolling pin nine times with the board. It was a tough remedy but it helped if you knew the right formula of words. Then the evil spirits would run away.[1]

But there were children who, even following this procedure and even with the most solemnly spoken exorcism, did not quiet down. Then the nursemaid would think about it. But God would help her and she found the right diagnosis: The child must have hairs on his back.

Once this diagnosis was made, the therapy followed quickly. The child was bathed and dried, and then little chunks of freshly baked, soft rye bread were rubbed back and forth on the back of the child until some of the little back hairs got attached to the dough. She would continue to rub with the flat of her hand until the little hairs stood up like bristles. And really, most of the time, the children stopped crying.

For miserably thin children, there was the following method: After the mid-day meal, the child was wrapped in the tablecloth with all the bread crumbs and closed up for a moment in a big trunk, which was opened again very quickly. This was done every day for four weeks, and tablecloth and all, the child was weighed every week. If it were going to get well, it must weigh a little more every week. When the first thin sickle moon was visible, the child was held up toward the moon so that it could see it, and the following words were spoken: "Mesiats, mesiats, wisokoss, da ityello nassej kosst." This means "Moon, moon, grow, put meat on these bones."

---

[1] The symptoms described suggest that the children were suffering from a form of rickets or, more likely, scurvy.–ed.

A child was weaned after eighteen, or sometimes after fifteen, months. When the mother was ready to offer the breast for the last time, she sat on the threshold and let the child drink until he stopped by himself and put down his tired head. This was a difficult, but also a festive, day as the child's dependence on the mother was loosened. There was also a day of unalloyed jubilation when the child stood on his own feet for the first time and began to walk. On this spot, the mother made a little cut in the threshold. This was called cutting the *pente* (fetters). Figuratively, the shackles had been cut from the child's little feet.

At the same time as the *bris* of my son, another great religious ceremony took place. For the whole past year, my still young mother-in-law, Cecilie, had a Torah scroll written, for which she paid several hundred rubles. This sacred scroll was to be dedicated and presented to the synagogue. This initiative of my mother-in-law was a very esteemed act, especially for a woman, and found much approval both in her house and in the little town. The *sofer,* the scribe who had written the Torah, a truly religious Jew who spent his life in prayer and fasting and was known as an honest man in Konotop, brought the holy scroll into our house. The ceremony of the dedication of the Torah was celebrated like a wedding. A *chuppeh* was brought and set up in one of the large rooms, and the rabbi had the honor of taking the Torah into his hands first, stepping under the *chuppeh* with it. And then everyone went to the synagogue, led by the rabbi, with the worthies and elders of the city following him, and last the women and girls, carrying silver candelabras with glowing candles. Even unmarried girls, who normally walked with uncovered heads, had to cover themselves in this procession.

Just as the parade began to move, a band struck up, martial music came ringing through the streets, and the entire procession skipped and danced. The men did a lively dance, clapping their hands passionately. Behind them skipped the women and girls, all rejoicing to honor the beautiful deed of this religious woman.

And so the procession arrived at the synagogue. Since the cere-

172

mony lasted into the afternoon, the entire crowd said *mincheh* there. The dedication of the Torah is one of the most solemn acts in a Jewish town, an event not easily forgotten. I was experiencing it for the first time, and it made a great impression on me. I had to watch the procession from a window, very sorry not to be able to participate.

After these festivities our guests from Poltava left us and everyone returned to his duties. The life in the house of my in-laws continued in its accustomed way, and I gradually recovered. I revelled in a new happiness, forgetting the worries of the time just past when I looked at the little boy, this tiny little creature sleeping so peacefully, hearing nothing, seeing nothing, knowing nothing of the young mother who stood hours together at his cradle gazing at him, smiling and dreaming of his happiness and greatness to come.

Months went by and my dear charming boy—he was blond and had blue eyes, very different from the Wengeroff type—grew and flourished and became a strong, healthy child. Every day my joy in him grew. What wonderful new content my life had now! My love was divided now between my husband and my child, and truly there was enough for both. Of course, the little one was the favorite in the whole household. Need I say that our married life became more tender and our attachment and true love for each other more intense through this child.

The time went by and our son was two years old. His intellectual development rushed ahead of the physical. He was alert and clever beyond his years. My husband and I were happy and proud of our firstborn. We made great plans for his future, but God planned differently and took our precious one to Himself.

Exhausted by the unbroken watching at his bedside, I left the bed of my sick child to lie down on the sofa in the next room and fell into a deep sleep. I dreamed I was in the dining room. Through the closed shutters, a little light penetrated into the half-dark room. Despite the closed shutters, I was conscious of everything going on outside. A huge black dog howled terribly, throwing his head back into his neck. Behind him stood a great crowd of musicians, playing violins covered in black cloth, which they held upside down in their hands. Astonished, I asked them why they played like this and received the dark answer: "We have to play like this today."

I awoke in great fright and rushed into the sick room, but they would not let me go to my child. He was no longer mine. Far from me up into Heaven he went, taking with him my young despairing mother's heart forever.

This was the first heavy blow that fate dealt me, and only the two little children that God gave me during the next few years comforted me a little and eased my pain.

In the meantime the conflict between my husband and his parents was exacerbated. He no longer found pleasure in studying Talmud with his *rebbe*. He brought the great folios into our living quarters and studied independently, and liked to see me sit beside him with a book or some needlework, and when he was tired we read together in a German work. His Talmud study had lost its religious character, becoming more a philosophizing, a critical examination. It no longer played the principal role in is life. He dedicated himself more to making a living, and used even my dowry to make independent business deals. But he lost all the money.

I had no voice with him in financial matters. He called my advice meddling and would hear nothing. It was his opinion that a wife, especially his, had no aptitude for this sort of thing, and that my "meddling" was a disparagement of his ability. This was the opinion among most Jews in Russia Minor, especially among the concessionaires. Each felt that he was his own boss, and brooked no advice.

OUT ON OUR OWN

I suppose none of my siblings heard the "Song of Wandering" so often and so clearly in their cradle as I did. The four years during which we lived in the house of my in-laws had passed, and now we were to begin an independent life. The in-laws got us a business, also a brandy concession, and we had to move to a different city. One morning a great comfortable carriage was at the door, ready to travel, a wagon with provisions beside it. The hour of farewell had come.

Sent off with blessings, my husband and I, our two children and two servants got into our carriage and went off into the world. We left this house, where for the last time we had lived the patriarchal Jewish family life together, forever.

Luben was the name of the place in which we were to establish our independent existence. The Jewish population in this little town in Russia Minor was more advanced than that of Konotop, especially in the externals of customs and habits. Its life-style was more European. The few Jews in Luben who were still loyal to the received religion played no large role. Life here was shot through with manners and customs of the Christian majority of the population. There were no Talmudists, no great Jewish scholars, not even a big synagogue. But it was not that irreligious character that in other places was an accompaniment of the Enlightenment. It was simply a lack of tradition, ignorance, and a dissolving into strange ways.

There was a small Jewish community, whose members were completely uneducated and ignorant people, and who considered us the intellectual aristocracy. We found a small apartment already prepared for us in Luben, which the in-laws had furnished with an eye to our needs and requirements. It didn't take long for me to know my way around my rather large household, and I conducted it expertly. My husband took over the business for which, as he had proved, he had some aptitude.

Now consideration for his parents was no longer required of him; he could arrange his life in accordance with his own wishes. His daily prayer in *tallis* and *tefillin* (phylacteries) ended at this time, although his interest in Talmud continued. With great pleasure he had long discussions with the rabbi of the town, who was often a guest in our house. But this interest in Talmud, as I have remarked, had taken on a strictly academic character.

The famed hospitality of Russia Minor reigned in our house. We were soon known and loved, and visits from relatives, friends and acquaintances never ended. Three times a day the table was richly set for eight to ten people. There was almost never a meal without guests. Our household increased in size from day to day, and of course it was

175

getting too big for our circumstances. The in-laws scolded us for this extravagance.

CHERISHED VISITORS

"There is news from Kathy." My husband came into my bedroom on a Saturday morning and handed me a piece of paper on which was written the following message in pencil: "Sister, send me something to eat. I and my child are hungry and we have nothing with us."

My compassion and shock were boundless, and I overwhelmed my husband with questions. The messenger, it seemed, was waiting in the kitchen. Quickly I threw on something and ran out to him. He was a young little peasant. I discovered that my sister's Jewish driver had stopped Friday evening in a village not far from Luben, and because of Sabbath rest and also because of some damage to his wagon had not been willing to go further, although he himself as well as his passengers were left on the road without food until the evening of the next day.

"This evening," the little peasant added, "she can be here."

I ran into the dining room and packed lots of wholesome food into a napkin: a Sabbath bread, cold cooked chicken, butter, cheese, some liqueur, and almond cake (which immediately reminded my sister, she told me later, of the days of our childhood and of our home). The peasant, who got a silver ruble for his trouble, was to deliver this package to my sister as quickly as possible.

After he was sent off I dressed and gave the necessary orders in the household while a nervous, joyous impatience would not leave me. What I would have really liked to do was have the wagon harnessed, travel to my sister and bring her back. But of course it was Saturday, and in those days religion controlled all we did in life. I could not give in to this wish of my heart. Even the coachman had almost allowed his passengers to starve because of the Sabbath.

At dusk I set the tea table, prepared for the dear visitors and waited. Finally they came, and what a hearty reunion we had! We were so happy to see each other. On this evening we went to bed very late.

I took my sister to the room that had been prepared for her, kissed her affectionately and invited her to have breakfast with us in the morning.

When we arrived for tea the next morning, my husband was expecting us. Immediately I noticed some embarrassment in my sister's manner, but could not discover the reason. My husband left us, and the two of us stayed a long time at the tea table chatting about our experiences. We forgot the present, lost in remembrance of the past. Then my husband came back from business and we ate our midday meal cheerfully and kept chattering until late into the night. The questions and stories were unending. We wanted to know everything about each other, after a separation of four years.

When I accompanied sister Kathy to her room on the second evening, again I invited her cordially to have breakfast with my husband and me. She hugged me and asked shyly whether she might have breakfast alone in her room. Taken aback, I asked for the reason. After a little hesitation, it came out: "Except for my husband, I've never seen a man in his robe. And so it embarrasses me to see your husband like this."

Although I found this embarrassment, which was typical of Jewesses of that time, a little strange, I did ask my husband to be considerate of my sister's sensibility. From then on, although he preferred to be comfortable, he appeared at the breakfast table fully dressed. And he remained considerate the whole time, showing his sister-in-law the greatest respect from the first day on. He felt it was quite in order that I gave her the best place at the table, even when very elegant guests were present. Her five-year-old little daughter was loved and cared for by all of us. ·

Three months had passed since sister Kathy's arrival when we received the news from our older sister, Marie, that she would visit us within the next few days. I was possessed by impatient joyful tension. But several days went by and she didn't come, nor was there any news of her. Our disquiet grew. There was no possibility, as there is today, of connecting with places at a distance quickly, so there was nothing else for us except to wait patiently until one day she surprised us.

There was a stormy, joyful reunion, and her stay in our house spread general celebration. We were more cheerful, more youthful, and the relationship between my husband and Marie developed in a much cozier and unembarrassed way than with Kathy. There was laughter and singing and joking all day long.

We made an effort to take advantage of everything, of every entertainment that Luben had to offer to amuse ourselves as best we could. These entertainments included a theater that played in our town once a year at the time of the annual fair. This wandering troupe was still very primitive. As in other provincial towns, they used a barn, the walls decorated with colorful bedsheets, a stage built of boards. Chairs, benches, and all the necessary furniture and even individual pieces of clothing were supplied by the well-to-do inhabitants of Luben, in exchange for free admission. But there were no actual free tickets, as is usual today. It was sufficient to announce at the cash box in a loud voice what article you had lent, and then without further ado you were admitted.

"A candlestick, three cotton blankets, twelve chairs, a skirt," a guest might call out. Immediately the borrowed cotton curtain was pulled back, and the guest could take a seat. The performances were supposed to start at nine o'clock in the evening, but they never really started any earlier than eleven, because the actors always waited for the honored officials of the town.

During the intermissions a band played, usually composed exclusively of Jewish musicians, *klezmorim*. They knew their public well, and often the audience called out requests.

"Yankel, play a polka," or a waltz, and so on. Yankel, of course, fulfilled the wish of his acquaintance, and then his colleague would fulfill the wish of *his* acquaintance, so that the intermissions became endless. It often happened that it was bright daylight by the time people left.

The theater was an event in the little town. It was always welcomed with great joy, and one attended every evening. Among the Jews, only the young people went to the theater. The old and pious never went there, but they let the young people go and kept a judi-

178

cious silence. Since we were considered the most well-to-do of the little town and had lent many objects, there were more places left for us.
And we went almost every evening with a large joyful company and
had a fine time.

We had much company, up to fifteen people were seated at our
three daily meals. We made sure that everything was strictly kosher.
Milk and meat dishes were strictly separate, both in use and when they
were washed. Friday evening in accordance with Jewish custom, two
challehs for *mautzi* (a blessing over bread) were placed beside each
gentleman's place; and the number of gentlemen in those fun-filled
weeks was not small. There was much to do. Marie remained with us
for several weeks and left us enthusiastic over our hospitable reception.

Solidarity among the members of a family was one of the greatest
Jewish virtues, and even under the influence of the entire *Sturm und
Drang* period, which destroyed so many of the good manners of Jewish family life, the solidarity of the family remained, although not
always to the same high degree. Like all morality among the Jews, it
was rooted in religious Law, which says, "Do not become a stranger
to your own blood."

Kathy remained our guest for fourteen months; she could not be
in her own home because of the Crimean War. These were long, long
months in which the poor woman had to suffer much sadness. Days
and weeks passed. Her confinement approached. My husband's
grandmother, whose skill I have described in detail, offered to come
to us in Luben. In November we received the news that this self-sac-
rificing woman was on her way to us. It was an unfortunate coincidence that there was not frost and snow as was usual at that time of
year in Russia, but rainy weather. Instead of a strenuous but quick trip
in a sleigh, the old woman had to make an uncomfortable and difficult
trip in a *postkibitka,* a very primitive carriage without springs. She
arrived exhausted after a very fatiguing, two-day journey. Fortunately
she was wrapped in an enormous fur, and did not catch cold.

The new member of the family did not keep us waiting long. It
was a son. After the *bris* my grandmother-in-law left, Kathy gradually

179

recovered, and we returned to our normal life. As before, no meal passed without guests. The cellar and the barnyard were always full, supplying the tastiest delicacies.

The year was 1855, an important epoch for the Russian Empire, the epoch of the Crimean campaign. The newspapers that came to Luben three times a week brought continuous horrifying news from the theater of war. There was one defeat after another. The Russian army, which was in the most incredible disarray, had to overcome many difficulties to which it was unequal, such as the transporting of the troops, munitions, provisions. The following spring whole divisions were found in the endless steppes of the Crimea who had been marched to the theater of war on foot, had been buried in snow and frozen stiff. The Russian aristocracy, the landed gentry, and business people armed entire regiments at their own expense. These were called the *ratniki*, mere untrained, undisciplined farmers who could be used on the battlefield only as cannon fodder.

If, once in a while, the Russian army won a battle, or a general had a clever idea, this could not change the outcome. It was not just a battle of enemy armies, but a battle between two systems. And the triumph went to the newer, better, more complete system that accompanied the achievements of European culture. The mood of the Russian population became darker and darker. Only those who had quietly been complaining against the regime got a sad satisfaction from this defeat, because they believed that the Empire could be healed of its faults only through external shaking up.

In April I became a mother again. My little son was given the name Simon and I recovered very quickly. Spring announced its arrival in that year with an unusual heat, and in addition, the newspapers brought the horrifying news that on the battlefield, and in its environs, cholera was beginning to rage. The population was warned to take care in eating and drinking. I had only a dim memory of this illness dating from my childhood. A terrible fear took hold of me so that no sensible advice was able to quiet me. The thought of the epidemic followed me like a ghost. It became an apparition in my head of which I could not free myself. My health suffered. I walked around the house cast down in melancholy. A stubborn fate decreed that I would come in close contact with the terrible disease.

Near the end of May we were invited by my husband's aunt to visit her in Kremenchug. We took our oldest child, Lise, with us on the trip to the south. There we were received with great joy. On the fourth day of our stay many relatives and acquaintances gathered to meet me, the niece-in-law. It was very cheerful and we spent our time in the most pleasant way.

On the next morning the aunt came to us in our bedroom and announced that the epidemic had moved into Kremenchug. With tears in her eyes, she told us that many of the members of yesterday's cheerful party were no longer among the living. I was horrified. We grabbed our things and within a few hours we left the city, sad and shaken. At the first post station we were no longer admitted into the waiting room, whence we heard the screams and groans of a cholera patient who was writhing in agony. We had to make camp in the open that night, a June night, warm and short. But although the sun rose at two o'clock in the morning, this night seemed an eternity. My fear and anxiety increased when my little daughter Lisenka began to complain of stomach pain. With trembling hands, I gave her medicine that we had taken along from the aunt. At great expense I got a little warm water from the farmers and prepared some peppermint tea for the child, and with a fearful heart awaited the coming day.

Finally we got horses and continued our journey, and the child felt better. The pain eased and by the time we got home that evening she was quite recovered. In Luben we found that cholera was already raging there. The doctor came and ordered a strict diet, and on the same evening my sister fell ill quite suddenly, a few moments after she had been partaking of the evening meal in the normal way. I went mad with fear, broke down and had to be put to bed. My sister recovered, but her child, whom she was nursing, caught the disease and died after a day of horrible pain.

With giant steps the epidemic spread from Sebastopol over the whole land. Thousands of people fell victim, many relatives and friends among them. No wonder; with the hygiene of that day, it couldn't be different. There was an absolute lack of rules and procedures. We can judge how favorable the conditions were for the spread of cholera in the 1850s, when even now, in 1908, cholera is raging all summer, fall and late into the winter, and people are dying in the street like flies. And yet there has been half a century between, a time during which Western European culture has made so much progress specifically against epidemics. But there is a rigid border between Western Europe and Russia, and progress only creeps into Russia, almost as if smuggled in. To this day St. Petersburg has no sewer system and the people don't believe in the little dangerous bacteria that are said to live in clear water.

It is not uninteresting that among the Jews the epidemic spread much less widely than among the rest of the population. Their life was ordered by law and was simpler, and given the many prescribed washings, and the strict rules about what was forbidden to eat, it was much more hygienic. I myself suffered terribly. I became much weaker and lay in bed for days at a time, apathetic and melancholy. My nature was shaken by the these happenings.

At last July arrived. One day my sister received the happy news that her husband would be coming. We were all looking forward to his arrival, and this joyful expectation brought a gleam of light into our dark life. During the presence of our brother-in-law Abraham Sack, who had a cheerful, sunny nature, my melancholy decreased a little and I breathed more freely. In the ten days that he stayed with us we conducted our old normal life. He left full of hope for an improvement in his material circumstances, and with him joy left our house again. I descended once again into a dull, melancholy mood.

My sister remained with us, continuing to wait and wait from day to day, from week to week, for news. She suffered inexpressibly and was fearing the worst. But God had mercy. The greater the need, the closer the help. The long-wished-for letter arrived. It was addressed to me and contained one note for me and a second for my sister Kathy. My brother-in-law reported a happy change in his affairs, so that he was finally able to send for his wife. We were full of jubilation all day long. My sister shed tears of emotion and gratitude. I helped her pack, and in a short time she was ready to leave. My husband and I took her as far as Poltava, where we helped her to buy an elegant carriage with three good horses and to hire a coachman and a Jewish cook, and sent her on her way.

My brother-in-law's hopes were fulfilled. He had become a rich man. This was one of the great vagaries of fate that the war year 1855 brought with it—the year in which the veiled, moody woman Fortuna turned the wheel of fortune in Russia most rapidly. With a mighty push, she rolled the highest down low and the lowest up to the heights.

My brother-in-law's genius carried him higher and higher. His self-confidence lent consistency and patience to his efforts, and the time was favorable. Alexander II had assumed the throne; a new era had arrived. Efficient and honest people could be active in all fields in Russia now.

We remained in Luben until 1859. In that year the three big *ot-kupsheriki,* the grandfather and father of my husband and Mr. Kranz-felt, took a lease on the brandy concession extending through the entire governmental region of Kovno, and appointed my husband chief of the enterprise. I could sing my wandering song again. We liquidated our business in Luben, packed all our possessions, and went to Kovno.

Before I relate my further personal fate, I wish to speak again of the year 1855 and its significance not only in the life of all of Russia, but especially in that of the Jews, as the beginning of a new epoch. It was the year of the ascendance to the throne of Alexander II.

ALEXANDER II

And God said, "Let there be light." And there was light.

A golden sun rose, and its warmth brought many a hidden bud to flowering life. Alexander II assumed the throne in 1855. This noble, far-seeing prince put one in mind of the royal Psalmist: "He raises the poor out of the dust and the needy out of the dung heap and sets him beside princes, beside the princes of his people. The stone that the builders rejected has become the chief cornerstone" (Ps 113:7–8 and 118:22).

Alexander II exemplified these words. With great generosity, he freed sixty million serfs; and he removed the most oppressive shackles also from the Jews. He opened the doors of his Residential cities to us. Swarms of Jewish youth poured into the capital cities to slake their thirst for Western culture.

In this glittering period the enslaved spirit of the Jews could stretch and expand, joining in the joyous excitement of the whole nation. The fine arts soared, along with a rapid development in the sciences, and the Jews contributed their share to the intellectual riches of the land.

The effects of the reforms of the 1840s became evident now, two decades later. There were a number of Jewish professors, physicians, engineers, writers, musicians, sculptors, who were recognized abroad and brought honor to their country.

Count Alexander Stroganov, Governor-General of New Russia and Bessarabia, and Count Vorontsov, Governor-General of the Crimea, were both energetic advocates of the emancipation of the Jews during the years 1856 to 1858. In those happy days, plans were in preparation for equality of the Jews. In a reply to Count Kiselev's Commission for the Solution of the Jewish Problem, Count Vorontsov and Count Stroganov gave their opinion as follows:

> If it is the case that the Jews are a bad influence upon the native population, then it is not advisable to confine them in the northwest of Russia on a small piece of native soil. Our opinion, based on experience, tells us that it would be more rational to distribute these few million Jews of Russia throughout our great empire, thus dissipating their harmful effect.
>
> Furthermore, the native population could learn much that is useful from the Jews: commerce, and restraint in drink, and modesty in eating, for example. It is unjust, in our opinion, to rob this historic, oldest people of all the rights of the

native population, at the same time demanding of them all duties: money, and human bodies for the protection of the country against its enemies.

Faults in a people cannot and must not be corrected through severity. Like the nations of Western Europe, let us give the Jews equal rights; then their reputed amoral nature will improve. Releasing them from the pressure of misery will be more efficacious than repressive measures. Since they are excluded from all higher offices in the country, they are forced to engage in trade—sometimes, also in deception—but no one can deny that they are diligent and able and steadfast in their old religious faith.

The Commission replied that there were far fewer Jews in Western Europe and that those Jews were much better educated. Here, in Russia, it was still difficult to introduce the Jews to Western culture.

As it turned out, the Jews gained an unimaginable influence upon trade and industry. Never before or after did the Jews of St. Petersburg experience a life as rich and refined as at that time. Much of the finance of the two capital cities rested in their hands. Jewish banks were founded. Jews founded corporations. The stock market and the banking industry grew to unexpected dimensions.

On the stock market a Jew could be in his element. It created wealth overnight. But while many people became rich, at the same time many were also plunged into the depths of poverty, and this kind of economic activity was something new in Russia. But the Jewish genius, trained up to now only in Talmud, was able to grasp it.

Toward the end of the 1850s the old brandy monopoly, the *otkup*, was reduced in scope. This was an improvement in some ways. Toward the beginning of the previous century many merchants—Jews, Russians and Greeks—had become rich in this business. Now the excise system turned over the entire brandy monopoly to the government.

Private initiative in this business disappeared as the introduction of the excise system made it unprofitable. The Jewish merchants invested their capital elsewhere, especially in the railroad field, which proved very lucrative for their practical, active minds. Their efforts were rewarded by enormous profits and much capital flowed into their hands.

A new way of life was now required, different from the old accustomed ways. Jewish religion and tradition began to be crowded out. Jewish employees had been accustomed to studying Talmud, observing all the strictures of their religion, along with their work. But the new economy made that almost impossible. Many Jews now worked for the *otkup*, the Excise authority (*aktsiz*), or the railroad construction firms. The terms "aktsiznik" or "shmin-defernik" (from the French *chemin de fer*) became household words. Jewish society was forced to tolerate a lack of observance from these young people as it had from bank employees who were required to ignore the Sabbath and the holidays and no longer could (or would) dedicate an hour a day to the Talmud. As the folk song had it:

Aktsizne youngsters are relaxed.
They shave their little beards,
They ride little horses,
They walk in galoshes,
And eat without [ritual] washing.[1]

MY WISE MOTHER'S PREDICTION

"Two things I can say for sure," my mother said. "I and my generation will certainly live and die as Jews. Our grandchildren will certainly not live and die as Jews. But what will become of our children, I can't guess."

The first two prophetic pronouncements have partly been fulfilled and the third one is also fulfilling itself, for our generation is a kind of hybrid. Swept along by the irresistible current of new Western European culture, we made the effort, even in our advanced years, to appropriate education in various fields of science and in foreign languages.

---

[1] According to Jewish tradition, one must ritually wash one's hands before eating bread.–ed.

But while other peoples and nations pick out only what suits their nature from strange, unaccustomed ideas, preserving their individuality and peculiar natures, the Jewish people are pursued by the curse that they can adapt to the strange and new only by abandoning what is most particular and most holy to them.

Into the brains of the Russian-Jewish men modern ideas tumbled in a chaotic tumult. Suddenly, irresistibly, powerfully, the spirit of the Sixties and Seventies penetrated Jewish life and destroyed its character. The old ways were discarded. The old family ideals disappeared, without being replaced by new ones.

The Jewish women of that time were deeply imbued with religion and tradition in their innermost being, so that they experienced the insult to the old ways almost as a physical injury sustained in a battle for tradition in the most intimate circle of their families. In this transitional period the mother, the natural educator, was allowed the right to educate her child only so long as the child did not require serious sacrifice or duty. As soon as the time for intellectual education arrived, however, the mothers were pushed brutally aside. The Jewish women who still clung to tradition with every fiber of their being wished to inculcate in their children the ethics of Jewish religion, the traditions of faith, the sacredness of Sabbath and the Festivals, the Hebrew language, and the study of the Bible—the book of books, a work for all times and all peoples. They wished to transfer all of these riches to their children in lofty and beautiful ways—together with the results of the Enlightenment, with everything new that was brought in by Western European culture. But their entreaties were rejected by the men with the harsh words: "The children don't need any religion!"

Jewish young men of that time knew nothing of constraint and measure, nor did they wish to know. In their inexperience, they tried to take the abrupt and dangerous leap from the lowest rung of culture to the highest. Many demanded of their women not only agreement, but submission and the abandonment of everything that only yesterday had been sacred.

Although preaching modern ideas such as freedom, equality, and brotherhood, these young men were the harshest despots imaginable

187

at home, toward their wives. They made the most inconsiderate demands. Their wishes must be fulfilled immediately. There were bitter fights in a family life that up until then had flowed along in a patriarchal and pleasant manner. Many a woman would not give in, yielding her husband complete freedom outside, but demanding that in her own house the old beloved customs be honored. Obviously, such a double life could not be maintained for long.

The spirit of the times won the battle, and with great pain in their hearts the weaker sex gave in. I will show in the next few chapters how this process played itself out in other families and in mine.

IN LITHUANIA AGAIN

I was very happy when fate brought us back to Lithuania in 1859. There life was more generous and richer in content, and the Jews were more intelligent. We settled in the town of Kovno, which at that time was a beautiful little provincial city. The majority of the population were Jews, speaking a mix of Hebrew and German. The Prussian border town of Tauroggen was not far away. Probably for this reason, the whole way of life in this town was influenced by German customs.

In the other cities of Lithuania Jewish tradition might still be completely untouched, but in Kovno the obligation to transmit tradition had been weakening. When we came the Enlightenment was in full cry there and the new ideas had enthusiastic advocates.

In advanced Jewish homes, especially among the rich merchants, where the fathers and sons had business connections in Germany and crossed the border many times, a falling away from tradition was rife. The only thing that was retained in many homes was the kosher kitchen. The men no longer kept the Sabbath holy and never interrupted the zeal of their business dealings.

Earlier, in the words of Heine, "A Jew might be a dog all week long, transforming himself on the Sabbath into a prince. At the *seder* table he was sovereign of his domain." It might be said that the men of the second generation lived all year round as dogs, without rest,

188

without peace, constantly worrying and working. Their spirit never rose to heavenly spheres, their bodies no longer gained power through the tranquillity of the Sabbath, never regained the strength they had lost in the work week.

There was a strangely mixed, unquiet mood on the Sabbath. The woman clung with her entire nature to the old ways. She still lit Sabbath lights on Friday night and recited the prayer. But the "enlightened" Mr. Husband lit his cigarette from the candles, so that her peaceful face was drawn into a pained smile.

The Master of the House welcomed his friends, who came to play a game of *préférence*, with the same hearty welcome that he used to offer the Sabbath angels. It is true that the *kiddush* cup stood on the table filled with wine, but no one sipped from it. It had become a symbol. But the pepperfish was there. The revolution had not progressed far enough to banish that from the Friday night table. There were also still *barches*, but they had been sliced and neatly arranged in the bread basket by the maid.

In the place of *zmiraus* (Sabbath songs) jokes were told. The entire gamut of Jewish humor, and the card games, lasted well beyond midnight. There was no *chevreh tehillim*—no congregation reading Psalms awaited the gentlemen for morning prayers. The Christian servants could go to bed; the men were not averse to blowing out the lights at the end of the evening.

They rose earlier than usual on Saturday morning because it was the day before Sunday and therefore there was more than usual to do in the shops and businesses. But they worked energetically on Sunday as well, for a remnant of nationalistic stubbornness prevented them from celebrating the Sunday in any festive way.

Of course relations between the sexes had changed radically. There were dance evenings in which not only the young but also married men and women of our generation took part. It had become a matter of course that young girls were taken home from these gatherings by young men. In homes with grown young girls you could always find young men as well. There was a freer tone in the conversation. The sincere praise for the *eishes chayil* (the woman of valor) had given way to enthusiasm for the *diva* of operetta—whichever one was the talk of the day. And cynicism was no stranger to the new generation.

In these "advanced" circles the study of Talmud had of course ended. Here and there a romantic who could not abandon the old ways continued his study of the Talmud and had his children educated in Talmud, but among the so-called cultured classes this was rare. Even the most devout and religious families saw the necessity to educate their children in European culture and allowed them to go to the capital to study. Only one thing they demanded of their sons: they must eat kosher.

Many anecdotes illustrate these strange conditions. For instance, one very religious couple sent their son to study in St. Petersburg. A Christian friend who was going to the capital was asked to spy on him, to ascertain whether the son was keeping his promise. When he came back he calmed the parents and assured them that their son was eating only kosher. He himself had been there for dinner.

"What did he serve you?" asked the parents.

"Rabbit," he replied, "but it was kosher. Your son told me it had been slaughtered by the *shochet* (ritual slaughterer)."

The conditions I am describing obtained, of course, in what are called the "upper" layers of society. Who knows what they will be called if Justice ever reigns! Mighty revolutions do not stir up the entire people at once. Cultural shifts are always most visible among the upper crust. The rest of society, if it adopts the new ways at all, does so hesitantly and in sometimes strange ways. That is how it was in Kovno as well.

At this time, there lived in this "enlightened" Kovno, in another part of the city, across the bridge over the Viliya River, people who reacted to the changing circumstances in exactly the opposite way. In this they found loyal fellow travelers in the Jews of the small cities of the province. These Jews turned to asceticism. They were plain people, but great human beings—great in their knowledge of Talmud, great in their sincerity of heart, in their love of neighbor, and in the greatest virtue, simple selflessness. In food, drink, and dress they lived at the lowest level, but their ideals were of the highest.

At first each group of these ascetics was composed of ten people. Tirelessly they watched over the young of the poor, over their studies and their lives, correcting them with good strict words. Later, they founded an organization that took the preaching of asceticism as its sacred task, scorning all enjoyment of life. For them, this life was only a passage, a stop along the way to a better, higher, purer existence. Every step, every action of the day must be well considered, and three times a day God must be implored to forgive the involuntary transgressions of even the purest person.

The Jewish working class in the ghettos, ground down by the struggle for existence, was drawn to these preachers. Especially the young talmudists and the *orim bochrim* (poor talmudic students supported by charity) were enthusiastically swept away by this movement. The early penitential sermons were preached at dusk. The synagogue would be jammed with old and young as though on the Eve of Yom Kippur. All wept and from the depths of their souls implored God for forgiveness of their sins.

At the head of this movement stood the famous Rabbi Israel Salanter (Lipkin), the greatness of whose soul approached that of Hillel. He was very hard on himself and full of indescribable love for others. He fought for a simplicity of manners, but was concerned that asceticism should never reach a stage where it would destroy life.

This was the year 1855, when the great cholera epidemic was devastating the land. The people fasted to do penance, for the uncanny disease was seen as a punishment from God. But Rabbi Salanter was afraid that the people would suffer injury through these self-imposed privations. During the very morning prayer of Yom Kippur he stepped up to the *almemor* (reader's desk) with a piece of cake and ate some of it in sight of all the people, encouraging them to do likewise.

Rabbi Salanter was a true teacher of the people. His own teachers had always been wonderful men. About one of them, Rabbi Hirsch Broide, the story is told that he lived on an unpaved street with his

191

aged mother. Once a great rainstorm turned the road into mud. So that his old mother would not miss her daily walk to the synagogue, Rabbi Broide went out at night and paved the way with bricks. Another story: He was surprised, and at the same time pained, that no beggars ever visited him. He thought that it must be the fault of the lock on his door, that it was too firm. So one day he just took it off. The good man did not imagine that the beggars knew quite well how poor he was himself, and avoided his house in order not to shame him.

Another of Rabbi Salanter's teachers, Rabbi [Joseph] Zundel [of Salant], used to study in field and woods, surrounded by the natural beauty of God's creation. One time he noticed that his student was walking along behind him. He turned to him with some wise words, concluding, "Israel, busy yourself with penitential sermons and fear God." These words worked their way deep into the soul of the young man and determined the course of his whole life. He soon laid down his work as head of a Talmud academy in Vilna, in order not to break faith with his ideal goal.

Where the Chasidim agitated against heaviness of spirit, he preached against excessive joy. It was the teaching of Chasidism that God is to be served with joy. The penitential preachers demanded that God be worshipped in all seriousness. "But heaviness of heart stands in the way of higher inspiration," argued the Chasidim. "Joy leads to frivolity," replied the preachers.

Redemption comes through deeds, Rabbi Salanter taught. He never tired of urging the community to practice works of love. Good deeds and repentance are the supports of the world. If a person were to spend just one hour a day in repentance, and this would keep him a single time from speaking slander, that in itself would be a great deed. His lectures and sermons exerted enormous influence. The charm of this pure personality was magic.

It is easy to understand why the Rabbinate of Lithuania was frightened by the growth of this movement. They feared that the preaching of asceticism could lead to the creation of sects, a thing that is strictly forbidden in Judaism. The rabbis went to the preachers and there were strange fights among them.

192

Of course, the "Enlightenment" made great fun of these battles. After all, the first disciples of the Lilienthal movement lived in Kovno. Among these, one of the most remarkable was the poet Abraham Mapu, who lived modestly there and earned his bread by teaching the Russian and German languages. He was a quiet and modest man, a teacher in his whole being, who came to life in his little study and became that Mapu who is honored by the Jewish world as the first writer of Hebrew *belles lettres.*

In this unremarkable-looking ghetto Jew, there lived a wonderful soul. From the narrow, crooked little streets with all their misery and poverty, out of the musky, sultry atmosphere of ghetto life, his imagination carried him to the great shining past of his people. Filled with enthusiasm he wrote his first novel, *Ahavath Tziyon* ("Love of Zion"). It was plagiarized by the translator Solomon Mandelkern, who published it under his own name in German as *Thamar* and, what was more insolent, "dedicated" the book to its actual author, Mapu.

This novel, full of the love of Zion, presented a Jewish reader with the contrast between his dreary present existence and the greatness and splendor of Jewish life as it was when the Jews lived on their own land. Mapu followed this romantic work with a powerful satirical novel, *Ayit Tzavua* ("The Hypocrite"), a grim protest against the old customs of the Jews. This novel was received enthusiastically by the young—and infuriated the old.

A storm arose against Mapu, and he and his work were scorned, ridiculed, banned, and persecuted. But he found his enthusiastic followers among the Jewish youth. He was a fighter for the enlightenment of the Jews, and he fought with a new, unprecedented weapon —with true poetry. He presented the Jewish young people with new thoughts, pointed out new ways for them, opened new horizons and new possibilities before them. He inspired many others to become Hebrew poets.

We had the opportunity to see this thoughtful man in our house, for he taught my eldest son German and Russian, and frequently also dropped in for an hour of cozy chat. My husband admired him very much and it was always a pleasure to listen to their lively conversation.

At first our life in Kovno was very pleasant. My husband felt that he was in his element here; and although I was put off by the new customs at first, gradually I came to enjoy the pleasant social life and the simple, free, and yet decent and harmless association of the two sexes. Gradually my shyness disappeared and I enjoyed taking part in entertainments. Sometimes I watched and sometimes I participated, depending on my mood.

I still wore my *sheitl*, my wig. All the other women, even the older ones in our circle, had given it up long ago and I felt uncomfortable; but I wasn't yet at the point where I felt my own hair would add to my beauty. It was not long, however, before my husband demanded that I remove the wig. I must adjust to the customs of society, he argued, and not become an object of mockery. But I continued to wear my wig for many more years.

Financially we were not well off in Kovno. This was 1859. There was a growing ferment in the population of Russia, Poland, and Lithuania. The Polish Rebellion was in preparation. The Christian preachers began to preach abstinence, to agitate against brandy, and since our business was tied to the generous use of brandy, we were threatened with ruin.

The concessionaires were taxed a monthly amount of 120,000 rubles, which we were soon unable to pay. The three families—Kranzfelt, Gorodetzki, and Wengeroff—partners in this large business, were financially destroyed. My husband could have hung on as an employee but his grandfather did not want him to take a subordinate position in a business in which he had once been the boss. He obeyed and became unemployed.

The political propaganda in Poland carried Jewish youths along with it, so that the Jewish young took part in the uprising as if they were fighting for their own cause, their own fatherland. They did not listen to the warnings of the famous Rabbi Meisel in Warsaw, who pleaded with them to return to the Jewish banner—that is, the Torah. They joined in the battle for Poland.

But their hopes were dashed. Russia triumphed. Cossacks raced through Poland and their *nagaikas* (whips) did not spare the Jews.

But the Jews were to suffer yet more. They had spilled their young blood and sacrificed, unafraid, in the ranks of the fighters, but they were scorned anyway. They were made to feel that they were "only Jews." Once again, the Jewish-Polish saying had come true: *Jak bida, to do Zyda, po biedzie za drzwi Zydzie* (In adversity go to the Jew. End of adversity, end of Jews).

Spring came, peace reigned in the land, but it was not the peace of fulfilled wishes and demands, the smiling peace of victory. It was the uncanny silence of horror, of blood and banishment, and we were faced with the void. It was time to start from scratch and look for a living.

Fortunately, my husband found a job with the telephone construction enterprise in Vilna. He did not hesitate for long and went there. I stayed in Kovno with the three children until, after a short time, we were able to follow him to Vilna.

VILNA

Vilna, the former capital of Lithuania, was a large city at that time, with impressive public and private buildings, an old town hall, a theater and grand, mostly Gothic, Catholic churches. Especially beautiful was the Ostro Brama, which had a portal of very great artistic value. Through this portal neither Christians nor Jews were allowed to pass with their heads covered. Frequently the faithful would drop to their knees there. Most observant Jews avoided this route, although the portal is in the middle of the city. Thanks to the magnates who lived on their estates very close to Vilna and engaged in commercial enterprises with the city, industry flowered in the capital.

At that time this city was still completely Polish in character. The Polish language reigned everywhere and the entire way of life was determined by Polish custom. But this changed in the early 1860s, after the Polish Rebellion, when the notorious Murav'ev became Governor General of Vilna. With unprecedented cruelty, this man tried to root out everything Polish in his district and Russify the entire land.

195

Although he was greatly feared, he himself was also afraid. He lived in his palace like a prisoner. Even the chimney in his study was walled off. He slept in his study and his food was prepared there, before his eyes, on a spirit stove. He lived so reclusively that the rumor began to grow that he did not exist at all, that he was a mythical person.

Let me give you a little anecdote. Some Jewish workers were fixing the roof of his palace and they were discussing the question whether there was such a person as Governor Murav'ev. They were itching to find the answer. So just as they were right above the single window of his study, they let down a young apprentice on a rope to look inside. Now, as he was swinging in front of the window, the Governor saw him and reared up in fright, fearing an attempt on his life. He raised an alarm, they cut down the horrified apprentice, but as Murav'ev saw this trembling, half-grown boy before him, he started to laugh and released him without a whipping. It was not often that Murav'ev was so mild.

The hangman took no vacations in his time. Almost daily, wretched people were drummed to the place of execution and there was always a large crowd accompanying the unfortunate victims, a crowd filled with pain and sympathy, and also rage.

One morning at the tea table we were startled by the drumming. Running to the window, we saw a primitive cart drawn by a single horse in which three men were being taken to the place of execution. This cart consisted of a board on four wheels, on which there stood a bench and a placard on which the names of the so-called criminals were written. This conveyance was called a *pranger*, a pillory. It moved through the streets to the great marketplace and stopped at the foot of the gallows.

The hangmen had to support the delinquents, already half-dead with fright, to lead them to the gallows. Sacks were tossed over their heads, the rope slung about their necks, and all three were put to death with one yank on this rope. Horror and shock fill me to this day when in my mind's eye I see the twitching bodies hanging before me. I don't think that I will ever forget the sight.

Understandably, living under this strict regime, and with their memory of the countless victims of the Polish Rebellion, the people lived in agitation and in sorrowful spirits. All, Christians and Jews, wore mourning for years. It was considered a crime to appear in bright clothing even at festival occasions, at the theater or concerts. But if someone did dare to wear bright clothing you could be sure that some Polish patriot would pour petroleum over him.

When we arrived in Vilna the city still had its old character: politically a proud city of Poland; culturally, so far as the Jews were concerned, a seat of intellectual aristocracy. Jewish society in this city, which was called "the Jewish Athens of Lithuania," consisted of many prominent, noble, rich and mostly still very conservative families, and a small group of progressives—the representatives of the new ideas. This "enlightened" group remained quiet, not daring to stand up against tradition like their counterparts in Kovno.

Here in Vilna the old generation ruled. Past leaders, such as Rabbi Elijah, Gaon of Vilna, and Rabbi Akiva Eiger were given the honorific, "The Patriarchs" by later generations. These names continue to live in Jewish memory. Vilna, the place of Talmud learning, the city of the great community with its many houses of learning (*Botei Midrashim*) and the famous *yeshiva* where hundreds of old and young men studied Talmud day and night. This Vilna was depressing for the moderns. They did not dare to take their "enlightened" irreligious stance in public here.

The new environment affected my husband in a positive way. I was happy to see that without any prompting, just following his own inclination, he returned to his learning of Talmud. He was turning back, at least a little distance, from the wrong path he had been following.

Now he tutored our son Simon in Hebrew and read Bible and Mishna with him, a thing he would never have done in Kovno; and decided to enroll the boy in the rabbinical school.

Here in Vilna I was reunited with my sister Helene, whom I had nursed through a severe illness during the year of my engagement, and whom I had left before she was fully recovered. Our reunion was very joyful, but did not last long.

197

HELSINGFORS[1]

Our financial circumstances got worse and worse. Finally, my husband was forced to decide to try to find employment elsewhere.

He went by himself to St. Petersburg, where he was made welcome by our wealthy brother-in-law, [Abraham] Sack. Substantial businessmen frequented that house, and through these connections work was soon found for my husband. In the fortress of Helsingfors, on a bay of the Finnish Sea in Sweaborg, an armory was to be built, and he obtained a good position there. He went to Helsingfors in March of 1866. Later that spring I followed with the children.

Since we were to live in the fortress, I was worried about the Jewish education of our two older children, and decided to take them to the rabbi of Mitau. I wrote to him. He agreed to all our conditions, and in his reply assured me that our children would receive a thoroughly modern European education in his home. But this prospect made me uneasy, and I wrote him back that I hoped that despite the modern education, he had a kosher kitchen. Otherwise, I would not be able to entrust my children to him. I received a satisfactory reply to this and began to carry out my plan.

But a strange coincidence interfered. I got into the wrong train with my two children, changed trains several times, and instead of arriving in Mitau, came to a completely unknown city and discovered, much to my disgust, that I was closer to Vilna now than to the goal of my journey. This coincidence became decisive, and my children did not go to school to the rabbi of Mitau. Small causes can lead to great effects. My husband was meeting us in St. Petersburg on a certain day, and that day was approaching. I had no more time left to try again. So I returned to Vilna. Soon we were reunited in St. Petersburg. I told my husband the story about the wrong trains and he laughed, glad that we would all remain together.

The next day we boarded the steamer for Helsingfors, once again hoping for better times.

---

[1] Modern Helsinki.–ed.

We arrived at Fortress Sweaborg. Foreign people, foreign manners and customs, a foreign tongue. I understood neither Finnish nor Swedish, and could converse with the native servants only through the mediation of the one Russian employee. But soon, after only two months, I had learned as much as I absolutely needed, using the Ollendorf method. Despite the raw North and the severe winter, which lasted seven months, there was a cheerful, lively community here made up of Swedes and Finns. In their appearance, these two nations are easy to distinguish. The Finns, men as well as women, are robust, blond, potato-nosed with small eyes. The Swedes are tall with fine noble features, wonderful strong blond hair, and healthy, large, broad teeth.

The people here lived very modestly. Although food was very cheap, they mostly ate herring, boiled potatoes and black bread. It was the custom, both among common people and among the bourgeoisie, to bake this black bread in the fall, enough for the entire winter. Each loaf was round, with a hole in the middle; the loaves were threaded on a rope and hung up to dry. The entire population gave credit to this dry black bread for their healthy, beautiful white teeth.

Even the wealthy people in this city led an extraordinarily modest life, and their meals were not much richer than those of the working class. On the other hand, they spent a lot on culture and on amusements. This city of only 20,000 had two theaters, three lending libraries, comfortable hotels, and many cafés. A free, proud people lived here: proud particularly vis-à-vis foreigners, vis-à-vis Russians. They called them *rüssene pergele*, "Russian devils." If you gave a beggar a coin he would press your hand gratefully. But a cab driver would refuse your tip.

The population was also very advanced intellectually and interested in everything that went on in the wide world. A farmer bringing his wares into town would never go back home without his newspaper, *Soimele* (Finland).

We lived in a mansard apartment of four small dark rooms whose walls consisted of mighty granite blocks about six feet thick, fitted together. Our bedroom was especially marvelous. The window sill was so wide that a table and chairs could be set on it. Of course, it was intended for other purposes. During a war a less peaceful piece of furniture would sit there, namely a cannon. But this bedroom had one advantage. Out the window there was a wonderful view of the Finnish Bay with its dark wooded shores. This was my favorite place. I used to sit there with the children, relaxing with some needle work, and there I could dream, gazing out at the wide sea for hours, listening to its eternal, mysterious murmur.

We lived very near the Commandant and the officers and soon became acquainted with them, and they frequented our home. One of them was prepared to teach my eldest son Russian. My husband plunged eagerly into the study of Finnish and Swedish, and made such rapid progress that he was soon able to use both languages in his business dealings. My daughter was studying English. Both older children attended a French school in the city. Every day they had to travel across the sea. I was proud to see such a desire for learning in my husband and in the growing young people. Proud, happy, and yet at the same time also sad, for their eagerness to learn did not extend to all that was most precious and sacred to me.

Here in Helsingfors we lived far from all that was Jewish. There was only one small community of old soldiers whose privilege to live here dated from the time of Nicholas I. They had a small synagogue and a so-called rabbi, who was also the *shochet*.

This was a community of so-called Nicholayevsker soldiers. Anyone in the know will understand what that means! In the 1820s, Jews had been drafted into the army in all sorts of ways, dragged away to serve for twenty-five years. This twenty-five year service in the army was considered worse than death, and the oppressed Jews tried in every way to avoid this living hell. Some of these Jewish boys were no older than twelve or thirteen. Capturing a runaway would earn you twenty or thirty rubles, and even among the Jews, there were scoundrels who made a business of this catching of runaways.

If such a *chapper* (catcher) were approaching a tailor shop, some good friend would quickly arrive to warn the apprentices, and there was an immediate flight as though the pestilence were coming. All sorts of hiding places were found. Those who were caught were called *poymeniki* (draftees). There was a little folk song: "Tailor sitting on the table, *oy, oy* sewing. And here comes a good little brother and says, the *chappers* are coming."

There is an enormous number of these folks songs, especially in a very moving collection by Ginzburg and Marek. I'll set down one of these from memory.

> *How bitter it is, my dear mother,*
> *A little ship on the green grass.*
> *So bitter, my dear mother, they've grabbed me like a rabbit.*
> *No crying, no weeping, my dear mother.*
> *It's not just me.*
> *Take it from me, and from my heart,*
> *I sit down and cry.*
> *It's so bitter, my dear mother.*
> *A tree without branches, so bitter, my dear mother.*
> *They're trying to make of me a Muscovite.*

Another song goes:

> *The grief and sorrow of Jewish children is as if they had witnessed the*
> *   likeh levoneh (eclipse of the moon).*
> *From then on they have no good, no nechomeh (comfort),*
> *They lead away Jewish children to the priem (draft board)*
> *And there is trembling in their neshomeh (soul).*
> *We pray to the reboineh shel oilom (Master of the Universe):*
> *Just give us for our tzar (suffering) a little nechomeh (comfort).*
>
> *Our life is so bitter, as bitter as death.*
> *Because we have to eat yevonishen (soldier's—i.e., not kosher) bread,*
> *Because we have to wear shatnez (linen and wool cloth).*
> *This is our terrible sorrow.*
> *He who is in heaven, He understands.*
> *God, God, why have You been porish (withdrawn) from us?*
>
> *You know that we cannot obey Your gzeyres (laws).*
> *This is our bitter breires (choice).*
> *Hence we ask the reboineh shel oilom (Master of the Universe)*
> *That You be moichel (forgiving) of our aveires (sins).*

201

Your punishment we are mekabel be-ahveh *(accept as just).*
When they cut off our beard and peyes *(sidelocks)*
It breaks our hearts.
If we did it on our own, we would be ashamed.
Hence we ask the reboineh shel oylom *(Master of the Universe)*
That You take us out of golus *(exile)....*

To get out of this *gzeyreh*, the usual remedy was available only for the rich: rubles. The poor had only one way out. Since only single men were drafted, the boys had to be married off in their early years. Often a little boy would be led away from the playground and put under his wedding canopy.

A rumor spread at that time that the government was going to draft Jewish girls for government factory work. It may be that this rumor originated in a desire to make the parents of girls willing to marry them off to these little boys. The business of *chapping*, of grabbing young boys, was called *behules* (The Terror).

It was a totally unnatural situation, and at that time no doubt the foundation was laid for the degeneration of a large part of Russian Jewry. These half-grown girls became mothers of children whose fathers were also half children. But the poor parents made this sacrifice. After all, a human being might be in danger, but the faith, Judaism, must not be damaged, and service in the army made it impossible to observe the Commandments. Only the lucky ones wound up in cities with Jewish communities, where at least they could receive kosher food.

There was only one advantage arising from these heavy years of military service. Those of the Jewish soldiers who did not succumb to the exertions and to the brutality of their commanders, and survived the twenty-five years of service with healthy bodies, could live wherever they wanted in Russia. With this advantage they often became quite rich later on. But the majority did not survive in good health.

Now I had to live in a community of Nicholayevsker soldiers. After Vilna—Helsingfors! It was very hard for me under such circumstances to run a kosher kitchen at all. The meat had to be brought from town. I myself had to see to all the work of the kitchen, since I would not depend on a Christian cook. And how these difficulties were multiplied at *Pesach* time only a religious woman, a true Jewish housewife, will understand. Through all of these difficulties I was sustained by my passionate wish to preserve the tradition for the children, and above all, by my love, my warm faithful love, for my husband. As the folk saying goes: "With a beloved man, even across the ocean."

We looked for a Jewish teacher for the older children but couldn't find one, so my husband taught our elder son himself. But he wasn't a teacher. He had little patience and often forgot himself. "You donkey, what's going to become of you?" he screamed at him. And sometimes his reprimands got physical, treatment not encouraging to a child, and this hour became torture. I often had to intervene. Soon this instruction ended, and we made an effort to engage a Jewish soldier who lived in the fortress. But, unfortunately, he was not interested in our proposal.

This Jewish soldier, who had been described to us as a saint by the captain, was an unusual and interesting figure. He was religious and modest, silent and quiet, and lived an almost ascetic life. Both his superiors and his comrades spoke of him as a man of God and treated him with special consideration. But despite this special treatment, he appeared punctually on the parade ground and fulfilled all his duties.

The rest of the time he spent bent over his Talmud in his own little room that had been assigned to him. He ate black bread, potatoes, and herring and drank *kvas* (a non-alcoholic carbonated drink). For religious reasons, he never ate from the common meal. He got Sabbaths off and went to town to eat properly once a week. His knowledge of Talmud was very deep, and my husband sat and studied with him quite often. No one knew anything more about his circumstances. He would not reveal where he came from. There in his tiny unheated little room, they sat and discussed Talmud, and these hours were among the most interesting for my husband on this lonely island. He always returned in a good mood and spoke to me with great admiration of this solitary man, who was known in the regiment as Arkadius Petrov. He refused our offer to undertake the education of our son because he said it would rob him of too much time.

203

A year and a half went by. Our life flowed on peacefully and pleasantly under a cold and distant sky. The fortress was almost complete, and my husband began to look for another position. He went to St. Petersburg and once again I remained behind with the children. It was December, short dark days followed by stormy northern winter nights. That was a sad time for me.

During the day I had little time to think because I was busy with the household and with the children. But at night, those endless lonely nights, I lay for hours with my eyes wide open and listened to the rushing of the wind and the howling of hungry wolves who were driven by the wild storm from the frozen shores into the sea. These voices became so familiar to me that I began to chat with them and to complain to them of my pain and sorrow. And the answer came back to me in a thousand voices, a murmur of complaint, weeping, keening. It tore my heart and made me forget my own troubles.

Gradually the sea became calm and then out of the depths a thousand joyful, soft tones arose and rang through the air like silver bells. And so the time went by. Finally, after several weeks—and even one week can be an eternity—my husband returned from St. Petersburg with the glad news that he had found a position as chief executive of a new bank. We remained in the fortress of Sweaborg until the building of the armory was complete.

Spring came. On the third day of *Pesach* God blessed me with a daughter, whom I named Zina. These were hard, hard hours. The armory was complete and was to be taken over by the Government. The two owners of the enterprise came from St. Petersburg for the occasion, a Mr. Hessin and a Mr. Klonski, an older gentleman who addressed my husband with the familiar 'du'. Although my husband was thirty-five years old, he did not resent this familiarity; respect for old age was in his flesh and blood. Nowadays you couldn't behave this way toward a young man. A single glance would remind the older man of the proper respect owed to youth.

My husband went to St. Petersburg. Once again I remained alone with the children, this time for a long, eternally long, ten months, during which my eldest son was *bar mitzvah*. He received a pair of *tefillin* (phylacteries), which he donned every day for his prayers. He became more and more eager to read. I had to allow him to read the daily newspapers in the sweet shop of the town, where the other customers were always surprised that such a small boy could read the Russian, German and French newspapers so quickly. He told me all the news.

Then once again I was prepared to travel with my children. We boarded the steamer that would take us to St. Petersburg and made ourselves at home in our cabin, where we were served a mid-day meal. It was a rich repast, but we could eat only half of it because, of course, I didn't eat the meat dishes, which were not kosher, and one look from me and the children left them untouched as well. After twenty-four hours we arrived in St. Petersburg exhausted.

ST. PETERSBURG

In the 1870s, during the reign of Alexander II, St. Petersburg was in its highest flower. The Nevsky Prospekt and the Morskaia are the main avenues of St. Petersburg, the setting of the liveliest and most elegant life of the city. Russian street life developed before our eyes, mirroring the very nature of the Russian people. Every time of day presented a different picture—each idiosyncratic and interesting: Eight o'clock in the morning the streets of St. Petersburg are dominated by young people hurrying to school from all parts of the city. The school hours all over Russia are from nine in the morning till three in the afternoon, with an intermission from noon until one. Here are school boys, of all different heights, hurrying along in their uniforms of gray and silver; university students in blue and black with gold buttons, their wide-visored caps worn on one side of their heads; girls in modest brown dresses with black aprons, unfashionably cut, outwardly looking all alike. All the boys and girls have brief-cases strapped on their backs in accordance with the rules of the school department. Calling greetings back and forth, chattering in loud voices, they hurry past each other to different destinations, joking, playing.

Even the most elegant streets are crossed by pack wagons in the mornings: Covered in mud and dirt, a huge horse pulls each wagon, a horse that has not felt a brush on its coat for many a year and day. The cargo is covered with a ragged blanket, and both wagon and horse are waiting for the benevolent rain that will someday free them of some of the dirt. The driver quite matches this wagon and this horse. He wears a green cap, and a sheepskin coat with ragged sleeves that is both his garment and his bed.

Noon. The Peter Paul Church bells ring the hour, a cannon is heard from the fortress, and the people in the Nevsky Prospekt pull out their pocket watches mechanically to correct the time. Now the streets present a different picture. Governesses, *nyanyas*, and well-dressed nurses in their national costumes, taking the children on their walks on the wide, beautiful Nevsky.

At four o'clock in the afternoon the *corso* begins in St. Petersburg, and especially in the winter this presents a marvelous sight. What luxury! The most wonderful sleighs, the rarest thoroughbreds, the most select toilette and costly furs pass in review.

The *corso* moves from the Nicholai railway station through the Nevsky, the long and wide Morskaia, all the way to the Posteluev Bridge. It's so wide that three rows of sleighs can ride comfortably side by side. All of them gorgeous, wide sleighs, mainly private sleighs, lined with sheepskin and carpets with a blanket of black bearskin.

The glittering, crunching snow, the neighing of the horses, the soft rustling of silken materials, the laughter and chatter, the luxury and splendor of the sleighs and their occupants—this is a sight that fascinates not only strangers but also the native population over and over again.

The move to St. Petersburg brought us changes and adventures surpassing anything we had ever expected. We entered a milieu of aristocratic, cultured people who lived in riches and luxury.

The Jewish community of St. Petersburg possessed a large, splendid synagogue and two rabbis, one learned in modern studies and one Orthodox. But it had distanced itself considerably from Jewish custom and tradition. The most distinguished of the Jews adopted many

206

foreign traditions and celebrated alien festivals such as Christmas. Of Jewish holidays they observed only *Yom Kippur* and *Pesach*—and even these were in a so-called modern manner. Many calmly arrived at the synagogue in a carriage and took their meals on *Yom Kippur* during the intermissions.

Pesach was observed even in the most advanced circles. It remained a festival of remembrance—not, to be sure, of the Exodus from Egypt but of one's own childhood in the little towns of Lithuania.

The *seder* evening was celebrated in an abbreviated form. Even baptized Jews could not forego the *seder*. They did not prepare a special meal in their own house, but they enjoyed invitations to the homes of their acquaintances who were not yet baptized. It was always very festive. The hostess dressed in her finest, the children dressed carefully, the guests in dinner jackets and white cummerbunds.

The table was embellished with a stack of *matzeh* heaped on a tray, a bowl of eggs, green salad, and radishes; and of course there was no shortage of good wine. And yet the gentlemen mostly preferred raisin wine, which reminded them so powerfully of their childhood homes. Prayers and the whole series of old symbolic customs were omitted. There was conversation until midnight, not about the Exodus from Egypt, but about questions of the day, events from the newspapers, news of the stock market.

The meal was lavish, beginning, of course, with eggs dipped in salt water. Then there was peppered *gefilte*-fish, broth with *matzeh* balls, and roast. It was a cozy supper with some special items but all it had in common with the *seder* evening was the name. There was no *Haggadah* on the table. The *Haggadah* was stored somewhere in an old wooden box where it rested peacefully along with yellowed volumes of Talmud, Bible and old Hebrew books. No questions were asked and hands had been washed at home with perfumed soap. Drinking the wine, there was no special emphasis on exactly four cups. And of course, a game of *préférence* took the place of *benshen* (the Blessing after the Meal).

What I describe here are the new customs of the thin layer, the top layer of the Jews of St. Petersburg. The majority—even many of the

207

élite—remained faithful to their tradition. But to live in this environment and to remain unaffected by its influence required a force of character and religious steadfastness that my husband unfortunately did not possess. As for me, I would have remained untouched by it all. My own strong faith, my upbringing, and the sincerity with which I clung to every Jewish custom would have preserved me. I would have passed proudly among all the weaklings, proud and happy to be still in possession of all the richness and fervor that they had lost long ago. I would have pitied their poverty of spirit.

Still, even in St. Petersburg, where Jews had abandoned so many of their traditions, I often saw how strong was the bond among Jews. If Jews anywhere in the provinces had a problem with the authorities, they turned to St. Petersburg for support, and the Jewish community spared no expense or effort to represent their coreligionists in the capital. They used their influence at the highest possible level to preserve the rights of oppressed Jews, with a zeal they saw as natural, as a matter of course. It is not for nothing that Jewish solidarity has become proverbial throughout the world. Even most of the baptized Jews were no exception in this respect. As a matter of fact, it was a requirement of polite Jewish society in St. Petersburg to organize philanthropic enterprises to house and educate hundreds of children.

Our home was similar to that of many other Jewish families in which the battle of tradition was waged. The man, the breadwinner, has the duty to support his family and therefore he is master. He can request, but he is also entitled to command. That was the rule of the day. My husband also began by requesting, and when this did not get him what he wanted he *demanded* the fulfillment of his wishes. He became despotic beyond all measure.

His modest, quiet, honest manner and boundless trust for other people did not fit into big city life with its haste and effort and conflict. Despite his knowledge and abilities he was not doing well financially. In the giant enterprises in which he took part he could not find advancement. This pained and tortured him, for in his memory lived times when he had been a big man, rich and elegant. At least in his own house, in the circle of his own family, he wanted to be compensated for this injustice. Here he must be complete master—and he was, in the fullest sense of the word.

It was not enough for him that I gave him complete freedom outside the house. I was compelled to reform myself and my household. First it was small, dear, comfortable little things, close to my heart, from which I had to separate. Soon more was demanded, and without consideration the foundation of our life up to then was destroyed.

At the very beginning of our stay in St. Petersburg, I had to give up my *sheitl* (wig). Despite the most strenuous resistance, I soon had to give up my kosher kitchen and gradually drive the old beautiful customs, one after another, from my house. No, I did not drive them out. I accompanied each one to the outermost portals of my home, sobbing and weeping. My heart bled as I watched them leave and I followed them with my eyes for a long, long time.

I was as sad as if I had accompanied to its grave all that was most precious to me. How much I suffered in that time. How many inner conflicts I endured. I had not dreamed of anything like this in my youth, when I lived a quiet, proud, beautiful paternalistic life in the home of my parents. Although I loved my husband as passionately as the first time we were together, it was impossible to surrender without resistance. For my own sake and for the sake of the children, I fought to preserve all those dear treasures. I fought a life-and-death battle for them.

Life in St. Petersburg was so designed that every one of a thousand different experiences brought me back each time to the one problem of Judaism. What heartbreak my son's high school years brought me! Simon was a student in the Fourth Gymnasium (high school). One day the boys in his high school were led into the chapel to take part in a religious service. All knelt before the icons; only my son remained standing. The supervisor of the class commanded him to kneel and my son refused. "I am a Jew and my faith forbids me to kneel before an idol." The supervisor left, furious. After the service Simon was summoned. He had been expelled. He was to pick up his papers tomorrow. That was bad news. Another worry.

I hurried to the *popechitel'*, the authorities. I begged and pleaded:

209

My son did not wish to ignore the school's discipline, he just wished to be faithful to his education, to all that he had learned in his home and from his rabbis. It was, after all, an important thing to honor and obey the authority of parents. If that were to disappear, it would lead to sacrilege! But Prince Livin remained obdurate. The interview was over. Pain closed my throat, tears poured from my eyes, for I saw my son's chance for a good life destroyed.

I ran away, but had got no further than the vestibule when the Prince called me back. Simon would leave this gymnasium, but he would see to it that he was accepted into a different one. And that is what happened. Once again I found peace, and was deeply pleased with the proud action of my son. He was blood of my blood.

But could I hope that with all these foreign influences the children would always follow their mother's example? They were growing up. They understood in their own way what was happening in their surroundings and sometimes they stood on the side of their father. Very often I was alone, with my husband and all of society against me. I surrendered, but no one can imagine the tragedy of those days for me.

THE DANGEROUS OPERATION: THE REFORM OF THE KITCHEN

A few yellowed pages to which I entrusted my feelings thirty-eight years ago in my despair remain as silent witnesses to my suffering. I will copy here the words I wrote on April 15, 1871, because I think they are of general interest. They express the pain, the desperate battle, which not I alone, but many a wife and mother endured during this period of transition in Jewish life.

> *The abscess has grown to such an enormous size that it threatens to choke me. What to do. Where can I find advice? Where will I get the strength for this battle? Oh, dear God, give me the strength of soul to survive this operation without permanent damage. I feel too weak to survive this. This is a fight to the death.*
>
> *I miscalculated my own strength. I did not believe that this last reform would throw me into such inner conflict. Why is it so hard for me to overcome my principles? I think the fault rests in my loyal nature. For me,*

honor and love for my parents are inseparable from honor and love for their religious customs. I am overcome by despair when I think of what I'm about to do. This act I must perform, upon which my future welfare, my peace and contentment, even the happiness of my children, are supposed to depend. It will wound my parents terribly. I've always been a dear, beloved daughter to them. Now they will have the right to curse me. Yes, I understand their burning pain. I'm a mother myself. But where are my own principles? Yes, they're here. I've been fighting for fifteen years to preserve them. They have become part of my heart, my flesh and blood. And now they have become a handicap and cause of dissension with those closest to me—every moment, more of our affection, respect and love for each other is shattered.

What makes me so unhappy about my present condition is my husband's behavior to me. He's never understood, or given himself the trouble to see, how he can view me as anything other than a necessary object. The thought has never occurred to him that I have my own principles, my own habits, that I came from my parents' house already filled with memories and even a certain experience and that the many changing circumstances of our life have built and strengthened and developed my firmness and resolve. He's never taken the trouble to approach my inner being, to recognize it. He demands submission from me. He demands desertion of my principles.

No, my friend, these last wishes I am not able to fulfill without demur. You should have prepared me for this gradually. Maybe then it would not have been so deadly difficult. But since you did not do that, since you remained a stranger to my inner life, my affection for my parents and my sense of duty to them has grown stronger day by day. I created a world of my own inside myself, from which it is so hard for me to separate now.

Oh, God in Heaven, only You can be an impartial witness of my suffering. To whom should I complain? Do you understand me, my husband? Isn't what you call stiffneckedness in reality a sign of my strength of character? Can't you see anything higher, purer, nobler in this? Only stubbornness, only selfishness? And what about the children? They're too young, but they'll take your side. They're children of their own time. The knife is sharpened. I have to decide. The operation must proceed because I'm choking.

Only I'm begging for time so that I can fight the fight first and foremost within myself and gather my spiritual strength. But who will help me? Nobody. So, it's back into my own world, into my heart, into the company of my own thoughts, into the world of my past, which is a rich

211

story, and into the impenetrable future. I will bring this terrible sacrifice on the altar of my hearth. Until I do this I won't be able to say that I have done my duty as wife, as mother. Not until I have acquiesced even in this wish of my family.

What is my life without love, without attachment? In a continuous quarrel with those closest to me? Every time this destructive question comes up I see death before my eyes. The bitterness that I always feel is enough to poison more than this life. It could poison three lives. All right, executioners, sharpen your knives. I'm ready.

With this deed, I am trying to end the continuous mocking of religion in my home. Better to commit the horror myself, and with this action preserve the true basis of religion, which is faith. Maybe I must hesitate no longer if I am to prevent the worst. Nowadays one has to be a mild and forgiving Hillel, not a strict Shammai. You have put something so unspeakably heavy upon me.

I am living in the most difficult time of transition. We Jewish women entered the married state without any personal rights. Our men view themselves as our masters or our servants, but never as our friends. Oh, dead paper, don't even you feel it? What words I have written here upon you. I feel so awful. I feel so faint. My hand will no longer obey me. I'm going to throw this paper far away from me. Should I even wish that someday it will fall into other hands?

This is how the *treif* (not kosher) kitchen was introduced into our house. In exchange for this sacrifice, offered for the sake of my family, I made one demand: Fifty-one weeks of the year I must live as they wanted. One week, the week of *Pesach*, belonged to me; no one was to stand in my way. We would celebrate this festival as I was accustomed to do in the home of my childhood. And that's how it was.

Of course, there was a good friend who hurried to acquaint my father with this reform in my home. My father listened to him calmly, preserving a wise silence. Then he said, "If my Pessele did that, she *had* to do it."

In addition to the religious struggles in our house, there was the struggle for existence. My husband's professional life was not going well. Whether as an employee in the bank, or as a stockbroker, he had no luck. He felt defeated and tired. His professional worries in St. Petersburg began to affect his health. The children were growing up, and their education cost more than we could afford. Our social life, as well, made financial demands that we could not meet.

I endured many difficult hours, but I did what I could to hide our financial situation from the children and from strangers. The hope for better times never left me. I worked and worked so that luck, if it should ever find us, would not find us a destroyed family.

This hope gradually took form and substance in my imagination. I foresaw that something wonderful would come to our home, bringing happy tidings. It would wait outside the door and then open it quietly. But it was opening it so quietly and so slowly!

At last the lucky change came. My husband was offered the position of Vice Director of the Commercial Bank in Minsk. We packed our things and moved. That was near the end of 1871.

Within a short time, my husband was made Director. From then on, we led a well-to-do, elegant life in Minsk.

THE THIRD GENERATION

Tsirl Waletzky

OUR CHILDREN

And there came the third generation, afraid of neither God nor the Devil. Above all, they worshipped their own will and deified it. They burned incense, erected altars and without embarrassment, without consideration, burned sacred offerings to this deity, their own will.

It was the tragic fate of this youth to have been raised without tradition. Our children carried no trace of the memories of an historic, independent Jewish people. They were strangers to the dirges of *Tisho be-Av*—strangers to the site of the grandeur of their past, expressed thrice daily in the prayers of longing for Zion. They were strangers to the rhythm of the Jewish holy days, with a joyous festival always following a day of sadness.

This generation found no inspiration anywhere. They became atheists. Maybe my youthful readers will feel that I see things too darkly. Is my memory dulled? Are my eyes dim? Oh no! I am a faithful chronicler. My bright sight sees only deep shadows because they are actually there, darkening the path of the new youth, the third generation. Show me happiness. Show me the nobility of your morality and I will bow to you.

Gradually, the fathers who had kept Jewish customs and Jewish ways out of their children's upbringing, who had had them educated exclusively in the "enlightened" European way, little by little these fathers saw their fateful error. They themselves, even though they had turned away from religion and tradition, in their hearts remained basically Jews. Good Jews in the ethnic sense of the word, proud of their past. The memories of their childhood were alive within them. But their children no longer had such memories, and their own parents—mainly these fathers—were responsible for this. Not infrequently the sensitive young, recognizing their inner poverty, complained to their parents about it.

Of course there was an opportunity to make up for the lack of home education. There was the regulated instruction of religion in the public schools. Good teachers could easily have turned the interest of Jewish youth to the great Jewish past, called their attention to old Hebrew poetry and to the history of the Jews, given them the proud certainty that they belonged to a people of old and inspiring culture and history.

Then Jewish youth would not have been lost at the first contact with the youth of other peoples once they went to school. They would not have felt so humiliated when they were "accused" of being descended from Jews. They would not have turned away with such rage from their own people, would not have forgotten their obligations, not have put their strength at the service of the others, as indeed they did. But, unfortunately, the Jewish teachers of religion are not everywhere and always equal to their high task. Only a very few of them understood their mission, their obligation.

In the 1860s the Russification of the Jews was initiated by the Government. In the first epoch of the "Enlightenment," at the time of the influence of Mendelssohn, the language of instruction in Jewish schools was German. Now the mood had changed. "Enlightened" Jews went along with the Government's demands to Russify because they expected political freedom in the future and desired unification with the great Russian people. The language question was resolved once and for all when, after the Polish Revolt, the Government made the Russian language obligatory in the Jewish schools of Lithuania.

Then the curriculum itself underwent the same process of Russification. Gradually the program of Jewish subjects was abbreviated, with the "general," that is to say the Russian, education favored until, for example, in the girls' schools it was forbidden to teach Hebrew script. These Government orders reinforced the tacit wishes of the younger generation and of the Jewish teachers, to give preference to the "general" subjects. In the end, these teachers themselves pushed Jewishness out of the Jewish schools.

It was no wonder then that the dark, cold, stormy period of the 1880s and 90s broke in upon us Jews and our children like a flood. It seized our fragile little ship and tossed it up and down in the tumultuous billows of life, hither and yon. People desperately sought a safe haven and thought they had found it in baptism.

Baptism—the heavy, horrible word reached like an epidemic, a plague into the innermost core of the Jewish people, tearing apart

218

those closest to one another. This word passed my lips very seldom. It cut too deep into the heart of a mother.

After the horror had happened, I never spoke about it with those closest to me, entrusting it only to pages that I wet with tears, preserving it deep in my memory until now. But today I will overcome my resistance. Today, I will speak of that dark night. And like everything I experience, this resolve, this task, shapes itself into a picture in my mind. I see myself as a little old grandmother sitting by the hearth, surrounded by the youth of today. They love to listen to me as I speak of times past, of Jewish life in those days. Their eyes grow wide, they shine. The children raise their heads proudly and listen. The miracle of shared blood: the children whose parents turned away from Judaism have at last returned. They long for the old, grand Jewish melody that they have never heard. All this I read in the clever eyes of the children, and to them I will open my wounded heart, and tell them of all the sorrow and horror of that night.

There was great enmity between the adherents of the modern school, whose leaders systematically estranged the children from their Judaism, and the great mass of the Orthodox Jewish population. This is easy to understand. The Hebrew language must not be abandoned. All permitted—and even many forbidden—means must be employed to continue Hebrew instruction. Punishment, fines, whatever—just so the goal is reached.

The old people were not going to give in easily. The *cheders* continued. The *melamdim*, scorned as they were, continued to drill their students. Even if the Government did mix into their business— what a poor opponent such interference was, pitted against the sacred zeal of the faithful! Even though the higher Talmud institutions, the *yeshivas*, stood under the control of the Minister for Public Education, such "supervision" was only theoretical. The power of the Government did not penetrate into the houses of worship. You couldn't achieve much there through force.

In the end the Government gave in, especially once (in 1863) the Society for the Promotion of Enlightenment among the Jews of Russia had been organized and, after a *Sturm und Drang* period, achieved a loving reconciliation with the old learning. This society worked quietly but stubbornly, finding support in the spirit of the age.

The wealthy classes sent their children only to the Government schools. The *cheder* was for working-class children. But even among the rich, the study of Hebrew language was not entirely neglected. A *melammed* came into the house for several hours a week. The goal now was Gymnasium (high school) and University. It was the exceptional rich man who would send his talented son to a yeshiva.

In these years of inner change, the Seventies, all sorts of terms became current in Russia. Nihilism, Materialism, Assimilation, Anti-Semitism, Decadence. These terms dominated the last quarter of the nineteenth century and stirred the Jewish as well as the non-Jewish youth of Russia into constant excitement. Turgenev's novel, *Fathers and Sons*, coined the word "nihilism." Enthusiastic youth found the echo of their own views and desires in Basarov, the hero of this novel.

Their battle with their parents became more and more bitter, reckless and inconsiderate. Not infrequently the young were ashamed of their parents, looking on them as mere money bags, created expressly to satisfy their desires. Honor their parents? For what? You can honor only those who are more educated than yourself. The gratitude, piety, and devotion of times past had disappeared from Jewish life without a trace, as though there had never been a time when they were the shining pride of a Jewish home.

In their eagerness to overturn what was old, to examine everything skeptically, to assert their own specialness by criticizing, the young generation broke all bounds. If life did not follow their wishes precisely, these "philosophers," even the girls, quoted Franz Moor to blame their parents for their own birth.[1] They might proudly declare: "If I saw my mother and a stranger both in danger, I would rescue my

---

[1] Franz Moor, a character in Friedrich Schiller's play, *Die Raüber* (The Robbers, 1782). The reference is ironic: the scheming Franz is a liar who demonstrates no loyalty to his family.

mother first," as though it could be any other way! The youth
1880s and 90s were so far removed from natural feeling that
thought they needed to prove what should be a matter of natur
blood and of instinct.

If I have described the scenes among parents and children in the
1840s and 50s in tragicomic terms, the battles in many Jewish families
of the 1880s and 90s were pure tragedies. Jewish youth had lost its
way along foreign paths. Their motto was "Assimilation," down to
their innermost core. Everything was topsy-turvy in Jewish life. It
was a true *tohu va-vohu* (unformed void) but the Spirit of God was not
floating over this chaos. Such was the general mood and composition
of Jewish youth when the dark, cold, stormy period broke out over
their life and their fate.

Va-yehi ha-yaum! And there was a day, March 1, 1881, on which the
sun that had risen over Jewish life in the 1850s was suddenly extin-
guished. Alexander II was shot to death on the banks of the Moika
Canal in St. Petersburg. Cold and rigid was the hand that had signed
the emancipation of sixty million serfs. The mouth that had pro-
claimed the great word of freedom was silenced forever. And the
grace imminently anticipated by the whole people was removed into
the far distance.

In a meeting, the City Government of Minsk had selected two
men as delegates to St. Petersburg to lay a wreath on the grave of the
humane Czar. The Mayor of the City, H. Golinevich, and my husband were selected. They took with them a document bearing the sig-
natures of all members of the community. This was the first time Jews
took part in such an act of mourning.

But now different times began, new songs were heard. The snake
that had not dared to show its face in the daylight now crept out of the
marshes. Anti-Semitism broke out, driving the Jews back into the
ghetto. Instantly the portals of education were shut in their faces. The
jubilation of the 1850s and 60s was turned to *kines*, to songs of lam-
entation. Hopes for the future were turned into the sorrowful plaints
of Jeremiah.

All remaining freedoms were taken from the Jews. Restrictions were piled upon restrictions, and these continue more or less sharply to this day, with no end in sight. The areas where Jews were allowed to live were more and more restricted. St. Petersburg and other Russian cities were forbidden to them; only certain categories of Jews—for example, merchants of the first rank who paid very dearly for this right, and who had earned an academic diploma in Russia—were permitted to remain.

Academic education itself was made harder and harder to get. Only a very small number of Jews were admitted to the high schools. Of the few who managed to graduate from high school, only a few would be admitted to a university. Inevitably there was corruption among both Jews and Russians. Jews used any means they could think of to enable their children to enter the high schools and universities, to circumvent the brutal ordinances.

Jewish parents would pay the tuition of poor Christian students so that there would be more Christians in the schools, thus enlarging the Jewish quota. Only a certain percentage of the students could be Jewish. Money and connections played a large role—sometimes the only role—when it came to the admission of Jewish students. That this was demoralizing even to the smallest children, is easy to understand. Sometimes the small candidates asked each other as they sat down to take the examinations, "How much is your father paying?" What bitterness this introduced into the hearts of children: that the rich could attain what the poor could not, that money determined justice.

Finally, when after unimaginable effort the parents had succeeded in bringing their Jewish boy to the point of taking the exam, even if he passed it at the head of his year, there was no certainty that he would get in, even into the high school. Once again, it was a question of the quota. How many Jewish students would be admitted depended on how many non-Jews were studying. By the time it came to admission to the university, many Jews were left behind.

The choice of profession for a young Jew in Russia was not determined by his inclination or his abilities, nor by his parents' plans for him, but simply and solely by coincidence, which would admit some

222

and cut off others, for no other reason than that they were Jews. And as in school, so it was in further life. The atmosphere surrounding the Jews became dark and threatening. They were scorned and ridiculed, even by the lowest levels of society, and persecuted.

I remember, for example, an episode characteristic of that time, something that happened to my husband in Minsk. He was in a crowded street, when suddenly he heard the command, right beside him, "Jew, get off the sidewalk!" He turned and saw a Russian with a face full of hate. The street was crowded with Jews.

One man lifted his cane and called out to the anti-Semite, "What are you thinking of, to speak like that, to speak so scornfully? The street is free for everyone."

In a moment the anti-Semite was surrounded by wrathful Jews. He disappeared very quickly.

A few days later, Governor Petroff summoned my husband and greeted him with the following words: "I hear that your command means as much as my own in this town. Maybe you'd like to take my job altogether."

My husband thanked him politely and calmly assured the Governor that he was very content with his position as Director of the Commercial Bank and wished no other. Only his high position and his connections in the bureaucracy prevented this incident from turning tragic. Anyone else would have been punished severely. Such episodes were repeated and became more frequent, harbingers of the bloody encounters that were not far off.

The new word, launched in the 1880s, was *pogrom*. First to suffer were the Jews of Kiev, Romny, Konotop and other places. They were helpless before the attack of the wild masses, and were brought down in the roughest possible way. We got detailed reports from newspapers, but chiefly from private correspondence. Panic spread very quickly. That was the beginning. It echoed from every corner of Russia, and among the Jews depression and despair began to reign.

But they did not remain numb and hopeless for long. They gathered their forces to defend themselves against the enemy, understanding that God would help them only when they were helping themselves. Fearlessly they made their preparations and rules, bearing in mind the words from *Megilles Esther* (the Scroll of Esther): *kaasher ovadeti ovadeti* (Since we are lost already, we might just as well defend ourselves).

In the city of Minsk the mood was dark. Business slowed down, the Jews left their stores, they hurried through the streets uneasily, casting suspicious glances about them. They were on guard. In case of a *pogrom*, they were ready to fight desperately. The air was charged; an explosion was expected any moment. The Jewish market women who came into my home, filled with fear and horror, told of the rough threats made against them by the farmers who brought their wares to market twice a week, speaking openly of an imminent attack and of the imminent murder of all Jews. My husband, too, brought such news from the bank, and the children brought it home from school. Enmity toward the Jews grew with every day, and even the street urchins had the nerve to throw stones through the window panes of the foremost families in Minsk, and to shout insults at the Jews in the streets.

Once there was a loud pounding on the street door of our apartment. The maid opened it and was astonished to see an insolent little street urchin before her, with a provocative expression on his face. Without taking off his cap, he asked the name of the master. The maid told him our Russian-sounding name, and the Russian-sounding first name.

He asked impatiently, "I want to know whether Jews or Christians live here!" And once he was given the answer he was looking for, he shouted into the apartment, "Jewish trash! Why do you boast a Russian name?" and ran away.

Hatred for the Jews smouldered in all layers of society. Hate-filled glances glittered around the Jews like knives as they moved about.

The Jews of Minsk armed for battle. Their homes became fortresses, everyone according to his way, whatever was possible for him. One might provide himself with strong clubs called *drongi*. Another might be mixing sand and tobacco to be thrown into the eyes of attackers. Boys as young as eight, girls as young as ten, took part in these terrible preparations and were courageous and unafraid in the streets.

One such hero called to his worried mother, "Be calm. When the *katsappes* (Russian hooligans) come to kill us, I've got a knife too." He reached into his pocket and brought out his little knife that he had bought for ten kopeks.

Nobody felt safe, even in his own house. The Christian servants, who had worked for us for some time, suddenly became impolite and impertinent so that we were forced to protect ourselves against enemies in our own home. After the servants had gone to bed every evening, I took all the knives and hammers out of the kitchen and locked them up in a cupboard in my bedroom. I put up a barricade, secretly, in front of the door, consisting of kitchen benches, chairs, a ladder, and other pieces of furniture. I smiled a little as I did this, for I didn't believe for a minute that in the case of a *pogrom* we would be able to save ourselves in this way. But I built this barricade over and over again, got up first every morning to take it down and put everything back into place, so that the servants would not notice our fear.

Things did not reach the stage of *pogrom* in Minsk. Accidentally, or perhaps not accidentally, this city was spared.

In these years of the 1880s, as anti-Semitism raged all over Russia, there were only two ways for the Jews. Either give up all that had become essential to them, in the name of Judaism; or take the other path, of freedom and of all possibilities, education, career. That path was the path of baptism. Hundreds of the "enlightened Jews" chose it. But the *meshumodim* (apostates) of this time were not baptized out of spite (*le-hachis*), nor were they like the marranos of earlier times who conducted religious services in their cellars. These were deniers of all religion. They were nihilists.

I challenge the greatest *zaddik* to come and declare that he has the courage, and the right, to demand of a young man without tradition, who had not been raised in Jewish ways, to sacrifice all that the future could offer him—happiness, honor, and fame for the sake of an unknown and empty concept. To demand that he resist all these temptations, to withdraw to the narrow darkness of a provincial town and lead a poverty-stricken life there—let such a *zaddik* tell me that he has the right and the courage to make this demand. *I did not.*

My children went the way of many others. The first one to desert us was Simon. When we heard of it, my husband wrote these simple words to our child: "It's not nice to leave an embattled camp."

The child of my heart, Volodya, who is no longer among the living, followed Simon's example. He had passed the final examinations in Minsk brilliantly and traveled to St. Petersburg to begin his studies at the university. He arrived at the office and handed his papers to the bureaucrat who was to decide about his admission. For Jews there were great restrictions. Only those who had won a gold medal were accepted, and not all of these but only up to ten percent of the entire student body.

The official returned the papers to my son and said harshly, "Those aren't your papers."

My son looked at him with astonishment. The official added, "You got these, you stole these somewhere. That's not a Jewish name but a Russian name, Vladimir. These aren't your papers."

On the same day this deeply wounded young man was forced to leave St. Petersburg, for as a Jew who was not a student he was not allowed to stay there for an entire twenty-four hours. He made the trip several times more, always with the same result. Finally he took the fateful step, and was immediately enrolled. Many other children suffered the same fate.

The baptism of my children was the heaviest blow I suffered in my entire life. But the loving heart of a mother can bear much. I forgave them and accepted the blame on our own shoulders as parents. Gradually, this sorrow lost the significance of a personal tragedy and turned more and more into a national tragedy. I grieved not just as a mother, but as a Jew, for the entire Jewish people, which was losing so many of its strong members.

But in that dark period not all "enlightened" Jews lost their way among the strangers. Many found their way back to Judaism, and for them these events became a cohesive force. One reaction to anti-Semitism was the organization *Chovevei Tziyon* (Friends of Zion) founded by Dr. Pinsker, Dr. Lilienblum, and others.

OUR VOCATIONAL SCHOOLS

My husband was depressed for a long time. But he revived once an opportunity arose to put his energy to work on behalf of the Jewish people, and was filled with a new spirit of joyful labor.

During the last quarter of the nineteenth century the question of the workers began to come to the forefront in Russia, gradually growing in significance. Among the Jews, the working class, mostly unschooled, was considered the lowest class of the population. No wonder, since the Jews are a people who honor learning above all else, whose aristocracy is of the intellect and spirit. Sarcastic expressions such as, "He understands *chumesh* (the Pentateuch) like a shoemaker," or "like a tailor," were common. Even today, it is not a rarity to see a Jewish father refuse to give his consent to the marriage of a daughter or a son if the proposed family are tailors or shoemakers. Despite all modern ideas, even to this day most enlightened Jews put a great deal of emphasis upon *yiches*, family history.

Now a ray of light penetrated the darkness and dinginess of the homes of this lowest class whose members had been left behind. They were awakened to a new, more beautiful life; intellectual ferment began to grow among them. The upper, wealthier classes of Jews furthered these tendencies among the proletariat, sparing no effort and money to support them.

These new ideas were accepted in our home with great enthusiasm, and my husband conceived the plan to found a technical school for boys in Minsk. *Oymer ve-oyseh*—no sooner said than done. He enlisted Rabbi Chaneles to work with him and asked the Jewish community to make a contribution out of the tax on kosher meat. The rest of the money would be paid by the members on a monthly basis.

With what zeal my husband got to work on this project! Every free hour now was dedicated to this holy work. The trades of the locksmith, carpenter and blacksmith would be taught, in addition to the elementary subjects required by the public schools. A building was rented and furnished with what was most necessary. And to his great joy, my husband was able to obtain it all very cheaply and sometimes without cost. The Jewish population of Minsk was very pleased with this enterprise, the wealthy prepared to further the good work with contributions of money. Not without reason did our Sages say: "Yisrael rachmonim bnei rachmonim" (the Children of Israel are philanthropists and the children of philanthropists).

A Board was selected from among the finest enlightened families of the city. They made my husband chairman. Everything was ready, and they began to admit the children, giving priority to orphans and the children of very poor parents. More than sixty boys were enrolled.

Room and board was arranged for the poorest and for the homeless. At first the children ate in the homes of various citizens of the town, every day in somebody else's home. But after a while the means were found to hire a cook and the poor children were fed three times a day in school. On weekdays the meals were very simple but fresh and wholesome—soup, a piece of meat, and vegetables. But Friday night and Sabbath the table was set in a festive way and the children were offered a traditional Jewish meal. There was no work on the Sabbath. It was a holy day on which the boys prayed in their synagogue.

These pupils, most of whom lived in cellars, were thin, pale children with great clever dark eyes. Of course their clothing was very poor. But they worked and learned with great energy. I often came there to enjoy the sight of these children hard at work at their studies. My husband spent at least an hour there each day. Rabbi Chaneles was very busy with this institution and instructed the children himself, without salary, in Bible and other subjects.

And so a year went by, and the school had enjoyed considerable success. My husband and Rabbi Chaneles organized an official report of their work; there was a celebration to which Governor Petroff was invited and several other officials, the director of the girls' high school, Madame Buturlina, and the teachers of the upper classes of the high school, as well as the foremost ladies and gentlemen of Jewish society. My husband read the report and everyone followed his speech with genuine interest. For the first time, in the rooms of a Jewish school, Jews and Christians discussed the affairs of the growing Jewish proletariat in solemn harmony.

228

The children, boys aged eleven through thirteen, were gathered in the large carpentry workshop, arousing much sympathy among the guests by their ragged appearance. Once the official part of the event was over, I turned to the wealthy ladies and told them that it was our sacred duty to see to the daily bread and appropriate dress for these poor boys, and my request was successful.

On the next day I invited several ladies to my home and we discussed our undertaking. We founded an organization, sending several hundred letters of invitation to the Jewish ladies. At the same time we asked them for either new or used underwear and clothing and small donations of money. In a few days there were large deliveries of clothing. I spent the money we received on woollen gloves and *bashlyki*—warm hoods.

We gathered all the pieces of cloth we had in the house, and my children's governess sat at the sewing machine for several days and made *bashlyki*. On my walks, I was always very happy to meet children in their warm hoods and gloves. The children were recognized among the people by these hoods and the school was at first called Wenger-off's Workshop. The members paid their dues with great regularity, so that we were able to provide the children, in addition to their meals, with strong, well-cut clothing made of good strong cotton.

It was a great satisfaction to my husband when the first generation of apprentices who had earned their diplomas in the school were praised wherever they were hired and acknowledged as good workers.

These first workers spread out through the country. Many left Lithuania and went to Russia, where they got permission to live since they were skilled workers. These were the first Jewish skilled workers in the northwest territory, and the first who had enjoyed systematic training in their own fields and also in Bible and in elementary subjects such as reading, writing, and arithmetic. Not long before, an apprentice had been treated by his master as a servant and was hungry all year long until he had learned something of his trade. Now it was possible for these apprentices, already schooled in their trade, to develop in a systematic, orderly way to become journeyman workers.

The children blossomed under these good conditions. They studied with great enthusiasm and made progress. Unfortunately, the budget was not sufficient. Our ladies' club decided to draw in the citizens of Minsk in a pleasant way to make a contribution, staging an autumn festival in which many non-Jews, even the Governor, took part. The festival earned between 2,000 and 4,000 rubles and became an annual event in the fall, always with great success.

But we needed more and more money, and many times my husband made up the deficit out of his own pocket. The school continued for about eight years under his leadership. A pleasant dance evening brought 3,000 rubles into the coffers of the ladies' club. At the next meeting my husband suggested that he apply for a loan from the treasury of the ladies' club, since the big treasury was empty. When this suggestion aroused objection, his feelings were hurt and he resigned as president. This was a blow both for my husband and for me, because we were robbed of an important sphere of our life. But, thank God, the school prospered without us and developed year by year, and exists to this day.

During this time a great tragedy came to the city. A fire caused two million rubles' damage. Our apartment, with all our furniture and new cupboards full of valuable clothing and furs, was destroyed. We were glad to get away with our lives. Through flames and smoke we struggled to an outlying part of the city with our children, where friends took us in. The fright of that night shook me so much that I fell ill and had to travel out of the country to recover. I took the children with me to Vienna.

The trade school, incidentally, did not suffer much fire damage.

Three years later I returned to Minsk, where my husband had built a new house in our absence. I brought completely new furnishings back with me from Vienna. Our home was fashionable and cozy. Our life became very pleasant.

Soon after my return a Mrs. Kaplan appeared, a very intelligent lady, a *gabete*, very knowledgeable about the needs of the Jewish people and filled with desire to meet some of these needs. She suggested to me the founding of a trade school for girls, a plan that I took up with great enthusiasm. I pressed her hand gratefully and our bond was forged.

From this moment on, I felt that my life was full once again with an intensive, I would say religious, coloration. We began work immediately. Mrs. Kaplan rented an apartment for the school. We selected a ladies' committee of young women and, as we had done with the founding of the boys' school, turned to the Jewish citizens of Minsk for contributions. I organized the first fund-raiser, an amateur theater production, which earned half of the necessary funds.

Every day the residents of attics and cellars and outlying parts of the city brought us their eight- to ten-year-old little daughters, begging us to accept them into the school. We bought three sewing machines on the installment plan and hired a seamstress for twenty rubles a month, a seamstress for underwear for ten rubles a month, and a *corsetière* for the same amount. We bought several hundred meters of simple cotton and all the necessary sewing materials, irons, scissors, and so forth.

The day approached on which we were to open the establishment. We all arrived at the appointed hour in the school rooms. Mrs. Kaplan, who had studied tailoring in Königsberg for several years, cut several pieces from a large bolt of cloth and distributed them among the girls, and instruction began in the three classes.

Before long several ladies and young girls came to offer their services. The young girls taught the children Russian and arithmetic free of charge. We hired a *melammed* to teach Hebrew. Lessons in the Russian language took place twice a week.

But we were troubled by the neglected appearance of our charges, and soon our wish to see them properly dressed was fulfilled. After a short time, we had the satisfaction and joy to see our sixty girls clean, with their hair cut short, dressed in simple, clean dresses and aprons and busy with their work. At my suggestion these children were taught the practical advice of the wise men of our people, the *Pirke Avot*, the Sayings of the Fathers. I was often present at these classes, and it gave me much joy to see with how much interest and understanding the children followed this instruction.

231

Because of the warm participation of the citizens of Minsk, who supported our undertaking financially, we were soon able to offer not only instruction but nutrition to these poor hungry creatures. The children learned very quickly and soon they were producing useful pieces of clothing. In the course of one year, they made so much progress that fashionable Jewish and Christian ladies had some of their clothing made in our workshop.

In the fall of the first year we organized a benefit festival that earned us two thousand rubles. These festivals became a tradition and continue to this day. Both the boys' and the girls' trade school existed for a long time without any privileges or rights. But gradually certain rights were granted by the Ministry for the Enlightenment of the People, for example, the right for holders of our diplomas to live in greater Russia. I myself passed a test for sewing underwear to get a permit to live in Kiev.

From then on, our Minsk schools were under the protection and supervision of the Office of Education since they taught Russian, furthering the aim of Russification. Ten years after the founding of the girls' school we organized an exhibit of things made by our pupils. The foremost residents of the city came; Jews and Christians, and even the Governor, Prince Trubetzkoi, honored us with his presence.

This was another beautiful day in my life. The girls, who just a short time ago had been poor, miserable, wild children, stood in the festively decorated exhibit room. They were clean and healthy, and surrounded by the leaders of the city, who examined and praised their work.

Our school gave the poor and neglected the possibility to earn their bread in an honorable and efficient way and gave them health, freshness of youth and, above all, human rights. Maybe some time soon the day will come again when Jewish *bal meloches* (working people) will stand on the same rung of society as the learned. In talmudic times, many of the *tana'im* and *amora'im,* like Rabbi Yochanan the bootmaker or Rabbi Hillel the woodcutter, delivered lectures even though they worked with their hands. With tears in my eyes I watched our Jewish children. A quiet joy filled me, for I knew at that moment that God had blessed our effort.

Despite the large contributions of money, the monthly contributions of our members, and the revenue of the festivals, our means did not suffice and we always worked with a deficit. Then we heard that Baron Hirsch had left several million rubles in his will for the trade schools of the Russian Jews. It sounded like a fairy tale, but soon it proved true. A representative of the trustees came to us from St. Petersburg, and after certain formalities both schools began receiving steady support—several thousand rubles a year for each to this day.

Years later, young girls whom I don't know still come up to me on the street, greet me with special friendliness, and call me by my name. And after I, surprised, ask them who they are, they answer: "Madame Wengeroff, I am Rivkeh or Malkeh, or so-and-so, from the workshop."

It takes me a while to recognize in this prosperous-looking girl the ragged little Rivkeleh of the past.

JEWS IN THE ARTS

The Europeanization of the Russian Jewish masses must really be seen as an evolutionary process, although it destroyed the old ways of the ghetto and caused a total shake-up and destruction among the weak and helpless. How could it be otherwise? Here was a spirit that for centuries had undergone the strenuous training of Talmud, which had sought to go beyond the everyday and achieve a higher Law, which had dedicated great effort to distinguishing between right and wrong. This was a life of the emotions lived out among gentle, blessed, and judicious practices and which had found refreshment from the difficulties of the everyday in the quiet gardens of *aggadah* (talmudic legends).

The richness of these spiritual values could not be destroyed outright through the new culture. That culture, which had lain in their blood, had been refined and heightened through centuries, sought and found a new field of endeavor and a new home in art. Of course, not many actually became very good artists. But the thousands of young writers who sought the light of day in the Sixties, the many who were sensitive and able to enjoy all the artistic creations of Europe, they all proved just one thing—that while the field of most personal and passionate interest had shifted, the intellectual and emotional energy was as great as it had been throughout the centuries.

Seen in this way, phenomena like Antokolski[1] are no longer surprising. There were always artists in the ghetto, but spiritual freedom was required to unshackle their creativity and free their hands. Antokolski was the son of a poor tavern keeper in the Vilna suburb of Antokol. From a very early age it was clear that he was very talented. He whittled wooden figures, and he produced all sorts of seals, whose handles were carved in various ways. While still a small boy he carved an amber brooch depicting Governor-General Nasimoff, which was a fine likeness, although he had seen the Governor only from a distance and only a few times.

He aroused much attention with his wood carving depicting a marrano family surprised at their celebration of the *seder* in their cellar. The whole tragedy of the situation was captured in this carving. The table was overturned, the *Haggadahs*, the dishes, the candlesticks, the candles, the wine bottles, everything tossed about, and the men pressed together in a corner. Against one wall a woman leaned with a suckling infant in her arms, and you could feel that she dared not breathe.

Clearly, in the ghetto this unusual talent would be left to starve, as so many talents had come to nought there. But there was a Mr. Gerstein in Vilna who took this young man under his wing and made it possible for him to go to St. Petersburg when he grew up. This was a long trip by wagon. All he had to eat was bread and herring. In St. Petersburg, the famous writer Turgenev noticed him and took him in, made it possible for him to be educated, made the culture of the time available to him, and cleared the path for him to the influential men of the city.

---

[1]   Mark Antokolski (1842–1902), the first internationally known Russian Jewish artist.–ed.

I had the great good fortune to meet this young master while he was working on his powerful work of Ivan the Terrible. Because of the size of the piece, Antokolski went to the Academic Council requesting a larger studio, but all he was offered was an attic on a third floor, which was reached by a small back staircase. He had to be content with this low, poorly lit room. But the work grew and grew, and all who saw it in the process of becoming were filled with enthusiasm. I still remember to this day the almost passionate excitement that possessed me on catching sight of this work. My brother-in-law Sack, who was friendly with Antokolski, had made it possible for me to visit his studio.

The work was still a clay model, but I felt as though I were standing, not before a lifeless statue, but in the presence of life. Behind the hard forehead, you could see great thoughts coming into being, ruthlessness directed towards a single purpose. Both arms were pressed on the arms of his chair as though he were about to leap from his seat. The Bible resting on his knees would slide off and soon his powerful hand would seize and raise the *paliza*, a scepter topped by an eagle, and drive the iron point through the boot and foot of his guard (*aprichnik*).

It was the most powerful work of sculpture that had ever been produced in Russia. Everyone spoke of it, in all layers of society, until word of it came to Czar Alexander II and he wanted to see it, too. Now this drove a fright into the academic bunglers. They begged the young artist to allow the model to be put into a larger room, for they were afraid that the Czar would surmise how shabbily they had been treating the young artist.

Antokolski refused, ostensibly because he did not want to risk his model. It could come to harm on that narrow staircase. But he also had the pride of the artist. Let the Czar see that great things can come from humble beginnings. And so, the staircase was covered with precious carpets and decorated with exotic plants.

It is true that the Czar felt uncomfortable on this labyrinthine path, whose exit was not readily visible. But when he stepped into the attic, he was overcome by the work. He shook hands with the artist, praised him, thanked him, and soon thereafter Antokolski received the title of Professor.

The number of artists making copies was much greater.

Music, of course, had always been popular in the ghetto. The *klez-morim* (instrumental musicians) could not read music, but they put their whole soul into their wild, untrammeled playing. They knew how to grasp you emotionally. The *chazonim* (cantors) had never studied music either, but their melodies, however informal, penetrated the deepest and most delicate meaning of each prayer and inspired the worshippers—and entertained them. There wasn't much variety in the ghetto. There were *chazonim* who traveled from town to town with their choruses, and the arrival of a new *chazan* was always an event. It fulfilled needs that are served these days by operettas and concerts.

Also an artist was the *badchen*, the entertainer at family parties who would set the mood with his *grammen* (verses), both serious and humorous. Many of the professional musicians all over the world—if you only know how to decipher their changed names—will turn out to be the descendants of *klezmorim, chazonim,* and *badchenim.* I can offer, as an example, the story of a man who is now Musical Director of the Czar's Opera in Moscow.

One afternoon, my friend N. Friedberg came into my study with two boys, one seven, the other six years old, and introduced them to me. "These are the children of the *badchen* Fidelmann." They were pale, thin boys who blinked at me with eyes black as coal, like little rabbits. "I'd like them to play for you. You'd like to hear them play, I'm sure, and I'm hoping that you will become interested in them if you hear them."

"Good," I said, "I'll do my best." While we were talking, the older child ran into the front room and brought in two little violins with a book of music containing only small Polish songs and dances, with which I was very familiar. The older boy screeched first one and then another of these, and I listened to the familiar melodies and was glad when he was finished. Now the younger one began to play. His

236

eyes sparkled, his face came to life, and I was moved by the rapid movements of his little hands and by his expressive face, full of understanding. At the end of this audition, I told Mr. F. that my friends and I would cover the honorarium of eight rubles a month. The boys had had to stop their lessons when their teacher raised his rates.

The children were dismissed peacefully and began instruction the very next day. My friend Friedberg, himself a very good musician, had seen talent in the younger one. The boys, especially the younger one, studied with great industry. It was my pleasure to have them instructed also by the Jewish *melammed* in Bible, writing, and Russian.

At first these housemates of mine kept running away, but after they had been studying for a year, they were happy to be examined. And even my husband began to take an interest in their playing. Often the little one would bring a basket of groceries into my kitchen, for his mother had no time on Friday to bring them to me herself. I scolded him for this. Under no circumstances did I want him to drag this heavy basket through the streets.

"I hope to God," I said, "that you will become a great, famous man and ride in carriages. I don't want anyone to see you with the basket."

He said, "For you, Madame Wengeroff, I can do anything."

Three years passed in this way, until the little one had learned all that his teacher could teach him. Since there was no other music teacher in Minsk, Mr. Friedberg and I decided to send him to St. Petersburg. I wrote to my sister, Her Excellence Sack, asking her to interest herself in the boy, of whom I had told her when I was last in St. Petersburg. To raise money for his trip and for the beginning of his stay in St. Petersburg, we organized a concert in which my protégé Ruvenkeh, later Roman Alexandrovich, performed as well. The concert raised the required funds and we began to prepare for his journey.

A great variety of people took part in outfitting him. He even got a silver watch from Mr. Syrkin, another benefactor of his. He was quite insanely happy about this gift. When he said goodbye, I

237

reminded him that in the coming good times he should always remember gratefully his old mother and all his donors and sponsors. I also asked him to report to me soon about his admission to the conservatory. He asked quite naively, "Where should I get a postage stamp?" I gave him a ruble for a postage stamp. He did not use it for this purpose.

Through the efforts of my sister and the recommendation of Anton Rubinstein,[1] the boy obtained a residence permit from Governor Grosser and tuition-free admission to the Conservatory. He studied with great success in the violin class of Professor Auer until he had to enter the military. Students in advanced classes helped him pass a high school diploma examination so that he would not have to serve as an enlisted soldier. What he needed to live on was provided by Mrs. Sack and Mrs. Anna Tirk, in whose homes he often played.

He entered the top Regimental Guard and wore a very picturesque uniform and a decorative hat. Two rooms in the barracks were assigned to him. He had his own orderly. In every way, he was shown great consideration by his superiors and won the hearts of the authorities.

The greatest of the gentry came to listen to him practice. When it suited him to be moody, he made them listen in the next room. He was chosen to play first violin in an orchestra sent from St. Petersburg to Paris. Still in the military in his glittering uniform, he played at the *Palais* before President Carnot with great success and received a valuable diamond ring from the President. He finished his studies at the conservatory. During his military service, he played concerts in St. Petersburg, Düsseldorf and Berlin.

THE DEATH OF MY HUSBAND

Softly and treacherously the specter of death approached our home. My husband began to feel worse and worse every day. His heart

---

[1] Anton Rubinstein (1829–1894). Composer, pianist, and founder of the St. Petersburg Conservatory, 1862. He converted to Christianity as a child.–ed.

began to give him trouble, and this was exacerbated by stressful circumstances at work. He would not dwell among the living much longer. But at that time, I had no inkling of how close his end was. In the last years of his life he had become calmer and milder, returning to the mystical moods of his youth when he had been absorbed in the study of Kaballah. I felt that he envied me for having retained my natural faith throughout our life. On the other hand, he still thought that mystical impulses represented a kind of weakness, and was covertly ashamed of them.

However, he let me be now, and no longer made fun of my religious approach to life and of my activities. Sometimes it even happened that he "visited" me in the synagogue. He himself did not attend to pray, but he would visit me there on the Holy Days and, with embarrassment, would explain that he just came to see that I was all right. But his visits came from a deeper impulse; it was his soul that drove him there, the atmosphere of Jews gathered together in solemn ceremony that drew him. He began to hesitate. Having once introduced a way of life, he did not want to change it. But the memories of his youth were mightier, grew stronger until they captured him once again. The tradition in his blood overcame all the modern *Sturm und Drang.*

More and more this inner conflict burst forth, sometimes quite suddenly. Once we gave a dinner for sixty people. My husband was in a good mood the entire time, chatted with everyone, played the gracious host until the guests had left our home late at night. Then suddenly, as if torn by great pain, he wrung his hands and cried, "Ach. Sixty Jewish children sat here together and ate *treif.*"

And so the prophecy of my mother was fulfilled. This mood regained its power over many men of our generation, for in the sacred hours when they dared to confront their true selves, they felt the gash torn across their souls. The intoxication fled. Awakened childhood memories regained possession of their eyes, claiming their rights in the most seductive way. These men were recaptured by the past, while at the same time the new times still beckoned.

My husband became more and more quiet and lonely. The one

remaining passion of the last years of his life was his garden, where he tended his flowers with fatherly care. In his idle hours he also liked to whittle, and to make copper plates. But this was not good for his lungs.

He stood up for the interests of his coreligionists to the very last moment of his life. He was eager to help, to do anything useful for them. My entreaties and warnings were useless. At times like that, he worked without consideration for his health. Every Jewish tragedy struck him as if it were his own, and any injustice, though other people's and not his own, seemed to bring him closer to death.

At that time the mayor of the city of Minsk was Count Chapskii, an aristocratic man of truly European culture, whose one goal was to Europeanize Minsk. He introduced trolley cars, he had a marvelous slaughterhouse built, he had the streets paved, and so on. He spent 100,000 rubles for these purposes, and not only out of the treasury; he also laid out large sums from his own pocket. When it came to his own person, he was simple and modest. His food and his dress were simple and almost poor, but to fulfill his plans he did not count on the means of the citizenry because most of them were poor people and could not afford much.

The result of all his zeal was a city debt of 200,000 rubles. And of course, it was the citizens who were supposed to pay this off. This burden was too heavy, especially for the Jews, and my husband felt that it was a matter of honor to fight against these plans. He prepared budgets covering the expenditures of the past few years; armed with these, he went to the last meeting of the city Duma (parliament or council), of which he had been a member for the past twelve years. He went in spite of my entreaties. I begged him and conjured him and implored him not to do this. His speech there lasted for two hours and made a strong impression. The papers reprinted it and it was the conversation of the day throughout the city. But on the very next day he broke down.

On the third day—it was a Friday—he went to work in the bank for the last time. But he came back very soon and called for the doctor, who calmed us and assured us that this was just a temporary weakness.

240

I was filled with foreboding but was pleased to allow myself to be fooled. My husband told me that he had invited a business acquaintance for the evening meal and asked me to prepare a good Jewish fish meal. And it was a pleasant evening. At their father's request, the children played piano and cello. The elegant rooms were festively illuminated; for the last time the mood of Sabbath filled our home.

But my poor husband could find no peace. Restlessly he jumped up from his place at the table and hurried about the apartment. He looked at the children playing, at the beautiful rooms, and I saw that through all his unrest a breath of happiness crossed his flaming cheeks. God had given him one more happy hour before his departure.

The guest took leave of us and invited me to come to Libau with the children. And my husband, accompanied by his servant, went directly to his bedroom. The children went to bed, the house became still. I was busy in the dining room alone. Suddenly the bell sounded shrilly from my husband's room, heralding the storm that would destroy our life together and separate us forever. I hurried to the bedroom and found my husband already very changed. The doctor came, prescribed medicines and comforted us as much as he could, remaining with me the whole night in the sick room. My husband was uneasy. He woke every other moment from his slumber, and each time, as he saw me still watching by his bed, asked me to go and rest.

"Take care of yourself, preserve yourself in good health for the children."

By morning he felt much better and asked to get up. He got dressed, drank his tea, went into his study, read a book, and even gave some orders to an employee of the bank. Once again hope crept into my desperate heart. But the fateful hour was drawing closer and closer. He began to complain again. The restlessness in him reached a climax. Now he sat, now he lay down, only to rise again in great haste. The clock struck six, the most terrible hour of my life.

It was a Saturday, the eighteenth of April, 1892. I was beside my husband, who had sat down on the sofa. I looked into his face fearfully. With tormenting worry, I watched each tiny change in his features. This upset him. He left my questions unanswered. I poured tea into his saucer for him, and he took a sip from it. And so we sat next to each other for another fifteen minutes or so, until suddenly he opened his eyes full of horror, took a heavy breath through his mouth and nose, and threw his head back. His strength left him. He fell back and remained motionless.

It became very quiet. For one moment that terrible stillness, when a thousand voices of despair and pain are suddenly silenced, reigned in the room. Half crazy, I threw myself weeping on my husband. I held his head, his hands. His eyes were closed. I called his name. All my love, all our dear memories were in that cry. I believed that it must wake him one more time, that his eyes would rest on me one more time before he closed them forever.

And he did look up. But these were no longer the eyes of my beloved husband. Vague, without light, his glance was strange, as though it came from far away. Perhaps from that place from which no one returns.

For the next few hours I was unconscious. Then, what an awakening! Emptiness opened before me. All the words of comfort and love from the children and friends and family who surrounded me roused no echo in my heart. Empty, empty, aimlessly empty, before me lay the rest of my life, which in that hour I would so happily have abandoned to follow the other path with my precious beloved. In that hour I understood so well the Indian custom of burning the widow with the dead.

Two old Jews and a *minyan* of *batlonim* (quorum of unemployed men) said prayers three times a day with the dead, and my precious Volodya said *kaddish* (the mourner's prayer). The funeral took place on Monday at noon. A large crowd gathered around our house. Many young boys who had been sent by the various *shauls* sang Psalms. Wreaths of flowers were brought but, at my request, these were left behind in the house and not taken to the cemetery.

My children and I tore our clothing over our hearts. The bier was lifted and they carried outside—the man, the father, the master of this house. At the cemetery, everyone who surrounded the grave said prayers. From among the crowd of the foremost Jews and Christians

Chonon Afanasii Wengeroff, Pauline's husband.

of the town the *maggid*, the city preacher, stepped forward to deliver a eulogy, which he concluded with the words: "Although he neglected many a Jewish custom in the course of his life, at his grave we must confess aloud that he was an *ohev amo Yisrael*, that he loved his people Israel."

243

APPENDIX

Lithuanian Jew with his wife and daughter (1846).
Léon Hollaenderski, *Les Israélites de Pologne* (Paris: 1846).

How Jews Used to Dress

Wengeroff devoted much of her original memoir to detailed descriptions of material life in the nineteenth century. The following is a particularly interesting description of Jewish dress.

Fashion is a tyrant, changing rapidly and not always for aesthetic reasons. When the Jews were forced to relinquish their old style of clothing (above p. 94) of dressing they sacrificed both a hygienic and a pleasing way of dressing.

The men wore a white shirt with sleeves ending in white wrist bands. Great care was taken with the selection of these bands. A certain amount of luxury went into the choice of materials for the ribbons that were used as a kind of necktie. Even older gentlemen from distinguished homes permitted themselves a certain vanity in the way they tied these ties. Later, wide black scarves appeared. But in the families that cared for tradition, these scarves were not used and were called *goyish* (non-Jewish). Even small variations in costume were matters of considerable sensitivity.

Their trousers were knee-length and also fastened with ribbon at the bottom. The stockings were white and rather long. On their feet they wore low leather shoes without heels. In place of a jacket, they wore a *chalat* of costly wool at home. The poorer classes wore a kind of cotton on workdays, but on festival days their clothing was made of *rissel,* a stiff wool material.

In the summer the poor dressed in *nanking,* a cotton material with narrow dark blue stripes. In winter they wore a gray, thick material. This *chalat* was very long, almost down to the ground. But this costume would have been incomplete if there had not been a belt around the loins. Special care was paid to this belt, for it fulfilled a religious commandment. It was to separate the upper body from the less cleanly functions of the lower, especially on the Sabbath and on Holy Days. This belt was fashioned in very luxurious ways; even men of lower station used to wear a silk belt in honor of Festivals.

The head dress of the poor on weekdays was a cap, with earlaps on the sides, which were mostly turned up but could be pulled down over

247

the ears in the winter. Over the forehead as well as on the sides, these caps had pieces of fur. These were called *Lappenmütze*. I don't know where this name comes from, maybe from the earlaps, maybe from the similarity to what Laplanders wear. Under this cap, every Jew of whatever station or occupation wore a velvet cap that never disappeared from his head, for it was sinful to go about bareheaded. As a matter of course, this little cap was not removed when one was a guest in a neighbor's house.

Summer and winter the well-to-do wore a tall hat of sable and a *streimel* on Sabbath and festivals. The tall hat was pointed in shape and always trimmed with strips of precious fur, even if not always sable. Peering out from under the hats, one could see the *peyes,* wide strands of hair snaking down to almost below the chin. Curly *peyes* were considered especially beautiful; men were ambitious to have not only curly hair, but also these stiff, beautifully curled *peyes. Peyes* were a prerequisite of a thinking man. Men could not have a serious discussion without curling their *peyes* about their fingers. And especially when they were learning Talmud, this play with their *peyes* was almost automatic. So often it has struck me that the study of Talmud has lost some of its intensity, and its logic and sharpness, because the *peyes* are no longer to hand for the scholar. Some men were pleased to grow their *peyes* very long, down to their shoulders.

The long jacket of silk, the belt, the fur cap and the famous *peyes* now had to be removed. The men found their fate very hard. Perhaps it would have been easier for them if at least they had been permitted to retain their side curls. They made a Jew, as it was thought in those days, resemble God. Now this *tselem elohim* was taken away from them, to be replaced by modern dress. The men had to wear a black coat that could not reach below the knee. Instead of their short knee pants, they wore long trousers down over their boots. In the summer they had to wear a hat, in the winter a cap of black cloth with a visor in the front. These were called *kartus.*

Jewish women of Lithuania and Russia had up until that time dressed in a somewhat Oriental fashion. Clothes were colorful and, among the rich, very costly. Large sums were spent on precious materials and on artistic jewelry. There was a very long shirt with a high collar made of finest linen. Even the women of the most aristocratic families knew nothing of petticoats or underpants. The long stockings of today were not customary then. The custom was knee socks, always white and, for the ladies of the richer families, in a lacy weave. There were no rubber bands at that time. The stockings were held up with wide satin sashes called *prinel,* often embroidered with cross-stitch embroidery. Also, knitted and crocheted bands were fastened with such sashes. The notions industry of the time did not provide the ladies of that day with any fasteners of tin or any other metal.

Their shoes were very similar to sandals, very low, without heels. They were held on the foot with narrow black bands, criss-crossing often up to calf height. These shoes were made of black wool or Morocco leather and were worn at all seasons of the year. No one had any idea of tall boots or galoshes at that time. Of course, even though shoes were very different then, female vanity still had its role. The sandals sported gold decorations, and were worn very small and very tight, so that many women walked with a sort of tripping gait.

Over the shirt women wore a silk corselet, pink and red being especially favored here. It was fastened in front with a wide silk ribbon, run through silver loops and ending in long silver points, sometimes as much as ten centimeters long.

The overshirt was very short and had three stuffed cotton rolls at the bottom, over which the skirt rested. But "rested" is the wrong expression; it was of a stubborn restlessness and had a natural tendency to slip off these rolls. And so just as the women wearing modern fashion today are forced to pull and tug at their blouses, so the Jewesses of that day were always trying to pull their skirts back onto these rolls. And it was not unusual to see these sufferers rub their fingers raw with the adjustments and readjustments of their skirts.

The sleeves were very tight and so long that they sometimes reached all the way down to the fingers. The entire upper garment was trimmed in fur, naturally as costly as possible. Rich women always chose sable. The throat was always closed with a standing collar, even in summer. This upper garment was approximately the shape of a modern bolero jacket. It was open in front, so that the corselet was visible unless it was covered with a scarf, and made of *karpo-volusk*, (that is—"fish scales"), a very apt name. They were little scales of gilt silver, so close together that one could hardly see the wool beneath. Nowadays you only see material like that in a fancy dress costume.

Special attention was paid to the scarf. Usually material embroidered in silver and gold was chosen, with a truly Oriental character. The favorite design was the half-moon. The upper part was covered in white lace from France, usually made of floss silk or cordoned silk, woven in extraordinarily artistic designs. The skirt was of a special cut, extremely tight, hardly the width of a step, and of course always ending above the feet. Satin was the favored material for this skirt, and spaced about two fingers apart there were ribbons down its whole length made of the finest materials worked with gold thread. I remember my mother's dress exactly. There were overlapping ellipses surrounding a tiny leaf on the borders. Only the front of the skirt, where it would be covered with the apron, lacked this gold border.

The apron was an absolute prerequisite for a complete costume. It was worn everywhere, in the street, and at all festive occasions. It was long, down to the hem of the skirt. Wealthy women wore aprons of colorful silk, or costly white cambric embroidered with velvet flowers and artistic patterns in gold thread. Poorer women made do with wool or cotton materials. The material of the skirt, with its alternating rows of dull and satin, was usually called *guldengestick*.

Over all of this there was a kind of coat, the *katinka*. The sleeves of this garment had a wide bell shape, bulky on top and narrow on the bottom. This *katinka* was very long and had a quite smooth, wide shape in front. The back was form-fitting. Usually satin was used for this, and since the *katinka* was usually a garment for the colder time of the year, it was stuffed and lined with wool stuffing and quilting. The richer ladies had them lined in satin.

I still remember that my mother, who laid great store by careful dress, wore a *katinka* lined in blue satin. But this coat was seldom worn as an outer garment, probably because it would hide the costly clothes underneath. So it was customary to toss the coat over your shoulders with the sleeves hanging down your back. Many women, especially the *gabetes,* the helpers of the poor, wore only one sleeve and let the other fall over their shoulders. Nowadays we would consider this *legère* careless and unworthy of a lady, but at that time it was acceptable. Times change and tastes change.

The greatest attention was paid by the rich to the headdress. In fact, among rich people the headdress was one of the most valuable possessions. There was a black velvet scarf very similar to the *kokoshnik* that Russian women wore. The edge of this was cut out into grotesque shapes and set with valuable pearls and diamonds. This headdress was worn above the forehead. The back of the head was covered with a smoothly fitting cap, called a *kopke.* In the middle of this *kopke* was a ribbon fastened with netting and flowers, and over the back of the neck, from one ear to the other, was a lace ruff. Near the eyes, on the temples, were little diamond "earrings." Of course, there were actual earrings also, and aristocratic ladies wore quite large diamonds in their ears. Pretty women looked especially nice with this adornment, but we must confess that those who were less beautiful also looked quite smart in these headdresses. This costly head scarf was the main article of clothing of a woman, and she was never seen without it.

About her neck she would wear long strings of pearls, sometimes with a beautiful silver-gray sheen. And of course after all this, it goes without saying that her fingers were adorned with diamond rings. Yes, it can be said that sometimes there was almost too much of these good and beautiful things. Sometimes the fingers disappeared beneath all this beautiful, artfully worked jewelry. Men did not wear even wedding rings; it would have been in very bad taste.

One might wonder at this ostentation of gems and pearls and precious metal, and think the Jewish women of that time vulgar and unendurably vain. Of course, they knew how to dress and how to adorn themselves. But partly this was for business reasons. The precariousness of the times, the nagging feeling of uncertainty, the laws that made it almost impossible to own real estate, meant that most of one's capital was invested in easily transported valuables. Also, the credit and the financial situation of the husband were gauged by his wife's jewelry. On festive occasions—the High Holidays and at weddings—this entire stock of valuables was exhibited.

The headdress of young women—the "veil"— was much more modest, but very colorful and almost adventurous: A yellow, green or red cap of wool or cotton with a net or muslin veil that was tied in the back of the neck into a bow, the ends of the bow, called *foches,* hanging down the back. Many old women wore big red woollen cloths wound around their heads like a turban, and this kind of turban cloth was called *knup.* There was always an ear ruffle on the "veil" of the young women. Right in the middle, over the forehead, there was a little silken ribbon attached with pins to lace in the shape of a little basket. This was called *koishel.* And even the poor had a ribbon of the color of hair above the forehead, and rings attached on each side of their eyes.

The head covering of girls was not very different from that of the women, except that the girls were still graced by their own hair. They wore a kind of narrow red wool ribbon, called *tezub,* with a bow of the same material. The cut of their dresses and aprons was like that of the women. They also wore the low sandals, but not the chest and throat lace, the *kreindel.* Rich girls also had a headband of black silk toile into which beautiful buds were embroidered with red, blue or pink silk. The shape of these headbands was the same for rich and poor. The simple ones were called *greishel* and the silk ones were called *vilnaer knipel.*

AFTERWORD
A LIFE UNRESOLVED

Pauline Wengeroff's daughter, Faina Vengerova.
(1877)

A Life Unresolved

PAULINE WENGEROFF AND HER MEMOIR

Pauline Wengeroff remains frustratingly difficult to know. At the end of her lengthy and detailed life story, we still sense lacunae—important events undescribed, powerful emotions unexplored. Was this Wengeroff's intention? Did she purposefully cover her tale of cultural crisis and personal loss with the affectionate, nostalgic tones of what she called in German a "Grandmother's Memoir"—(*Memoiren einer Grossmutter*)? Or is our frustration more the product of our own expectations, our own (mis-)perceptions of how a nineteenth-century East European Jewish woman should have told her own story? There is always that temptation to look between the lines of an old woman's memoir, to claim to have discovered those things that Wengeroff left unspoken, to historicize or feminize or psychologize her tale in our own terms. But there is also the dignity we owe any author, our obligation to try to understand the tale as it was presented. Wengeroff's memoir provides a marvelous entryway into a world whose complexities and subtleties historians are only beginning to appreciate. But as we follow the transformation of the schoolgirl Pessele Epstein into the banker's wife, Pauline Wengeroff, we will have to pick our way most cautiously if we want to imagine *her* world rather than a pale reflection of our own.

The interpretive challenge is presented to us immediately: the book's German title makes it clear that this "Memoir of a Grandmother" was also intended as a set of "Pictures from the Cultural History of Nineteenth-Century Russian Jews." In writing her memoir Pauline Wengeroff made her own life into a chronological framework on which to hang a larger ethnological tale. And this was not unintentional. Especially in the original one-volume German text (pages 1–104 of the current edition) Pauline carefully pasted the gently hued wallpaper of her childhood reminiscences onto an underlying solid architecture of ethnography and cultural pedagogy.

Of course, every memoir is the product of artifice and craft. As Frank Kermode noted about his own autobiography: "Absolute fidelity to historical fact is inaccessible; the minute you begin to write it you try to write it well, and writing well is an activity that has no simple relation to truth."[1] Memoirists recount the events of the past while keeping one eye on the present. They know, before we do, how the story will come out, who will win and who lose, what will succeed and what will fail. Inevitably, therefore, they "cheat" as they tell their tale, privileging those memories that lead to the inevitable result, and downplaying or ignoring those that do not. They have no choice but to select from among myriad details in order to shape a purposeful and directed story.

But Pauline's memoirs are doubly crafted, for she writes to shape not only herself, but also the world from which she came. Hers is a pioneering effort to create a "usable Jewish past" for women and men like herself who felt uprooted by modernity. This book is at least as much a public as a private memoir, and Wengeroff's public purpose allowed her—indeed, it demanded of her—to skip over the personal and familial details that we might have expected to hear.

I. Nostalgia for a Complex Jewish Past

Like many East European Jews over the last century, Wengeroff wrote her memoir out of a sense of profound cultural crisis and religious loss. The crisis could be explained differently by various authors. Yehezkel Kotik, who was born a few years after her and a few miles from her home in Brest-Litovsk, blamed immigration to America as well as the harsh conditions and anti-Semitism in Russia for the decline of the *shtetl*.[2] Writing in the midst of World War I, A. S. Sachs—also a *Litvak* (Lithuanian Jew)—blamed the dislocations and horrors of the war for a loss from which he felt the Jewish people would never recover.[3] For Wengeroff, the main causal factor had been modernization itself: the Haskalah or Jewish Enlightenment and the assimilatory pressures from the outside society. But however they explained it, all of these writers shared an awareness that the world in which they had grown up had irrevocably disappeared. It was the self-imposed task of these aging eyewitnesses to recall the lost world, to evoke it on the written page, and thus to preserve at least a taste of it for generations to come.[4]

Each memoirist had to decide for himself which particular aspects of the lost Jewish world were worthy of remembrance. For Pauline Wengeroff the decision was easy: that world had been shaped by a set of religious norms and practices, and it was these that had to be recalled. She therefore devoted the bulk of her original one-volume book to a highly idealized representation of "a year in my parents' home" built around the annual cycle of Jewish holidays as seen through the eyes of a seven-year-old girl.[5] Her focus was on the warm spirituality of the Jewish holidays and, in particular, on their domestic context. Her child's-eye Jewishness was full of bright candles and good tastes and the wonderful odors of constant cooking and baking. The stringencies of Judaism were softened by wealth and luxury. The rigid repetitiveness of halakhic ritual was transmuted for her into structure, stability, and security.

But make no mistake. There is a careful pedagogical purpose behind the ostensible naiveté. Even the briefest comparison of her memoir to others of this genre makes clear how carefully Wengeroff inserted a wealth of halakhic and ritual detail into her narrative. Thus, A. S. Sachs also built much of his 1917 memoir around the holy days of his *shtetl* youth, and Bella Chagall anchored her 1935 account of Vitebsk in holiday tales as told by a child. But Sachs' accounts emphasized the interesting characters and quaint situations of small-town Jewish life rather than the minutiae of observance, and he felt free to mock a "barbarous, disgusting" custom like *kapporos shlogen* (swinging a tied chicken over the head before Yom Kippur) or to replace a religious with a national explanation for a holiday like Passover. In Chagall's stories there is almost no halakhic detail at all. For her the holidays have become times for family gathering, occasions for the rough and tumble of siblings, and stimuli to the curiosity of a child slowly emerging into self-consciousness.[6]

Wengeroff, on the other hand, put all of her effort into recording the religious rituals of her youth and imbuing them with emotional and spiritual significance. She was a religiously sophisticated Jew with a strong sense of the individual meaning and importance of each ritual, and she recorded them with sometimes astonishing detail and accuracy. Thus she carefully notes down the different ways that "challeh" (the portion of bread dough that was symbolically broken off and burned) was taken from the Sabbath bread and from the Passover *matzehs*.[7] For each holiday meal she gives us the lighting, the menu, the bread shape ... *and* the halakhic requirements: the second *seder* could not begin until three stars had appeared in the sky but had to be completed before midnight; the *seder* meal could include fowl but not meat[8]; the third Sabbath meal had to include both fish and meat; and so on.[9]

Pauline's ritual knowledge was not limited to the kitchen and the serving of food. She knew that her father took care to recite the afternoon prayers early (*mincheh gedoleh*) rather than following the more common practice of saying them close to nightfall and combining them with *maariv*. His *kiddush* goblet, she tells us, had to be a certain size; it was held specifically in the right hand; her father and the others drank more than half the goblet's contents at once (Hebrew: *rov kos*). She knew that the *shehecheyanu* blessing recited on the second day of *Rosh Hashonoh* had to be recited over a new fruit, that there was a special name (*in gotts nomen*) for morning prayers on the day after *Yom Kippur*[10] and a special way to take leave of the *sukkeh* on the last day of *Sukkos*.[11] Pauline delights in citing folk explanations for practices—explanations drawn from the broad arsenal of kabbalistic, magical, and superstitious beliefs that underlay East European Jewish culture—but she knows the difference between popular custom and halakhic principle: her mother and the children cast away bread crumbs (symbolically, their sins) on *Rosh Hashonoh* but her father dismissed this ceremony (*tashlikh*). She similarly recalls her father's (futile) objection to their noisemaking at Haman's name during the Purim *megillah* reading.[12]

There is no way to know how much of her halakhic knowledge came to little Pessele through formal instruction and how much was so deeply embedded in the day-to-day of her home life that she absorbed it unconsciously. We know she went to a girl's *cheder* but she does not tell us for how long she went nor, for that matter, exactly what she studied there. But the depth of Wengeroff's ritual knowl-

edge is quite extraordinary; almost every one of the customary practices and halakhic rulings she mentions, even if they are no longer well
known today, can be tracked down in anthologies specifically devoted
to *minhag*. It was very important to her to pass on this knowledge to
her readers: hence her great stress on even the smallest details, and her
great pains in the second edition to correct a few terminological and
technical errors even where these would hardly have been noticed by
her likely audience.[13] We must remember the high level of Wengeroff's ritual knowledge if we want to appreciate her intense sense of
personal loss and shame at the end of her life.

The Jewish values and practices that Pauline learned as a child were
those of the powerful *misnagdic* (anti-Chasidic) stream of nineteenth-century Lithuanian Judaism. Pauline's father proudly linked
himself with that constellation of values associated with the Gaon of
Vilna (Elijah ben Solomon, d. 1797), and R. Hayim Volozhiner
(1749–1821): punctilious observance of the commandments; a rigorous intellectualist approach to their significance; and primary religious emphasis placed on systematic Torah study (for men).[14] Sometimes we catch a glimpse of just how *misnagdic* halakhic rhetoric may
have penetrated into the young girl's consciousness. The Gaon, for
example, placed great emphasis on the requirement to sleep and to
eat all meals in the *sukkeh* on *Shmini Atzeres,* a practice that was not
then followed by most Jews. So insistent was he on this point that the
Gaon ordered people to dress warmly and sleep in the *sukkeh* on
Shmini Atzeres even when it fell on a day cold enough to exempt people from that obligation during the main part of the holiday. He
argued that this extra stringency "would underscore the halakha for
the students." No wonder then that Pauline stressed that her family
ate all of its meals in an often uncomfortably cold *sukkeh* on this day
and that she associated their practice with the strict discipline of her
parents' household (p. 61).[15]

But the Judaism presented in this book is not merely an account-
ing of Pauline's youthful observations. She was familiar with other
important strains within nineteenth-century traditional Judaism, and

in the second volume of her memoirs she devoted several pages to the Chasidic world (which she had encountered in her father-in-law's home) and another few pages to the "musar" or ethicist movement, a pietistic offshoot of Volozhin talmudism associated primarily with Rabbi Israel Lipkin Salanter (1810–83). Admittedly, her treatment of these movements does not indicate any intense personal contact. She relies primarily on well-known hagiographic anecdotes and much of what she wrote may have come from books rather than her own experience. (This is why we have omitted some of this material from the present edition.) Still, Pauline was clearly not unsophisticated in her understanding of traditional Judaism. She pointed out important religious concepts behind each school and emphasized the differences between them. She did this as part of a sustained effort to introduce and defend traditional Jewish practice to her modern readers.

Wengeroff has a good eye for the quaint and curious, but on the whole her portrayal of Judaism focuses on mainstream practice and she tries to present the customs and usages in a fashion that will make them intelligible and even soul-stirring to her readers. She never indulges in the kind of social criticism, historicizing relativism, or appeals for religious reform that were then the stock-in-trade of so many maskilic writers and memoirists. This child of a *misnagdic* household even muted her criticism of Chasidism.

By the time she wrote her book, Wengeroff's religious life had undergone a significant change of locale—it was now a religion she (and many other more "modern" Jews) practiced especially in the synagogue. As a child, on the other hand, she seems to have experienced Judaism in an almost exclusively domestic context. Synagogue was a male activity, certainly not intended for a seven-year-old girl. Pessele was left behind even on the High Holy Days when, she remembers, her busy mother did attend services.[16] As a result, Wengeroff was probably not very familiar with the details of everyday synagogue ritual, and she made several errors about it as, for example, when she tried to describe the timing of the *sliches* (penitential) prayers before *Rosh Hashonoh*.[17]

But Wengeroff, as any writer, shaped her picture of the past to fit with her adult experiences and values. She therefore included translations of a number of moving passages from the High Holy Day liturgy, probably taken from the translation in the prayer books she used as an adult. (We have omitted them from this edition.) Here, as in other places in the text, we are reminded that these lonely memoirs of an elderly woman are more than nostalgia. Wengeroff was trying to articulate a synthesis of what she now believed to be the essence of Judaism. As much as it was a fond reminiscence of a world gone by, her book was also an attempt to make Judaism available and meaningful to the new generation. If this book is not a halakhic manual, it is a very early example of the "Introduction to Judaism and Jewish Practice" that remains a popular genre of Jewish writing to this day.[18]

II. A FAMILY IN FLUX

Like any family, the Epsteins of Brest-Litovsk must have had their own dynamic, their points of conflict and congruence, their areas of balance and dysfunction. But it is not easy for the reader to discover any of this behind the warmth and stability of Pauline's nostalgia, especially in her original first volume, which focused on the years of her childhood and adolescence. The Jewish literary conventions she inherited, the strict rules of propriety under which she lived, and the idealized image of the past that she was trying to create all dictated that she speak of her family in pious stereotype, downplaying friction and change and painting a picture of faith and harmony under the direction of stern patriarchal wisdom and godly maternal guidance.[19] But there are hints of deeper currents, of underlying tensions that may help to explain the disaffection and rebellions of later years. If we read carefully, noting especially those details that Wengeroff omitted or glossed over, we may be able to nuance our understanding of the family that shaped her world.

The dominant figure in the Epstein family during Pessele's years at home was undoubtedly her paternal grandfather, Ziml Shimon. This was not the kindly old *zeydeh* (grampa) of Yiddish folk memory; even Pauline's nostalgia could not make Ziml Epstein into that. In his two brief appearances in the memoir, Ziml leaves us with a powerful impression of enormous personal wealth, an austere aristocratic bearing, and an insistence on formal respect as his due.

Born into a distinguished rabbinic family, Ziml Epstein early turned his attention away from his studies towards the world of business. He made his initial fortune in Bobruisk, where construction of a major Russian fortress and the supply of its garrison had become important sources of Jewish income.[20] In those days Bobruisk Jews were so prosperous that people joked they would soon have to import some Jewish paupers lest the biblical prophecy "For the poor shall never cease out of the land" (Deut. 15:11) be proven false.[21] The gradual Russian acquisition of large parts of what had once been Poland-Lithuania provided enormous opportunities for Jewish entrepreneurs who knew how to seize them. Ziml was soon assuming government contracts all over White Russia and Poland, specializing in the building of fortifications as well as in laying out the new macadamized (gravel) roads that linked the towns of Poland and Lithuania with the Russian interior. In 1832, after the failure of the Polish Revolution and the imposition of more direct Russian control on Warsaw, Ziml joined the stream of Jewish entrepreneurs who moved to that city and who quickly came to dominate its economy in sectors ranging from construction and government supply to finance, manufacturing, and commerce.[22] Ziml's links to the Russian authorities no doubt help to explain why he, by then the first "Litvak" on the Warsaw community's Council of Wardens, was seen to be on the side of "enlightened" proposals and refused to oppose the government decree that required western dress.

For much of his life, Yehuda Epstein, or Yudl as he was usually called even in his books, remained in the financial and personal shadow of his authoritarian father. There can be little doubt that the brickyard in Brest and the contract to supply bricks for the fortification there were Ziml's doing. When that endeavor failed, Yudl did not undertake some new business venture. Rather, he fell back on his father's generosity (which, judging from Pauline's accounts of their reduced living conditions, was not unlimited) and remained studying

Torah in Brest. There are hints that Yudl suffered psychologically from his reversal of fortune: Pauline mentions his personal loss of resiliency, and the fact that he began attending a *chevreh tehillim,* a "working man's synagogue," suggests that he may have felt excluded or uncomfortable in wealthier circles.[23] His once controlling presence in the family eroded in these years: the older children no longer lived under his roof; Ephraim left for America; the children's more modern ways of dressing and behaving took over; and the practical details of Pauline's marriage were now taken over by a "family council" (pp. 124ff.). By fifty, Yudl was an old man.

His father's death in 1854 brought Yudl a considerable inheritance (although he complained that it was "not what it should have been"). That sum, combined with the more than 80,000 rubles he received in settlement of his law suit with the government, allowed him to live once again in luxury, devoting himself to study and welcoming guests into his house as he had when Pauline was a child. But good fortune was not to be his for long. The Polish Revolution of 1863 caused him considerable financial losses, his first wife died soon after, and, he tells us, he lost his entire remaining capital to "men as cruel as panthers" with whom he had invested. It seems that only then did he settle in Warsaw, dependent on family charity from his children and sisters, and spending the rest of his life trying to publish his scholarly book. The consistency with which Yudl failed in business suggests, at least, that the fiasco in Brest may have been as much the result of his own incompetence as the fault of an apostate lawyer.[24]

There is a fascinating family story that may reveal something more about Yudl's relation to his father and how the old man felt about his scholarly son. Writing during World War I, Pauline's distant cousin Barukh Epstein reports that Ziml and his partner had occasion to appear before Rabbi Moses Ze'ev Margolin, then rabbi of Bialystock, for adjudication of a disagreement. Ziml was overwhelmed by the integrity and saintliness of the rabbi and left with the sensation that not only was money the root of all evil but also that, compared to Torah study, money-making was a trivial pursuit, little more than a child's game. Ziml's response was characteristic.

That very day he announced his decision

> ...to dedicate one of my sons completely to the Torah. I will not bring him into my business, and I will not familiarize him with my situation or any of my affairs. He will be a nazirite, totally separated for the Torah and the religious message [cf. Isaiah 8:20].... I have chosen my son Yudl to dedicate to this holy purpose. His abilities, his qualities and his temperament make him appropriate to be sanctified to heaven. Moreover, he is already clearly devoted to Torah study, and I can see that his soul is rooted in the Torah. He also likes to attend the Sages and study their ways.

Ziml immediately directed his nephew to find an appropriate tutor-companion for his son.[25]

Of course, we should not take this account too literally. By the time Barukh Epstein recorded the events, almost a century had passed, some of the details may have been mis-remembered, and the tale, raised to the level of family mythology, had been adorned with motifs drawn from the biblical story of the prophet Samuel.[26] Still, the tone of the story rings true: the sense of new wealth and opportunity competing with old values of Torah study and piety fits well with Ziml's times and personal history, and with the career of his son. Yudl of course did eventually go into the family business and then failed miserably. Ziml may have well regretted not following his earlier intuition about his son's qualifications.

What also rings true in the story is the capsule portrait of Ziml as an authoritarian *pater familias* who could so freely decide the fate of his children. Yudl laid claim to the same authority, and one of the dominant themes of the memoir is Pauline's lament that patriarchal control had passed, that in the modern world parents were now forced to follow the wishes of their children. But obviously, not all of the young people in this society appreciated the heavy hand of their fathers, and Ziml's rulings could lead to personal tragedy, as we shall see.

What can we say of Yudl Epstein's talmudic scholarship? By his own account as well as in the memory of his children, Yudl was happiest when he could devote all his waking hours to the text of the Talmud.[27] What does not come out clearly, however, is that on many levels Pessele's father was a transitional figure in the intellectual history of traditional Russian Jewry, and his style of talmudic scholarship had been passed over in favor of new approaches and methods.

Yudl Epstein was enormously proud of his rabbinical forebears and took great pains to publish (and then correct and re-publish) a list of them in his books.[28] But times had changed, and in the early nineteenth century the new type of "straight study" (*limud yashar*) advocated by R. Hayim Volozhin had come to dominate Lithuanian talmudism. Yudl himself was not trained in this approach. Rather than attend the new yeshiva at Volozhin, he had studied with private tutors at home in the small town of Glusk near Bobruisk, where his grandfather David had been the rabbi for some twenty-five years. The tutor whom Ziml hired for him was trained in the new approach, but stayed only long enough to leave Yudl with a strong sense of his own inadequacy. "I know," Yudl wrote, "the limits of my intelligence, the meagerness of my learning, and more important, the perverted educational system that was customary when I was a youth. Students wasted their days and years in twisted *pilpul* and did not study in the logical order."[29]

Even a brief glance at his two publications tells us much about Yudl Epstein's scholarship. The *Kinmon Besem* is actually no more than a pamphlet-sized appendix to a much larger work on talmudic *aggadah* by Abraham Schick. The pamphlet is something of an oddity in that it is clearly an unfinished work—no more than a selection of those of Epstein's study notes on the Babylonian Talmud that dealt with aggadic (non-legal) passages and thus could logically be included in Schick's work. Epstein claimed that he submitted his materials at Schick's request, but Schick seems less than enthusiastic about the inclusion: there is no reference to the *Kinmon Besem* on the title page of any of the four volumes, and in his brief introductory letter Schick seems not overly familiar with Epstein's background since he errs in describing the other man's education. In light of what we shall see below concerning the publication of Epstein's second, larger work, we cannot help wondering if the *Kinmon Besem* was published only because Yudl Epstein made a generous contribution to the printing costs of the larger work.[30]

The publication history of the *Minchas Yehuda* tells the story even more clearly. Pauline was wrong when she stated that the book was written in the 1840s (p. 3). In fact it was not until many years later, when he was already in his seventies, living in Warsaw, impoverished and dependent on his children and sisters for financial support, that Yudl Epstein dreamed of publishing the notes he had made over a lifetime. "For what am I, and what has my life been? ... Who will remember me in the tents of Torah, where every man who loves God and His Torah prays to dwell forever?" And so Yudl hired an editor and, after fifteen months of work and at a cost of over one thousand rubles, he finally had his book printed in two hundred fifty copies.

He put a brave front on this collection of study notes. It seems he could not obtain the standardized letters of rabbinic approval, which were regularly printed at the head of such religious works, and so instead he republished those that had prefaced his earlier pamphlet, *Kinmon Besem*. The limited size of the print run was, he claimed, "because I am not interested in a business venture. I won't sell even one. Rather I shall donate them to Houses of Study and schools." This, of course, is the same generous rhetoric we heard from Pauline, but it does little to hide the fact that no commercial distributor would invest in the book. In desperation, the old man demanded that the copies of his book be kept permanently available in the *batei midrash* to which he had sent them; they should not be lent out under any circumstances. By the end he was almost pleading for the memorial he sought: "I have my reasons...." Yudl died 20 Tishri, 5640 (1879).[31]

What of the younger generation, the teenage boys and girls already married with their own children, who lived and grew into adulthood together in the extended Epstein household?[32] Jewish autobiographical and fictional literature of the nineteenth century is replete with tragic stories of too-early marriages that failed, sometimes on their own and quite often because of a sudden decline in the fortunes of the parents, who were supporting the young couple. Among the

Epsteins we know of only one failed marriage, that of Pauline's brother Ephraim, who abandoned his wife and son, traveled to America, and eventually converted to Christianity. But we still wonder about the impact of the arranged marriages and about the pressures each young couple faced when suddenly forced to set up its own home in the "new city" of Brest. How did the young people cope with all this under the family's far less positive financial circumstances in the 1840s and early 1850s, and what did it do to the relations between the generations?

Almost at the end of Wengeroff's original one-volume book she tells us the story of her sister Chaveh's marriage in 1848. She presents this marriage as the last in the family that followed the "old ways." Her own just two years later, she assures her readers, was already quite different: more romantic, and with far greater attention to the rights and feelings of the young couple. Something she doesn't stress at all is the fact that marriage had a radically different impact on her day-to-day life than it had had for any of her older siblings. Each of the earlier marriages—her sisters' and her brother's—resulted in the new couple being added to the Epstein household. Even though the family was already in reduced circumstance and had to accept a divorcé as Chaveh's *beshert* (intended one), the girl was still able to live within the Brest circle with her new husband. Two years later in 1849 seventeen-year-old Pauline would be shipped off to live in a distant Ukrainian village with her husband's family (and a Chasidic family at that).

The close tie between marriage and finances in this society is made even clearer when we realize that at least two of the Epstein children married first cousins: her sister Kathy (who married Abraham Sack; above p. 109) and her brother Ephraim Menachem. Ephraim's laconic comment reinforces what Pauline has already told us of the alliance (above, p. 114.):

> At my seventeenth year of age [1845–46] I married my first cousin, this being at the behest of my paternal grandfather, who bestowed the dowries on all his grandchildren and did not want to have this wealth to leave their circle. I will say that this kind of benevolent tyranny works neither health of body nor of mind.[33]

*Pauline Wengeroff's brother, Ephraim Epstein,
as an adult in America.*

We do not know how much the dowry was, but it was not enough to keep the young man in Brest-Litovsk. When an uncle decided to move to America in 1849, Ephraim seized the opportunity to leave with him, effectively abandoning his wife and infant son.

The issue was not merely money, of course. Pauline tells the stories of her brothers-in-law experimenting with modern literature and science in a largely humorous vein, but she also acknowledges that families—including her own—were torn apart by the new ideas. As a child, her brother Ephraim had been a brilliant product of the traditional Jewish educational system. Taught his Hebrew letters and prayers from the age of four in a *cheder,* able to sing the synagogue readings from the Prophets and Five Scrolls from the age of eight, he had presented a Hebrew ode on the marriage of Crown Prince Alexander in "the grand and ancient synagogue of Brest ... in the presence of a great audience and the Christian municipal authorities." But while still a youth, he reports, his "mind became liberated from the trammels of talmudic haughtiness that makes its devotee presume himself to be superior to the common laborer." He studied Russian and German "by stealth," and, he hints, his relation with his father became less than warm: "There was little sympathy and affection between us."[34]

Like his sister, Ephraim chooses to downplay any familial conflict in his narrative. In his memoir, therefore, he writes of "an inextinguishable affection" between him and his mother. He assures his reader that "there is nothing in life I would not and did not give up for her," presumably a reference to his return to a Jewish way of life while she remained alive. (He adds that he would have done the same for his father, though out of a sense of "duty" rather than love.) Writing for an audience of American (mostly Christian) physicians Ephraim could conveniently ignore the obvious fact that his conversion to Christianity must have been seen by his parents as the most strident form of rejection and a cruel expression of overt hostility. It is also significant that, at least in Pauline's account, he granted his wife a formal divorce only because of pressure from his parents. He must have known that without an official Jewish bill of divorce from him, his wife could never remarry and was unable to have a life of her own. His harsh treatment of his wife (and child) underscores the tremendous anger he bore towards his entire Jewish family and the strictures they had imposed upon him. But though he changed his religion in America, Ephraim retained one lesson that his Jewish upbringing had taught him well: rage was not an emotion to be easily revealed.

III. Ambivalent Modernization

Like so many other Jewish memoirists of the twentieth century (and their readers), Pauline lived a life fundamentally different from the one she so deeply missed. She could feel guilt over her life's dissonance, but she could not resolve it. She was, after all, a product of the very modernization process she decried.

It is important to remember that Pauline was born into a Jewish family not yet polarized by the ideologies of Jewish modernity—or at least into one that did not perceive all calls for change as automatically illegitimate. These were the years of what has been called the "conservative" haskalah in Russia, when calls to educational reform like Isaac Baer Levinsohn's *Teuda be-Yisrael* (1828) could still be published with the public approval of Vilna's rabbi, Abraham Abele. Among the Lithuanian *misnagdim* in particular, the conservative haskalah was understood as complementing, rather than undermining, traditional Judaism. As Pauline tells us, her own father took his son and sons-in-law to meet the reformer Max Lilienthal when the latter visited Brest-Litovsk in 1842. This helps to explain why Yudl was willing to publish the *Kinmon Besem* as an appendix to the work of a conservative *maskil* like Abraham Schick of Slonim.[35] Epstein's magnum opus, his *Minchas Yehuda*, is certainly not a breakthrough in form or content, but it does, working from within the tradition, ask what must have seemed bold questions about the historical accuracy of the talmudic accounts.

When, many years later, she wrote her memoir, Pauline Wengeroff was still trying to evoke the early haskalah's naive dream of religious continuity combined with cultural evolution that had shaped the Jewish environment of her youth. That is why her account, for all its emphasis on religious observance, also presents the haskalah in positive terms, why she emphasizes the benefits Jews had derived from modernization, and why, instead of demonizing modernity, she tends to blame cultural breakdown on the excesses of inexperienced youths. It is also why Pauline clings to the image of Czar Nicholas I as an "enlightened monarch" who wished only to help and improve his Jewish subjects. The Nicholas who lived in her memory was the glo-

rious monarch, chest covered with medals, who planned the fortifications at Brest-Litovsk, not the despot who imposed a brutal con-
scription policy on thousands of young Jews. In this Pauline was simply echoing what one historian has called the "tragicomic" error of
the earlier *maskilim* who put their faith in the government's good will.
Of course, those earlier writers had had little choice but to look to the
government for support; it is somewhat surprising that Wengeroff, so
many decades later, continued to reiterate such long-rejected assumptions.[36]

One central question remains that Pauline does not readily
answer. Her account of cultural change always emphasizes the young
men—her brothers-in-law, her brother, and her husband—who were
too immature to "find the middle way" between tradition and modernity. But what of Pauline herself? Was she not also swept up in the
enthusiasm of her generation for German literature and western learning? As a teenager was she offended by the boys' stealing time from
their talmudic studies to read forbidden books, or did she join them
and other young people who met secretly in the fields outside of town
to read Schiller and share their hopes and dreams? She admits that as
an adolescent, she received private tutoring in both German and Russian and that she read and memorized German and Russian literature
with enthusiasm. Her mother had pored over the traditional Yiddish
ethical tracts, but Pauline mentions reading only the stirring and emotional literature of the German *Sturm und Drang* (Storm and Stress)
period—the stories, poems, and plays of Heinrich Zschokke and
Friedrich Schiller. At sixteen, as she prepared for her imminent marriage, she concentrated on her German and Russian studies so that she
could tutor her small-town husband in these skills so necessary for
financial success (and personal enlightenment). The success of her
studies is attested to by her memoirs, written in flowing German and
addressing knowledgeably so many themes of modern Jewish life.

Although Pauline presents herself as an unwilling victim of modernization, her rhetoric of disappointment does not completely hide
the fact that she, her husband, and her family successfully forged what
we recognize as a modern Jewish identity. Over a twenty-year period

271

and with the help of his powerful brother-in-law Abraham Sack, Chonon had transformed himself professionally from a Jewish concessionaire of the old school into Afanasii Wengeroff, the director of a major bank in Minsk.[37] He, like Sack, was part of a growing urban Jewish bourgeoisie in Russia. Though most of these men and women newly arrived from the *shtetl* abandoned traditionalist observance—indeed, an increasing number actually converted to Christianity—their Jewish ethnicity linked them into a network that served social, cultural, philanthropic, and professional needs simultaneously. They helped each other to find jobs, they raised money from each other to help less fortunate Jews, they joined together to sponsor promising Jewish artists, and most of all, they were each other's company and refuge in the intimidating excitement of modern Minsk and St. Petersburg. Pauline complains that there wasn't Jewish content at her dinner parties. She doesn't mention, because she took it for granted, that all the guests were Jewish and Jews continued to socialize largely with each other.

The old Jewish values did not disappear; rather they were adjusted and transformed so that powerful memories could be expressed in the new cultural context. Jewish holy days lost their halakhic impetus, but they became important opportunities for remembering and re-enacting the past through rituals of food and fellowship. Pauline is not speaking ironically when she says that "the mood of Sabbath filled our home" (p. 241) after a Jewish business acquaintance had come to enjoy *gefilte* fish and be entertained by her children playing piano and cello on Friday night. No doubt it was the hope of economic advancement that drove so many young Russian Jews to seek higher education, but the old maskilic idealization of western culture retained its power and attraction. We should not dismiss Pauline's lengthy encomia to successful Jewish musicians and artists as the prattlings of a "society lady."[38] She is proudly articulating her vision of a continued life of the Jewish spirit in the new, broader marketplace of ideas. Though she does not mention it, we are not surprised to learn that Pauline's children—that "third generation," which she berated for "fearing neither God nor the devil"—would almost all make their marks as distinguished literary critics and translators, political essayists and musicians.[39]

In St. Petersburg and Minsk as in London, Paris and New York, it was the practice of charity that provided the central arena for modernizing Jews to express and elaborate the old identities. Individual beneficence now became a commitment to mutual responsibility and collective progress. What Wengeroff remembered as the obligation of the housewife to hand out a few coins on *Rosh Chodesh* was now expanded into a new kind of "religious" duty. Pauline, her husband, and their friends stood up for the rights of Jews and involved themselves directly in establishing ambitious charitable institutions for the vocational training of the Jewish lower classes. Pauline internalized a new definition of "the deserving poor"—her arguments at the end of her book for the dignity of manual laborers (*bal maloches*) are taken from the powerful rhetoric of social reformers, socialists, and Zionists all over the Jewish world.[40]

Pauline and her husband were Jewishly well-educated and well-informed members of a generation engaged in making a new order out of the images and ideas they had inherited from their youth. Talmudism was now expressed in a broader cultural interest in Jewish history, philosophy, and literature. Chonon never completely lost his taste for the stimulating give-and-take of talmudic study, and he sought out opportunities to discuss Jewish themes and ideas, whether with a lonely talmudist in Helsingfors or with the Hebrew novelist, Abraham Mapu, in Minsk. Remarks scattered throughout the memoir indicate that Pauline too was sympathetic to this process of translating the past. She speaks favorably of a broad range of contemporary Jewish cultural endeavors: the Society for the Promotion of Enlightenment among the Jews of Russia, modern biblical and folkloristic scholarship,[41] Hebrew belles lettres and poetry, and the growing interest in a Jewish homeland.

Pauline Wengeroff was not a scholar. Though she read the German-Jewish press and Russian-language works on Jewish ethnography, there is no evidence that she could read Hebrew literature in the original.[42] She was strongly committed to modernizing values, but she lacked a consistent terminology, a set of ideological *topoi* with which to validate the new Jewish practices and values that made up her life. This is why, as we shall see, she framed her cultural history in terms of loss and failure rather than creation and accomplishment. But her very act of composing a memoir—the very first written by a Jewish woman from Eastern Europe—gives eloquent expression to the fact that her life was motivated and undergirded by new concerns and values.

IV. THE WRITER AS A WOMAN

One of the most striking features of this memoir is the consistency with which Pauline Wengeroff uses gendered terminologies to articulate both her past and her present.[43] At first this does not seem surprising. After all, traditional Judaism assigned very different religious roles to men and women, rigidly controlled contact between the sexes both in and out of marriage, and reserved the public sphere almost entirely to men. Pauline's gendered understanding of family structure and social change would therefore seem an accurate reflection of the realities around her.

But Pauline uses the categories of male and female not just descriptively but also polemically to make what can only be called a "political" statement. Over and over, she returns to one central argument: the spiritual impoverishment of Jewish life that accompanied modernization is completely the fault of men. Her mother objected when her father took his son and sons-in-law to meet the reformer Lilienthal, and correctly foretold the terrible results of the new studies. Pauline's first quarrel with her husband was over the latter's gradual abandonment of religious belief and practice (pp. 164ff.). Jewish women "were deeply imbued with religion and tradition in their innermost being," and the "insult to the old ways" was for them almost a physical insult. They desperately fought their husbands' tyrannical demands for change, and desperately tried to maintain tradition at least in their homes (pp. 187–88). In the end, however, the women lost the battle and had to watch every precious Jewish custom disappear from their lives. There are few passages in modern Jewish literature as moving as Pauline's despairing notes to herself when, in 1871, her husband required her to introduce non-kosher food into their home (pp. 210ff.).

In and of itself, this radically gendered understanding of Jewish modernization raises fascinating questions for the cultural historian. What factors allowed for the woman, formerly so excluded from the religious leadership of her community, to be seen now as the true guardian of tradition? Did women assume this role because they were less acculturated than men, or was their religious role itself an expression of the particular forms that modernization assumed for women? Was the home the last sacred haven for tradition, or had tradition lost its status by being relegated to the domestic sphere? How does Wengeroff's portrayal fit with the view of so many male reformers of the age who presented the woman as victims of tradition and the modernization of Jewish society as their only salvation? Indeed, was it always true, as Pauline suggests, that it was the man who sought to acculturate and the woman who sought to preserve the past? Were there not as many cases in which women rejected the gender roles and values of the past in favor of new definitions of success? All of these questions are germane to Pauline Wengeroff's book but unfortunately lie beyond the scope of the present Afterword.[44]

We must content ourselves with addressing a narrower, but still tantalizing question: how does Wengeroff's sense of her own gender role help her to explain the larger changes going on around her? To put the question in another way, why does gender appeal to her so strongly as an explanatory category? After all, she knew of other explanatory factors. At one point or another, she herself mentioned the difference that geography, class, and the rising virulence of anti-Semitism made to the nature of Jewish acculturation. And she is hardly what we today might call a feminist: the highest praise she can offer for the stable and pious world of her youth is to call it "patriarchal"—a term she uses consistently and with not the slightest hint of self-consciousness or irony. And why does she not see as causative her own love of German and Russian literature, her own role in teaching Chonon German, her own consistent support for maskilic and modernizing Jewish values? Why does she continually return to her central argument that immature and weak-willed men destroyed the world of Jewish tradition?

Her attitude can certainly not be attributed to a lack of strong female role models in Pauline Wengeroff's life. Undoubtedly the most powerfully drawn figure in the entire book is her grandmother-in-law, under whose influence the young girl lived during her first four years as a married woman. Pauline's unbounded respect for the old woman is clear. Bella Wengeroff had saved Pauline's infant daughter by an arcane medical procedure. Bella Wengeroff had made a lengthy and uncomfortable trip to help with the delivery of Pauline's sister's child. Bella Wengeroff was a tireless worker and an aggressive business-woman, a renowned cook and household manager, a repository of folk medicine and folk wisdom for the entire community. For Pauline, Bella Wengeroff was the archetype strong Jewish woman, easily on a par with the young women of the twentieth century who "crowded the university lecture halls and clinics, smoothing the way for the equality of women in society and in science" (p. 161).

Pauline's picture of her own mother is more complicated to assess.[45] We are given the overwhelming impression of a sedulous household manager and sternly religious woman who insisted on the strictest observance of every commandment and pious custom (*min-hag*). Pauline leavens her stories of her father's learning and piety with fond memories of his personal vitality, his fascinating stories, and his personal handsomeness. Her mother, on the other hand, is remem-bered for ensuring that cabbage was checked for worms and that fowl were checked for *chometz*, for mocking Pauline's sisters' attempts to be fashionable and for a stern lecture on the repentance required just before marriage. In retrospect Pauline admires her mother's fervent way of praying and her pure faith—but she never once mentions a maternal hug or kiss. Indeed, she never even tells us her mother's name! (It was Zelda, as we discover in a brief mention of her death in the introduction to Yehuda Epstein's *Minchas Yehudah*.)

There are interesting suggestions in the text that Zelda Epstein may actually have grown more deeply pious, more rigorous in her observances, as she grew older. In telling the story of her mother painting the wallpaper with black paint as a sign of mourning before *Tisho be-Av*, for example, Pauline seems to indicate that this was a new, unexpected practice in their household. During Pauline's teenage years, when the family lived under straitened circumstances, Zelda is portrayed as withdrawn into the sacred books and as attending the synagogue with her husband, while the details of household management now fell to Pessele. Is it possible that the teenager resented the obligation but was unwilling to express her feelings openly? However titillating, such questions must remain in the realm of speculation.

It has been suggested by more than one scholar that modernization was particularly difficult for East European Jewish women (and their daughters elsewhere) because it was accompanied by economic marginalization and a loss of real power within their families and their society. According to this theory, the Jewish woman, who had once played an active role in the family economy, was now, through the process of *embourgeoisement* and the internalization of non-Jewish family values, forced into the role of homemaker, thus losing her status and her voice. Some scholars have gone further, suggesting that in traditional East European society wives had actually held the dominant role in family finances since they supported their talmudist husbands. Once the husbands abandoned talmudic study and "went to work," the wives lost the status that being the primary breadwinner had yielded. There is growing evidence, however, that the image of such a dominant economic role for women is exaggerated, an erroneous extrapolation from a very limited number of cases to East European society as a whole. This is clear even in Wengeroff's memoir: she obviously mentioned the dedicated wives of the *prushim* of Eishyshok as an exceptional case of marital devotion.[46] While it is certainly the case that Jewish women took an active part in family businesses both small and (as in the case of Bella Wengeroff) large, there is no reason to believe that Pauline's mother was ever anything but a housewife or that Pauline herself was ever expected or prepared to take any active role in business.[47]

One possibility that deserves further exploration is that the experience of modernization was so different for Jewish women because the nature of their traditional piety had been so different from that of men. The study of "women's religion," though still in its beginning stages, has already shown us that traditional Jewish women defined and practiced their religion in ways that overlapped with, but also diverged from, those of their male counterparts.[48] Pauline Wengeroff's memoir provides us with a remarkably detailed and varied picture of this women's religion, one that is not restricted to the texts of the *tchines,* and the perspective from the women's balcony. Zelda Epstein's religion was complex and layered: domestic practice was built upon extensive knowledge and deep concern for halakhic rigor, and her "folk" beliefs were intricately interwoven with aspirations to spiritual experience and personal transcendence.

The pattern of women's practice and faith that our memoir reveals may itself be part of the reason for Pauline Wengeroff's gendered approach to modernization. The religion of her youth had been overwhelmingly a religion of practice. We have already stressed her extensive knowledge of ritual detail and the way in which she privileged halakhic rulings in her account. Ritual practice was not routine or burdensome for her; it inspired in her (as in her mother) deep emotional responses and religious exaltation. Her father provided the intellectual underpinnings for that ritual, but it was her mother (and women generally) whose hands wove the stable fabric of domestic piety, who maintained its routine, and who structured the safe world for which she so longed in her later years of wandering and loss.

What traditional women's religion did not contain in those years was the intellectual quest characterized by the new yeshiva learning of Volozhin on the one hand, or the mystical yearnings of Chasidism on the other. Pauline knows that Chonon had been struggling with issues of faith before their marriage, and she knows that it was a crisis of faith that prompted him to visit the court of the Lubavitcher *Rebbe* soon after their marriage. But she cannot tell us of what that crisis consisted or even what happened to Chonon while he was away. Her brother Ephraim seems also to have gone through a wrenching personal quest for faith. From the obituaries written about him by colleagues in America, it is clear that Ephraim's conversion to Christianity was not prompted by mere opportunism. He devoted three years to the study of theology at Andover Theological Seminary, held a number of teaching, missionary and pastoral positions in Christian institutions, and actively pursued a life-long interest in mystical thought.[49] The path that led these two young men towards Jewish mystical thought and then to a break with traditional values was not at all atypical; it is echoed in the biographies of many of the maskilim of the nineteenth century. But it was an exclusively masculine path.

If Wengeroff's experience is at all representative, the women of her elite circle were not driven from tradition by failed ideology or religious crisis. Pauline talks of her brother and brothers-in-law fighting with their parents about ideas; she speaks of her sisters seeking permission to adopt new fashions in clothes. Wengeroff was not trying to trivialize her sisters. Rather, they (and she) simply did not see the conflict between the old and the new as necessarily total. They believed that limited change was possible, and tried to fight the battle for modernity on restricted and marginal battlefields. This was the dream of the earlier optimistic stage of Russian Haskalah: to purify Judaism of obscurantism and to modernize Jewish education and occupational structure in the expectation of gaining access to the larger culture. In this vision, it would be possible to assimilate to Russian culture, to become loyal and equal citizens of the czar, and yet to remain proud, loyal and creative Jews.[50] Women like Pauline Wengeroff had felt comfortable with that vision and held onto it long after it had crumbled for men.

We have already noted that in her memoir, Wengeroff goes beyond the nostalgic to the prescriptive. Armed with the vision of an integrated identity that she had learned as a young woman, Pauline Wengeroff could adopt the new, westernized rhetoric of poetic beauty, social concern, family warmth and spiritual uplift to justify the old prayers, practices and values of her mother's religion. Her book is arguably the first statement by a Jewish woman of Eastern Europe of the new "women's religion"—of Judaism as she believed it should be.

V. GENERIC MODELS/PERSONAL CHOICES

We began by suggesting that Pauline Wengeroff's memoir was a public, as much as a private, document, that it was an attempt to articulate a view of the Jewish past and future as much as it was an account of her own life. We may therefore legitimately ask how our author went about creating this image of the Jewish past for public consumption. Where did she find terms for tradition that would appeal to her modern readers? The literary devices and images that Wengeroff used to portray her remembered world—the child's point of view, the emphasis on piety and domesticity, the warm family ties, the delicious food, the folksongs, and the mixture of quaint and inspiring religious practices—nowadays these all seem rather trite and obvious. But Wengeroff was the first woman, and indeed one of the first writers, to adopt these conventions and shape them into what we mean today when we refer generically (and incorrectly) to "the culture of the *shtetl*."[51] How she went about framing her story may tell us a great deal about what it was she was trying to say.

Pauline did have at least limited models for her task. First there were the stories she had heard from her father, an oral tradition that would develop over the nineteenth century into a library of hagiographic books with its own canons of pious significance and historical authenticity.[52] Yudl Epstein actually contributed to, and helped to publish, at least one of these hagiographic/historical volumes. Pauline shared her father's belief in a pious rabbinic past as well his sense of an urgent need to preserve that past before it was lost.[53]

Pauline could also draw on another emerging form of Jewish historical writing—the so-called "second track" of Hebrew (and then Yiddish) historiography, less formally academic and more religiously conservative than western Jewish scholarship. These writers promoted a *maskilic* program of enlightenment (which they understood as a positive result of Russian rule) while, at the same time, seeking "to curb religious erosion, extreme acculturation and assimilation."[54] In local histories as well as in more comprehensive works, they also stressed the importance of East European communities in the overall development of Jewish history. Wengeroff knew of this literature at least indirectly, and her description of the relocation of the Jewish cemetery of Brisk is a contribution to this sort of local history.[55]

Finally her memoir was part of a rising ethnographic impulse among Russian Jewish intellectuals that had led to the formation of the Historical and Ethnographic Society in St. Petersburg, the establishment of Jewish documentary archives, and the publication of important historical journals and anthologies. The dream of preserving a vanishing Jewish folk culture had already inspired Piotr (Pesach) Marek and Saul Ginzburg to publish the anthology of Russian-Jewish folksongs to which Pauline referred twice (pp. 52 and 201). S. Ansky, most famous for his play "The Dybbuk," published his essay on "Jewish Ethnopoetry" in 1908, the same year that Wengeroff's book first appeared, and it was while she was working on her second volume that he organized the ambitious Jewish Ethnographic Expedition of 1912.[56] Wengeroff's reports on folksongs, beliefs, and customs were a self-conscious attempt to participate in this secularized and "modern" form of Jewish identity.

But in the final analysis, we must not forget that Pauline Wengeroff wrote not a history but a memoir. Sometime around her seventy-fifth year, by then already a widow for some fifteen years, this strong and eloquent woman decided that her life story was worth preserving for her family and the world at large.[57] How she approached the autobiographical task tells us a great deal about Pauline's intentions.

By the start of the twentieth century, Jewish autobiography was already replete with its own set of conventions. The first Jewish memoir written for public consumption was composed more than a century before in 1792 when Solomon Maimon published the story of his life—from Talmud prodigy in rural Poland to recognized philosopher in Berlin. As Alan Mintz has pointed out, Maimon's was a "seminal" work that imported the autobiographical norms of Rousseau's *Les Confessions* and shaped them into "the first and freshest telling of ... a story that became the very cornerstone of modern Jewish literature: the narrative of acculturation." By the time Wengeroff was writing, this narrative convention had already yielded up several important Hebrew-language accounts of the transition from tradition to modernity, most especially Moses Leib Lilienblum's self-critical and despairing *Sins of Youth* (*Hat'ot Ne'urim*; 1873).[58]

Even if Wengeroff never read any of the autobiographies written by Jewish men, it is still noteworthy that the memoir she wrote is so different from them in its fundamental assumptions. She completely changed the central direction of the masculine narrative. There is no story of a personal loss of faith. Instead of a religious crisis and "apostasy," Wengeroff, as we have stressed, idealized ritual observance and traditional faith, and she rigorously externalized any religious falling away, displacing and projecting it onto others.

Equally important, Wengeroff's picture of marriage is radically different from the one conventionalized in the Jewish autobiographical genre. Whereas male writers from Maimon on had seen their traditional, arranged marriages as oppressive traps, Wengeroff presented her sister Chaveh's match as yielding stability and happiness *because* it was of the old-fashioned variety. Marriages were happier in those premodern times, she tells us. "The high moral character of the young couple hallowed their union and safeguarded their faithfulness to each other. They did not become tired of each other, and did not chase after novelty." Modernity had changed Jewish marriage, but not for the better. "The Enlightenment shattered the sacredness of this marital life and destroyed many dear treasures" (p. 80).

And here we come to a contradiction central to Wengeroff's book and to the task she set herself as a writer. In keeping with her idealization of the Jewish past, Pauline Wengeroff had elevated traditional marriage over modern. But as a teenager she herself had absorbed the modern romantic dreams that informed the books she read, and she had desperately wanted her own courtship to be free and loving according to the new model. Though today's reader might be hard put to see Pessele's marriage as different in any significant way from that of Chaveh two years before, Pauline needed to believe that it was. She never lost this dream, and over half a century later, she still treasured all the loving letters Chonon had sent. She was still delighting in the deep affinity that had, she was sure, immediately sprung up between them.

Perhaps it was because she perceived of her marriage as more "modern" that Pauline could not help but be disappointed by its reality. The couple's relationship was stormy at best. Even leaving aside their religious disagreements for the moment, it is clear that financial insecurity, the lengthy separations involved in Chonon's search for work, and the repeated family relocations all left deep marital scars. During hard times, Pauline labeled Chonon a domestic tyrant, and she accused him of taking out on her the frustration he was feeling at work. Even after they were well-established in Minsk, however, Pauline tells us that she took the children and moved abroad for three years. She says she went to seek medical help (*zur Kur*) after a traumatizing fire, and it may be that the rising anti-Semitic atmosphere of the time convinced Chonon that his family would be safer outside of Russia. But whatever the ostensible reason, such a lengthy separation could not have contributed to a close relationship between husband and wife. It is against this background that Wengeroff wrote that modern marriages did not generate "the truly divine spark of love" that might "sustain the shivering soul" in old age when the fire of passion had long burned out.

Perhaps here we have a final key to the public format of Wengeroff's personal memories. Wengeroff lived most of her life in relative privilege and comfort. Her husband and children achieved considerable status and fame. How then could she write a memoir whose overall tone was one of decline and failure, of regret and resentment? May we not argue that, on some level at least, Pauline Wengeroff focused her memoir on broad historical change because it provided a legitimizing venue for the public expression of her own, very personal disappointments and frustration? The broader terminologies of religious and national tragedy provided what Wengeroff needed—a perspective on her own wanderings and isolation, her difficult relations with her husband, and her resentment of her "tyrannical" children.[59]

We began by stating that Pauline Wengeroff remained frustratingly difficult to know. In the end, the problem remains because we can never separate the private from the public, the personal from the ideological. Ultimately, we cannot know Pauline Wengeroff's heart. She did not want us to.

NOTES TO THE AFTERWORD

[1] "Memory and Autobiography," *Raritan* 15 (1995), 36–50:37. Kermode's essay that centers on the argument for the existence of an evolving "self" basic to the autobiographer's craft highlights the absence of any such claim by Wengeroff.

[2] Yehezkel Kotik, *Meine Zikhronos* (Warsaw: 1913–14; second edition, Berlin: 1922); annotated Hebrew edition, ed. David Asaf, *Ma She-Raiti. Zikhronotav shel Yehezkel Kotik* [Tel-Aviv: University of Tel-Aviv, 1998], p. 87. An English translation is currently being prepared for Wayne State University Press.

[3] A. S. Sachs, *Horeve Velten* (New York: 1917; second edition 1918). The reference is to the English edition, *Worlds That Passed* (Philadelphia: 1928), pp. 1f.

[4] This goal—passing something evanescent down to the next generation—is so commonly articulated in Jewish autobiographical writing that historians and readers often take it for granted, ignoring the complicated emotional and ideological stance it implies. The memoirist's sense of loss comes out of, and reinforces, an awareness of the great distance between one's own childhood and one's own current lifestyle, and the realization that it is the present (with which the author does not feel completely comfortable) that is molding his or her children. Alienation from both past and present leaves the author with a sense of shame and of desperation. Bella Chagall was, in her own words, "tormented" by the thought that her daughter would not be able to understand the message she was sending through her memoir (*Burning Lights*, [New York: 1946], p. 11). Pauline Wengeroff would have immediately empathized with this anxiety.

[5] Gauging the age of the child observer is a little complicated. In the German original, when describing the Passover *seder* Wengeroff notes that her brother Ephraim was then 12 years old. By his own testimony, Ephraim was born on the day before the Fast of Esther (12 Adar), 1828—a day that

fell that year on March 17; "Why Do I Live So Long?" *The American Journal of Clinical Medicine* 15 (1908), p. 522. Thus he would have been twelve at the *seders* of 1840. This dating also fits in well with Wengeroff's comment that her sisters were then dressed in the fashion of the 1840s. Granted that she was born in 1833, this means that Wengeroff was remembering/reconstructing herself and her experiences at age seven. Wengeroff's father and mother were then about forty. See below, n. 28.

[6] Sachs, *Horeve Velten*, pp. 105, 172 and passim; Bella Chagall, *Burning Lights*, pp. 220ff.

[7] For Sabbath *challehs* (what Pauline calls *barkhes*), a small portion of dough was separated and burned *before* the baking of the bread; for Passover, a piece was broken off from one already-baked *matzeh* chosen at random from the entire lot. On this distinction, see J. D. Eisenstein, *Otzar Dinim u-Minhagim* (reprint, Tel Aviv: 1975), p. 131, *s.v.*, "hallah," and *Shulhan Arukh, Orah Hayim* §457.1.

[8] Wengeroff mentions this in connection with the second *seder* and explains that they ate chicken rather than roast—that is, meat like beef or lamb—in the presence of the *zro'a*. The custom of not eating meat at the *seder* applied to both *seders* and was intended to avoid the impression that the food was actually considered the Paschal sacrifice; see e.g., Danzig, *Hayei Adam*, §130.9.

[9] It is interesting that Pauline recalls her house being decorated with greenery on *Shvuos*; this was a practice which the Gaon discouraged (Danzig, *Hayei Adam*, §131.13). One of Wengeroff's few misstatements about ritual law is that in her house after Passover people did not eat *yoshen* but waited for the *chodesh* (*hadash*). In fact the rule is that one may *not* eat *hadash* until the evening of the eighteenth of the month of *Nisan* (the fourth day of Passover). What Pauline may be remembering is the custom initiated by the Gaon to eat *matzeh* made specifically from the new grain on the eighteenth as a way of marking the commandment (Danzig, *Hayei Adam*, §131.12).

[10] Cf. Josef Lewy, *Minhag Yisrael Tora* (Brooklyn: 1994), III, p. 137 *ad O.H.* §624.

[11] See ReMA *ad O.H.* §667.1 cited in Lewy, *Minhag* III, p. 185 *ad loc.*

[12] The popular practice of trying to drown out the reader at each mention of the name of Haman actually presents halakhic problems. In order to "properly" fulfil the commandment, one must be silent from the time of the recitation of the opening blessing through the entire reading and the recitation of the final blessing. Any utterance during that period would be considered a "hefsek" (interruption) and invalidate the entire process for the person who made the noise. Moreover, one is obliged to hear every word of the *megilla* clearly; even noise produced by stamping the feet or with noise-

makers could prevent the congregation from hearing some of the words. In many traditional communities today, the name of Haman is repeated by the reader after the noise of the *graggers* has died down.

[13] Changes in the spelling of Hebrew terms between the first and second editions include *Schalssude* to *Schalosch Suda* (p. 78; Hebrew: *shalosh se'uda*), *awdole* to *hawdole* (Hebrew: *havdala*), *jehorek* (p. 187) to *yehoreg*. Wengeroff corrected fine details, such as the text in which Zelmele Volozhiner would have found the laws of honoring one's father and mother (not the Talmud but the *Shulhan Arukh;* p. 8). The question, of course, is whether she was making these changes in response to suggestions she received from someone else, or whether she caught the errors herself. Only very rarely did an error in ritual detail escape her notice.

[14] On the issue of women's religion, see below. On misnagdim in general, see now Alan Nadler, *The Faith of the Mithnagdim. Rabbinic Responses to Hasidic Rapture* (Baltimore: The Johns Hopkins University Press, 1997). On the Vilna Gaon, see Immanuel Etkes, *Yahid be-Doro. Ha-Gaon mi-Vilna—Dmut u-Dimui* [The Gaon of Vilna. The Man and His Image] (Jerusalem: Merkaz Zalman Shazar, 1997), and the useful presentations included in *The Gaon of Vilnius and the Annals of Jewish Culture. Materials of the International Scientific Conference. Vilnius. September 10–12, 1997* sponsored by the Community of Lithuanian Jews and Vilnius University and published by Vilnius University Publishing House, 1998.

[15] On the Gaon's position on this issue, see Abraham Danzig, *Hayei Adam* (Jerusalem: 1958), §153.5.

[16] Well known is the Vilna Gaon's advice, in a letter written home during a trip to the Holy Land, that a "daughter not go to the synagogue for there she would see garments of embroidery and similar finery. She would grow envious and speak of it at home, and out of this would come scandal and other ills" (Israel Abrahams, *Hebrew Ethical Wills* [Philadelphia: Jewish Publication Society, 1926], p. 321 and cf. p. 316). It seems unlikely that this extreme view was followed widely even in circles close to the Gaon. But even if Pauline accompanied her family to services, she clearly did not feel this was worth mentioning.

[17] See *Memoiren einer Grossmutter,* first edition, I, p. 96. Wengeroff tried to correct her presentation in the second edition (I, 100) but still erred. We omitted the passage from this English edition.

[18] Compare, for example, Arlene Rossen Cardozo, *Jewish Family Celebrations. The Sabbath, Festivals, and Ceremonies* (New York: 1982) or the classic *Jewish Catalogue,* Richard Siegel, Michael Strassfeld, and Sharon Strassfeld, eds. (Philadelphia: 1973–80).

[19] On the idealization of the pre-modern Jewish family by modern writers, see Paula E. Hyman, "Introduction" to Steven M. Cohen and Paula E. Hyman, eds., *The Jewish Family. Myths and Reality* (New York: Holmes and Meier, 1986) and Hyman, "The Modern Jewish Family: Image and Reality," in David Kraemer, ed., *The Jewish Family. Metaphor and Memory* (New York: Oxford University Press, 1989), pp. 179–93.

[20] According to his tombstone, Ziml Epstein was born in Lithuania (Yiddish: *Lite*) (Samuel Yevnin/Jevnin, *Nahalat Olamim* [Warsaw: 1881–82; reprint 1967–68], p. 33). Wengeroff's statement that he moved there in the 1820s to work on the fortifications is probably erroneous. In the parlance of the time, *Lite* included large parts of White Russia and Polesia and it seems more than likely that Ziml, like his son and granddaughter, was born in Bobruisk.

[21] Barukh Epstein, *Mekor Barukh* (Vilna: 1928), p. 907.

[22] The rise of these economically powerful Jews and the explosive growth of the Warsaw Jewish community, especially in Congress Poland after 1815, provide a crucial context for Jewish modernization that is only slowly being analyzed by historians. For now, see Jacob Shatzky, *Geshikhte fun Yidn in Varshe* (New York: 1947–53) and Bina Garncarska-Kadary, *Helkam shel ha-Yehudim be-Hitpathut ha-Taasiya shel Varsha ba-Shanim 1816/20–1914* [English title: The Role of Jews in the Development of Industry in Warsaw 1816/20–1914], Publications of the Diaspora Research Institute of the Haim Rosenberg School of Jewish Studies, Tel-Aviv University, 54 (Tel-Aviv: 1985). For the date of Ziml Epstein's settling in Warsaw, see his tombstone as above, n. 20. There were apparently two Ziml Epsteins in Warsaw and it is not always certain about which Shatzky is writing (*op. cit.*, II, 86–87; III 78). On Bobruisk, see Y. Slutsky, ed., *Bobroysk* (Tel Aviv: 1967).

[23] There were fierce struggles within the Jewish community over the construction of a new grand synagogue to replace the one torn down in the 1830s. See Aryeh Loeb Feinstein, *Ir Tehilah* (Warsaw: 1886; reprint 1967/68). Yudl no longer had the means to compete (even if he so desired) in such an acrimonious and crippling fight over personal status.

[24] One of the most common themes of Jewish literature and ethical tracts in this period is the vagaries of fortune, and Jews are often portrayed going suddenly from great wealth to the depths of poverty. Such radical decline could have terrible effects on people. Ephraim Epstein, Pauline's brother, reports that one member of his family committed suicide over his financial losses. The details of Yudl's life are taken from his introduction to *Minchas Yehuda*.

[25] *Mekor Barukh,* pp. 830ff.

²⁶ The chronology of the story is somewhat problematic: Rabbi Moses Ze'ev ben Eliezer of Grodno did not become head of the rabbinical court in Bialystock until 1824 (*EJ* [1972], *s.v.*), but from Yudl Epstein's own words it seems that his father acquired this companion tutor for him in 1816–17; see below, n. 28. Yudl mentioned meeting Rabbi Moses Ze'ev when the latter once stopped at his father's home for lunch (*Minchas Yehuda*, "Introduction").

²⁷ Pauline's brother, Ephraim, repeats her account: "In his sixties my father withdrew from business and gave himself over to the study of the Talmud, to which he gave from twelve to fourteen hours a day"; see Ephraim's memoir cited above, n. 5. In the Introduction to his *Minchas Yehuda*, Yudl emphasized his study, mentioning only in passing that "for a few years he had engaged in commerce." The Warsaw historian, Samuel Yevnin, and Yudl's cousin, Barukh Epstein, also portray him as a great talmudist.

²⁸ For the family tree, see below, Appendix II. A younger cousin, Yehiel Mikhl Epstein, was among the most influential rabbinical authorities of the day. Rabbi Yehiel Mikhl b. Aaron Isaac ha-Levi Epstein (1829–1908), author of the comprehensive, multi-volume code of Jewish law *Arukh ha-Shulhan* (1884–1907), was the grandson of Yudl's paternal uncle. His son, Barukh ha-Levi Epstein (1860–1942), was the author of the popular *Torah Temimah* as well as of the memoir, *Mekor Barukh*, which we have already cited.

²⁹ On Yudl's education, see his detailed remarks in the introduction to *Minchas Yehuda*, p. 4, as well as his epistolary appendix to *Saarat Eliyahu*. It is not irrelevant that Yudl studied at home and that he provided the same sort of private education for his son and sons-in-law. In 1802, R. Hayim Volozhiner established his new yeshiva as an antidote to this kind of private scholarship, which he saw as a sign of cultural crisis: "For some time now the great scholars of the Torah in our land each builds himself a separate room to himself and says, 'I will save myself' and withdraws from a generation that does not love the Torah" (Simha Asaf, *Mekorot le-Toldot ha-Hinukh be-Yisrael* [Sources for the History of Jewish Education], 2nd edition, vol. IV [Tel Aviv: 1947], p. 170). Yudl's education was old-fashioned in form as well as in content.

³⁰ On this work, see below, n. 35.

³¹ Yevnin, *Nahalat Olamim*, §145, p. 72f. We have no firm indication of the year of Yudl Epstein's birth. He himself says (Introduction to *Minchas Yehuda*, p. 4) that he was a few years younger than his teacher, R. David Tevele, and that the latter was 24 in 1817. That would mean Yudl was born a little before 1800. A similar conclusion comes from Pauline's remark that her father was 40 at the Passover *seder* she described in her memoir, above, n. 5.

[32] The personal tensions and cultural strains implicit in the marriage arrangements of this period have been studied in a number of path-breaking articles. See for example, Immanuel Etkes, "Marriage and Torah Study among *Lomdim* in Lithuania in the Nineteenth Century," in Kraemer, ed., *The Jewish Family*, pp. 153–78; David Biale, "Childhood, Marriage and the Family in the Eastern European Jewish Enlightenment," Cohen and Hyman, *The Jewish Family*, pp. 45–61. It might be noted here that early marriage was a continuing tradition in the Epstein family. According to their son, Yudl Epstein was himself only fourteen when he married his thirteen-year-old bride Zelda. Their first child was born a year later (Epstein, "Why Do I Live So Long?" p. 523).

[33] Ibid., p. 524.

[34] Ibid., p. 523.

[35] Schick's life work, which has to my knowledge not yet received scholarly attention, was devoted to the exposition of various midrashic and aggadic texts to which the author appended lengthy essays on major topics of the Jewish religious understanding, written under the acknowledged influence of western authors, both Jewish and non-Jewish. The *Kinmon Besem* was appended to the volumes of Schick's commentary, *Eyn Avraham*, to Jacob ibn Habib's classic anthology, here entitled *Agadat Bavli ha-nikra be-shem Eyn Yaakov* (Königsburg: 1847–48).

[36] On the maskilic attitudes of these years, see Immanuel Etkes, "Introduction" to Isaac Ber Levinson, *Teuda be-Yisrael* (Jerusalem: 1977), pp. 4–5. On the positive attitude of the early Russian maskilim towards the government, see Israel Zinberg, *A History of Jewish Literature* (New York: 1978) XI, pp. 22, 29f., 36f.; XII, pp. 117ff. The comprehensive Hebrew anthology of scholarly articles ed. by Etkes, *Ha-Dat ve-ha-Hayim. Tnuat ha-Haskala ha-Yehudit be-Mizrah Eyropa* [English title: *The East European Jewish Enlightenment*] (Jerusalem: 1993) includes a useful bibliography by Samuel Feiner. For a recent treatment of government Jewry policy in this period, see Michael Stanislawski, *Tsar Nicholas I and the Jews. The Transformation of Jewish Society in Russia 1825–1855* (Philadelphia: JPS, 1983).

[37] It is not irrelevant that Pauline, her husband, and her sisters all adopted Russian given names. In her tale of the rise of anti-Semitism in Minsk she is clearly aware that the fact that the Wengeroff name sounded non-Jewish could be advantageous. In America, her brother, who actually converted to Christianity, changed neither his biblical-sounding given names, Ephraim Menachem, nor his very Jewish-sounding family name, Epstein. On the extent to which Pauline's daughter Faina tried to hide the family's Jewish origins from her son, see Nicholas Slonimsky, *Perfect Pitch. A Life Study* (Oxford and New York: Oxford University Press, 1988), p. 14f.

[38] On Roman Alexandrovich, his grandmother's protegé, see Slonimsky, *Perfect Pitch*, p. 7.

[39] Pauline's son Semyon (Simon) was well known as a literary critic and professor of literature. Zinaida (Zina) made her mark as a translator and promoter of modernist writers. Later in life she married the poet Nicholas Minski. Yet another daughter, Isabella (b. 1877) was a world-famous pianist and teacher, whose pupils included Leonard Bernstein. Faina (b. 1857) studied medicine and married Leonid Slonimsky, a well-known journalist, essayist, and political writer.

[40] Abraham Greenboim, "Disparagement of the Working Class among East European Jews up until 1914" (Hebrew), Shmuel Ettinger, ed., *Uma ve-Toldoteha* (Jerusalem: 1984), pp. 49–54.

[41] She proudly footnotes, for example, the studies of Jewish and biblical history published by her cousin, Israel (Abraham Sack's brother), as well as the Zionist work by Grigory (Joshua) Syrkin (1838–1922), the Sacks' step-brother. See the German *Memoiren*, II, p. 26.

[42] On the whole, Wengeroff's citations of Hebrew words are accurate, but she makes a number of mistakes about the dates and nature of her father's books. She also refers to a local history of Brest-Litovsk, *[Brisk] Ir Tehila*, by a German title and mistakes the book's publisher for its author. This suggests, at least, that she could not herself read these books. Though she praises the Hebrew novels of Abraham Mapu, she gives no indication that she was able to read them in the original Hebrew. It might also be noticed that she gently mocks her husband's stepmother as pretentious about her bit of Hebrew knowledge.

[43] The importance of Wengeroff's gendered perspective has been stressed by several historians including Shulamit S. Magnus, "Pauline Wengeroff and the Voice of Jewish Modernity," in T. M. Rudavsky, ed., *Gender and Judaism. The Transformation of Tradition* (New York: New York University Press, 1995), pp. 181–90, and Monica Rüthers, "Tewjes Töchter. Lebensentwürfe ostjüdischer Frauen im 19. Jahrhundert" (Cologne: Böhlau, 1996).

[44] For a thoughtful introduction to the study of gender and acculturation, see Paula E. Hyman, *Gender and Assimilation in Modern Jewish History. The Roles and Representation of Women* (Seattle and London: University of Washington Press, 1995), especially chapter 1, "Paradoxes of Assimilation," pp. 10–49; for Wengeroff see p. 72. For maskilic attacks on the place of women in traditional Jewish society, see for example, J. L. Gordon's poem, "The Tip of the *Yud*" (*Kotzo shel yud*) (1876) as conveniently explained in Michael Stanislawski, *For Whom Do I Toil? Judah Leib Gordon and the Crisis of Russian Jewry* (New York and Oxford: Oxford University Press, 1988), pp. 124ff.

[45] Pauline's brother, Ephraim, described their mother as "a blond of quiet, unresisting, unpretentious nature and in every respect bodily and mentally different from my father" ("Why Do I Live So Long?" p. 523).

[46] A convenient popular treatment of the Eishyshok *prushim* is available in Yaffa Eliach, *There Once Was a World. A 900-Year Chronicle of the Shtetl of Eishyshok* (Boston: Little, Brown and Co., 1998), pp. 184ff.

[47] Pauline did make special (and resentful) note of the fact that, from the start of their married life, her husband rejected her advice in financial matters (p. 181). But this does not demonstrate that she had expected to take an active role in the conduct of affairs. Indeed, she indicates that in Russia Minor, at least, women in wealthy families were usually kept out of business completely.

[48] A useful English introduction to the theoretical issues is provided by Chava Weissler, *Voices of the Matriarchs. Listening to the Prayers of Early Modern Jewish Women* (Boston: Beacon, 1998), especially chapter 2: "Studying Women's Religion," pp. 36–50.

[49] Epstein's brief memoir and the several memorials published about him are consistent in stressing the seriousness of his conversion to Christianity. A. S. Burdick, editor of the medical journal to which Epstein contributed, reported:

> He was essentially a mystic, seeing in the books that he read and in the greater book of nature many things of subtle significance which most of us, imbued with the material philosophy of the age, could not perceive; yet to him they were alive with messages from the Infinite. Next to the Bible, which he read constantly, I think his favorite author [was] that rare old middle-age mystic, Jacob Boehme, of whom the average twentieth-century man knows nothing. (*American Journal of Clinical Medicine* 20 [1913], p. 255.)

[50] The dream was still clear in J. L. Gordon's famous poem of 1862/63: "Be a man in the streets and a Jew at home/ A brother to your countryman and a servant to your king." See Stanislawski, *For Whom Do I Toil?* especially pp. 49ff.

[51] On the historiographic trope of the *shtetl* and its centrality to modern Jewish self-consciousness, see recently David Roskies, "The Shtetl in Jewish Collective Memory," in idem, *The Jewish Search for a Usable Past* (Bloomington: Indiana University Press, 1999), pp. 41–66; Steven J. Zipperstein, *Imagining Russian Jewry. Memory, History, Identity* (Seattle and London: University of Washington Press, 1998), Prologue and Chapter I: "Shtetls There and Here. Imagining Russia in America," pp. 15–39; Barbara Kirschenblatt-Gimblett, "Introduction" to the paperback re-issue of Mark Zborowski and Elizabeth Herzog, *Life is With People. The Culture of the Shtetl* (New York: Schocken Books, 1995).

52 To my knowledge, the first publication in this new hagiographic-historical genre was a biography of R. Shlomo Zalman of Volozhin, the very Reb Zelmele whom Pessele heard about as a child (Yehezkel Feivel ben Ze'ev Wolf, *Toldot Adam* [Dyhernfurth: 1801–9] republished together with a nine-page appendix [called Part III] by Shlomo Zalman's grandson, R. Shalom of Yanishek). In a reprint of the entire work (New York: 1949–1950), a story very much like the one told to Pessele appears in Part III, p. 58. On the work and its author, see now Edward Breuer, "The Haskalah in Vilna: R. Yehezkel Feivel's *Toldot Adam*," *The Torah U-Madda Journal* 7 (1997), pp. 15–40. There has been considerable scholarly interest in recent years in the various "schools" or "streams" of nineteenth-century Jewish historiography. To my knowledge, no one has yet taken account of works like *Toldot Adam*, which, for all their hagiographic form, do pay careful attention to issues of verification and historical logic in a manner quite in tune with the methodologies of modern historiography.

53 *Saarat Eliyahu* (The Storm of Elijah), a biography of the Vilna Gaon written almost immediately after his death but published only in 1875–76, with careful annotations by Epstein's relative, Samuel Yevnin. (Yevnin was also the author of *Nahalat Olamim*, the collection of Warsaw tombstone texts that we have cited already.) Yudl Epstein's appendix, framed as a letter to the author, appeared together with critical historical footnotes from Eliezer Lipmann Rabinowitz and a detailed note from Hillel Noah Steinschneider, historian of the Vilna Jewish community, on pp. 38–42 of the edition issued together with other biographies of the Gaon as *Sifrei ha-GRA mi-Vilna* (Jerusalem: Levin-Epstein, 1954).

54 Shmuel Feiner, "Nineteenth-Century Jewish Historiography: The Second Track," in Jonathan Frankel, ed., *Reshaping the Past: Jewish History and the Historians* [=Studies in Contemporary Jewry, X] (New York: Oxford University Press, 1994), pp. 17–44.

55 Wengeroff's sense that she is writing a "history book" led her to include more than one account drawn from secondary sources, newspapers, and journals. We have generally omitted these passages, especially because they often include erroneous generalizations or assumptions.

56 Saul Ginzburg and Piotr (Pesach) Marek, *Evreiskiia narodnyia piesni v Rossii* [*Di Yiddishe Folkslider in Rusland*—Yiddish Folksongs in Russia] (St. Petersburg: 1901; reprinted with extensive translations and annotations with an introduction by Dov Noy, Ramat Gan: Bar-Ilan University Press, 1991). On Ansky see David G. Roskies, "S. Ansky and the Paradigm of Return," in *The Uses of Tradition. Jewish Continuity in the Modern Era*, ed. Jack Wertheimer (New York: Jewish Theological Seminary, 1992), pp. 243–60, and idem, "Introduction" to S. Ansky, *The Dybbuk and other Writings* (New York: Schocken, 1992).

[57] Pauline began writing a memoir as early as 1898. According to the Russian Jewish Encyclopedia, portions of Wengeroff's book were published as early as 1903 in the Russian periodical *Voskhod*.

[58] Alan Mintz, *"Banished from Their Father's Table." Loss of Faith and Hebrew Autobiography* (Bloomington: Indiana University Press, 1989). The quotes about Maimon are on p. 10f.

[59] The relation between Wengeroff's presentation and the values espoused by her children deserves separate treatment.

The following tentative reconstruction of Pauline Wengeroff's family is based on the sometimes contradictory text of the memoir as well as various genealogical jottings by her father and brother, the notes of her cousin Barukh Epstein, the autobiography of her grandson, Nicolas Slonimsky, as well as encyclopedia articles. I have accepted Ephraim's statement that he was one of 11 children—8 girls and 3 boys —ed.

The (Ha-Levi) Epstein Family

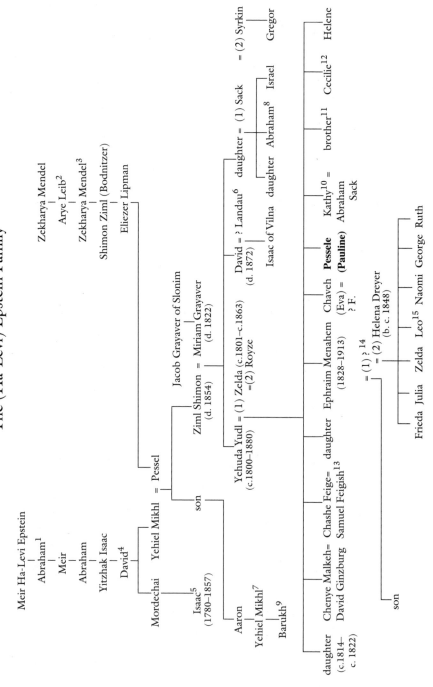

The Wengeroff Family

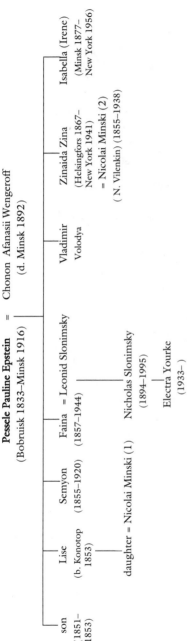

Pessele Pauline Epstein = Chonon Afanasii Wengeroff
(Bobruisk 1833–Minsk 1916) (d. Minsk 1892)

son (1851–1853)

Lise (b. Konotop 1853)

Semyon (1855–1920)

daughter = Nicolai Minski (1)

Faina = Leonid Slonimsky (1857–1944)

Nicholas Slonimsky (1894–1995)

Electra Yourke (1933–)

Vladimir Volodya

Zinaida Zina (Helsingfors 1867– New York 1941) = Nicolai Minski (2) (N. Vilenkin) (1855–1938)

Isabella (Irene) (Minsk 1877– New York 1956)

---

1 Head of the rabbinical court of Brest-Litovsk (Brisk). Signed a responsum in 1637.

2 Head of the rabbinical court of Cracow.

3 Head of the rabbinical court of Belz, author of *Be'er Heter*, a commentary on *Shulhan Arukh, Yore De'a*.

4 For approximately the last 25 years of his life, rabbi of Glusk, a town near Bobruisk, where Yudl Epstein spent many years as a teenager.

5 A follower of the Lubavitcher *Rebbe*, who authored a number of books on that branch of Chasidism

6 David Epstein's wife was the daughter of Ezekiel Landau, rabbi of Vilna

7 Yehiel Mikhl Epstein (1835–1905), leading halakhist and author of *Arukh ha-Shulhan*. According to his son, Yehiel studied with Abraham Sack, Pauline's brother-in-law, in the *cheder* in Bobruisk (Barukh Epstein, *Mekor Barukh*, p. 854).

8 Bobruisk 1828/29–Berlin 1893/94. On him see Epstein, *Mekor Barukh*, pp. 854ff. Abraham Sack married Pauline's sister Kathy. According to Wengeroff (p. 176), they had a son in 1855, but he may have died young since Barukh Epstein says that Sack was left with only one daughter, who predeceased him.

9 Barukh Epstein (1860–1904). Born Bobruisk. Author of popular biblical commentary *Torah Temima* (1902). Settled in U.S.

10 I assume that Kathy was younger than Pauline from a number of comments in the memoir, but if so, she was born no earlier than 1834 or 1835 and was at least six or seven years younger than her husband (and cousin) Abraham Sack (b. 1828). In the introduction to her second volume of memoirs, Pauline says she was writing them in Heidelberg, where she had been reunited with her sisters Helene and Kata. The latter may be Kathy, whose husband had died in Berlin in 1893/94.

11 Born c. 1842.

12 Mentioned by Wengeroff as coming to her wedding. It may be that Cecilie was the Russian name of one of the older sisters and that this child was a boy; Ephraim Epstein is quite clear that there were three sons.

13 This identification is based on the fact that Pauline says she was accompanied to meet her prospective bridegroom by her older (or oldest—*ältere*) brother-in-law Samuel Feigish as well as her most recently (or youngest —*jüngst*) married sister and her husband. I assume that the sister is Chaveh, whose husband is identified only as F. (although Pauline does refer to a sister that was with her as Cecilie). Earlier, Pauline had identified her oldest brother-in-law in 1840 as David. This leaves Samuel Feigish as the husband of Chashe Feige.

14 Ephraim married one of his first cousins c. 1849. The union ended in divorce.

15 d. age 5 from an accidental overdose of morphine.

*Ephraim Epstein, Pauline's brother,
in his eighties.*

Semyon Wengeroff, Pauline's eldest son.

*Leonid Slonimsky, Pauline's son-in-law,
while a law student
at the University of Kiev (1870).*

GLOSSARY

aggadah talmudic material not considered legally binding; thus, *aggadah* includes historical, mythical, legendary, and other sections

Akdomus (Heb. *akdamut*) first word of Aramaic hymn recited on Pentecost

almemor reader's desk in the synagogue; also called the *teva*

amora'im, s. *amora* scholar of the Talmudic period who lived after the closing of the Mishna

apikoros heretic; *apikursish* heretical

arba kanfos (Heb. *arba kanfot,* lit. four corners) garment adorned with ritual fringes (*tzitzis,* Heb. *tzitzit*) worn by males in accordance with the biblical command Deut. 22:12.

aveg away

ayin ho-ra (Heb. *ayin ha-ra*) evil eye

badchen (Heb. *badhan*) jester

bar mitzvah term for Jewish boy who reaches the age of 13 and is therefore "a son of the commandments"—i.e., obliged to perform them as an adult

barches (pl.) rich white bread traditionally served on Sabbaths and other religious festivals (also called *challeh* from Heb. *hala*)

bas tovim (Heb. *bat tovim*) lit. daughter of good people; young woman with a good pedigree

bchor eldest son

bedecken veiling (of a bride before the marriage ceremony)

behelfer assistant

behules (Heb. *behulot*) tumult

beis midrash, pl. *botei midrashim* (Heb. *beit midrash,* pl. *batei midrash*) House of Study (publicly maintained library and study area for students of traditional texts)

beize angry

benshen lit., blessing; Grace after Meals

bocher, pl. *bochrim* (Heb. *baḥur, baḥurim* lad, young man) *yeshiva* student

borchu (Heb. *barkhu*, lit. bless) opening words of evening prayer: "Bless the Lord who is blessed."

bris (Heb. *brit*) circumcision

bsures (Heb. *bsorot*, s. *bsora*) news

busheh (Heb. *busha*) shame

chapper grabber; bounty hunters who seized Jewish young men and boys for army service

chas ve-sholem (Heb. *ḥus le-shalom*) God forbid!

chasid, pl. *chasidim* (Heb. *ḥasid, ḥasidim*) lit. holy one; term for followers of a pietistic movement that swept East European Jewry from the late eighteenth century

chazonim, s. *chazen* (Heb. *ḥazan*) cantor

cheder (Heb. *ḥeder*, lit. room) elementary school conducted in a room in the *melammed*'s home

Chevreh-Tehillim Beis-HaMidrash (Heb. *Bet Midrash shel Ḥevrat Tehilim*) chapel or study hall for Psalms Society (a society, characteristically made up of non-scholars, which met regularly to recite Psalms)

chodesh (Heb. *ḥadash*, lit. new) grain from the new crop

chol ha-mau'ed (Heb. *ḥol ha-mo'ed*) intermediate days of Passover and Tabernacles

chometz (Heb. *ḥametz*, lit., leavened) food unfit for Passover consumption

chossen (Heb. *ḥatan*) bridegroom

chumesh (Heb. *ḥumash*) Pentateuch

chuppeh (Heb. *ḥupa*) wedding canopy

churben (Heb. *ḥurban*) destruction

davenen to pray; (as a noun) a prayer service

dayanim, s. *dayan* judge

deitelholz thin wooden rod used for pointing

dobry den' good morning; *dobry vecher* good evening

dovor min ha-chai (Heb. *davar min ha-ḥai*) lit. anything from a living being

droshe, pl. *droshes* (Heb. *drasha*, pl. *drashot*) sermon, learned speech

dzhigitovka burdiuk trick riding

efsher (Heb. *efshar*) maybe

Eishes Chayil (Heb. *Eshet Ḥayil*) Woman of Valor; opening words of

Prov. 31, traditionally recited by a husband in honor of his wife on Friday evening before the meal

eretz yisroel (Heb. *eretz yisrael*) Land of Israel

erev evening, eve. In Jewish tradition, the day begins at sundown of the day before. Hence, *erev yom tov* holiday eve, is actually the start of the holy day

esrog (Heb. *etrog*) citron

Estertanes (Heb. *Taanit Ester*) Fast of Esther

gabete pious woman engaged in public charity

gazeta pantoflowa unofficial newspaper

golus (Heb. *galut*) exile

goylem (Heb. *golem*) statue

gragger noisemaker used on *Purim*

gram, pl. *grammen* (humorous) verses

gzeyreh (Heb. *gzera*) harsh edict

Haggadah lit. telling; book of recitations and prayers used at a Passover *seder*

hakofes (Heb. *hakafot*) circling; marches around the synagogue on *Simches Torah*

hamanohren (lit., Haman's ears) *kreplach* associated with *Purim*

hamantashen (s. *hamantash*—a play on *mohntash* [poppyseed pocket] and the name of the arch-villain Haman) poppyseed pastries served on *Purim*

Haskalah Jewish Enlightenment; (usually in the sense of education in western, as opposed to traditional, disciplines)

havdoleh (Heb. *havdala*, lit. separation) prayer recited to mark the end of the Sabbath or Holy Day

hesebet (from Heb. *heseba* [reclining]) couch on which to lean while eating the Passover meal

hoshanes (Heb. *hoshanot*) bundles of willow branches used on *Hoshano Rabbo*

hoshano (Heb. *hoshana*, lit. please save) first word of set of prayers recited on Tabernacles

Hoshano Rabbo (Heb. *Hoshana Raba*) seventh day of Tabernacles

Issru Chag day following a religious festival

kaddish prayer of praise; prayer recited by mourners; hence, the male offspring who will recite the *kaddish*

kalleh bride

kasha groats; buckwheat

kasher made kosher; made to conform with Jewish ritual requirements, especially regarding food.

katsappes (lit. goats) Ukrainian slang for Russians with big beards.

kiddush (lit. sanctification) prayer recited, usually over wine, before certain meals on Sabbaths and Holy Days.

kinos (Heb. *kinot*) lamentations, dirges; mournful prayers recited on the Ninth of Av

kittel white robe worn on High Holy Days and other specific solemn religious occasions

klopfer (commonly in Yid. *klapper*) knocker

kneidlach (s. *kneidel*) dumpling

Kol Nidre lit. all oaths; opening words of the prayer service on the Eve of the Day of Atonement

kosher (Heb. *kasher*) ritually fit

koved (Heb. *kavod*) honor

kreplach small filled pockets made with a noodle or pasta dough akin to ravioli and wontons

krias shma (Heb. *kri'at shma*) set of biblical texts, required to be read daily both morning and evening

kriyeh (Heb. *kri'a*, lit. tearing) tearing of an item of clothing to signify mourning

ksubeh (Heb. *ktuba*) marriage contract; read out during the wedding ceremony

kugel pudding

kundesim (s. *kundes*) mischievous boys

kutshmeh high, tapering fur hat

kvas non-alcoholic form of apple cider

latkeh pancake

lernen to study (used especially for study of sacred texts)

Litvak Jew from Lithuania

lulov (Heb. *lulav*) palm branch tied together with myrtle and willow branches

maariv evening prayer

magidim, s. *magid* preachers

mah nishtanah (lit. why is it different?) opening words of the "Four Questions" asked at the start of a Passover *seder*

malkes (Heb. *malkot*) lashes

matzeh, pl. *matzehs* (Heb. *matza*, *matzot*) unleavened bread eaten on

Passover

mauchel (Heb. *moḥel*) forgive

mazel tov (Heb. *mazal tov*, lit. good luck) congratulations

megilla scroll; the biblical Scroll of Esther

mehuder (Heb. *mehudar*) ornate; especially beautiful

melammed (pl. *melamdim*) teacher of Jewish subjects; usually, teacher of elementary subjects though P. W. uses it for more advanced subjects as well

melaveh malkeh (Heb. *melave malka,* lit. accompanying the queen) joyous meal to mark the conclusion of the Sabbath

meshores (Heb. *mesharet*) servant

meshuggene (m. *meshuggener* from Heb. *meshuga*) crazy

meshulach (Heb. *meshulaḥ*) emissary; f. *mishelachas* (Heb. *meshulaḥat*) often, divine messenger; P.W. translates "plague from God"

meyuches (Heb. *meyuḥas,* lit. attributed to) of illustrious birth

mezumon (Heb. *mezuman*) lit. prepared, invited; the form of the Grace after Meals used when at least three adult males are participating

mezuzeh (Heb. *mezuza*) small parchment scroll inscribed with biblical passages and mounted on the doorpost in accordance with Deut. 6:9

milchig dairy

mincheh (Heb. *minḥa*) afternoon prayer; *mincheh gedoleh* (Heb. *minḥa gdola*) roughly the first half of the afternoon time period within which it is permissible to recite the prayer

misnaged, pl. *misnagdim* (Heb. *mitnaged, mitnagdim*) lit. opponents; term for opponents of Chasidism

mitzveh, pl. *mitzvehs* (Heb. *mitzva, mitzvot*) religious commandment; good deed

mohel ritual circumcisor

mohnelach (s. *mohnele*) small candies made from poppyseeds and honey and served on *Purim*

moraur (Heb. *maror*) bitter herbs

more horoes (Heb. *morei hora'a*) official rabbi of a community

nebech alas

nveileh (Heb. *nevela*) dead body (of an animal not properly slaughtered and therefore unfit to eat)

nyanya nanny

omer Abbaye (Heb. *amar Abaye*) Abbaye (an often quoted talmudic rabbi) says

omer lit. sheaf, biblical unit of measurement. According to biblical law

Jews were to bring an *omer* of newly harvested grain to be waved in the sanctuary (Lev. 23: 10-14); P.W. uses the term to mean the period from Passover to Pentecost, when there is a ritual "counting of the *omer*"; cf. *sfireh*

oneg shabbes (Heb. *oneg shabat*) enjoyment of the Sabbath

oren ha-kodesh (Heb. *aron ha-kodesh*) Holy Ark where the Torah scrolls are kept in the synagogue

orev (Heb. *arev*) surety; guarantor

oylom (Heb. *olam*) world; audience

parnuse (Heb. *parnasa*) livelihood

pasken (from Heb. *posek*) decide; issue a judicial ruling

Pesach (Heb. *Pesaḥ*) Passover

peyes (Heb. *peyot*) earlocks

pidyon lit. redemption; gift of money from a Chasid to his *Rebbe* in exchange for the latter's prayers and blessings

podriadchik (pl. —*i*) contractor; entrepreneur

poter (Yid. derivative of Heb. *patur, ptura*) exempt

pripetshek hearth; lower part of the stove

pruteh (Heb. *pruta*) small coin

pushkeh charity box

Reb form of polite address to a male, prefixed to either the given or family name and akin to Eng. "Mr."

rebbe teacher, rabbi; Chasidic leader; respectful term of address to a teacher or rabbi

rebbetzin rabbi's wife

Rosh Chodesh (Heb. *Rosh Ḥodesh*) first day (or two days) of the Jewish month

Rosh Hashono (Heb. *Rosh Ha-Shana*) Festival of the New Year

sandik person given the honor of holding the child on his knees during a circumcision

sarverkeh waitress

seder lit. order; ceremonial meal eaten on the first and second evenings of Passover

sfireh (Heb. *sfira,* lit. counting) ritual counting of each of the forty-nine days between Passover and Pentecost (*Shvuos*); the forty-nine day period which is marked by ritual practices associated with mourning

shabbes (Heb. *shabat*) Sabbath; *Shabbes Chazon* Sabbath before the Fast of the Ninth of Av, so-called because the synagogue reading from the prophets (Isaiah 1) begins with the word *ḥazon* (vision); *Shabbes Nachmu* Sabbath after the Fast of the Ninth of Av, so-called because the synagogue reading from the prophets (Isaiah 40) begins with the word *naḥamu* (be consoled)

shadchen matchmaker

shailes (Heb. *she'elot*, s. *she'elot*) questions concerning religious issues

shammes (Heb. *shamash*) synagogue beadle

shatnez clothing of mixed linen and wool, forbidden by Jewish Law

shaul (commonly in Yid. *shul*) synagogue

shehecheyanu (Heb. *she-heḥeyanu*, lit. who kept us in life) blessing of thanksgiving recited at the start of important festivals

sheitl wig worn by pious women to cover their hair

shikseh non-Jewish girl

shlach (Heb: *shlaḥ*) send

shlachmones (Heb. *shlaḥ manot,* commonly *mishloaḥ manot*) sending of gifts, a religious obligation on *Purim*

Shmini Atzeres (Heb. *Shmini Atzeret*) Eighth Day of Assembly, the last day of Tabernacles

shmoneh esreh lit. eighteen; central feature of all Jewish prayer services, so-called because its original form contained eighteen benedictions

shmureh (Heb. *shmura*) guarded

shneider tailor

shochet, pl. *shochtim* (Heb. *shoḥet*) ritual slaughterer

shtender lectern upon which to rest the large Talmud folios while studying

shtreimel soft fur-trimmed hat worn especially on Sabbaths and Holy Days

Shulchan Aruch (Heb. *Shulḥan Arukh*) sixteenth-century code of Jewish law composed by Rabbi Joseph Karo

shures (Heb. *shurot*, s. *shura*) lines

Shushan Purim day after Purim; a holiday in some places

shver father-in-law

shviger mother-in-law

Shvuos (Heb. *Shavuot*, lit. weeks) Pentecost, the festival seven weeks after Passover

Simches Torah (Heb. *Simḥat Tora*) Rejoicing in the Law, holiday that follows immediately on *Sukkos*

sliches (Heb. *sliḥot*) penitential prayers recited especially during the week before *Rosh Hashana*

sudeh (Heb. *se'uda*) large meal associated with religious observance; the obligatory *Purim* meal

sukkeh (Heb. *suka*) temporary booth used on Tabernacles
Sukkos (Heb. *Sukot*) holiday of Tabernacles

talles (Heb. *talit*) prayer shawl
tana'im, s. *tana* scholar mentioned in the Mishna
tashlich (Heb. *tashlikh* lit. you shall cast) ceremony performed usually on
    the first day of the New Year
tchines (Heb. *tḥinot*) Yiddish-language prayers of supplication printed in
    small booklets intended especially for women (and men) who
    were not trained in the intricacies of the Hebrew liturgy
tefillin phylacteries (black leather boxes holding parchments on which
    biblical prayers are written that are worn during morning prayers
teivolim (s. *teivel*) demon
tikun lit. repair; fixed sets of prayers offered at night as in *tikun shvu'os*
    and *tikun hoshana raba* often published in small booklets
Tisho be-Av ninth day of Heb. month of Av—a fast day in memory of the
    destruction of the Temple in Jerusalem
torgi auction
treif (Heb. *taref*) not kosher, not ritually acceptable
tzores (Heb. *tzarot*) troubles, woes

yehoreg ve-al yaavor let him be killed but not transgress; traditional
    description of commandments that must be observed even on pain
    of death
yiches (Heb. *yiḥus*) pedigree
Yom Kippur Day of Atonement
yom tov (lit. good day) Holy Day; *gut yom tov* happy holiday; see also *erev*
yomim nauro'im (Heb. *yamim nora'im*) Days of Awe, High Holy Days
yoshen (Heb. *yashan*, lit. old) grain from the old crop

zaddik righteous person; also, Chasidic leader
zeicher le-churben (Heb. *zeḥer le-ḥurban*) remembrance of the destruc-
    tion [of the Temple in Jerusalem]
zmiraus (Heb. *zmirot*) hymns sung during meals on Sabbaths and festi-
    vals
zoger, f. *zogerke* reciter
zro'a (lit. [upper part of] the arm or foreleg); piece of roasted meat set
    out on the *seder* table

STUDIES AND TEXTS IN
JEWISH HISTORY AND CULTURE

Bernard D. Cooperman, General Editor